MY SERMON NOTES

115 SERMON NOTES

MY SERMON NOTES

CHARLES H. SPURGEON

VOLUME 4
ROMANS TO REVELATION

BAKER BOOK HOUSE
Grand Rapids, Michigan 49506

First published in 1884
Reprinted 1981 by
Baker Book House Company
VOLUME 4
ISBN: 0-8010-8206-4
FOUR-VOLUME SET
ISBN: 0-8010-8201-3

Eighth printing, January 1990

PHOTOLITHOPRINTED BY CUSHING - MALLOY, INC.
ANN ARBOR, MICHIGAN, UNITED STATES OF AMERICA

PREFACE

THIS is the concluding portion of " My Sermon-Notes." There are many more skeletons in the tombs from which these have been brought to light, but I have no idea of summoning any more of them from their retirement. I have no desire to become the rival of Mr. Charles Simeon; and yet, if I should copy any man's outlines, I should prefer him for a model. Notwithstanding the depreciatory remarks which I have frequently read from witty writers who have referred to that great sermonizer, I believe that no one has done better service in that line than he. His helps were needed at the time when they were prepared. In much the same way as the Homilies were necessary to the preachers of the Reformed Church in its infant days, Simeon's outlines were needed by a newly-converted clergy who had begun to feel the glow of the great Methodist revival. It may be that these Sermon-Notes may be just in time for a return of zeal for the doctrines of grace, and a restoration of spiritual ardour, when young men shall feel called upon to speak at once for Jesus, and shall hardly know how to shape their thought's expression unless some man shall guide them.

It was never my design to help men to deliver a message which is not their own. It is ill when prophets steal their prophecies from one another, for then they are likely—all of them—to become false prophets. But as the young prophet borrowed an axe of a friend, and was not censured for it so long as the strokes he gave with it were his own, so may we refrain from condemning those who find a theme suggested to them, and a line of thought laid before them, and with all their hearts use them in speaking to the people. This should not be their custom : every man should have an axe of his own, and have no need to cry, " Alas, master! it was borrowed "; but there are times of special pressure, bodily sickness, or mental weariness, wherein a man is glad of brotherly help, and may use it without question. For such occasions I have tried to provide.

I am more than ever impressed with the conviction that men must not only preach that which they have themselves thought over, and prepared, but also that which they have themselves experienced, in its life and power. The seed of our teaching must be taken alone from

Holy Scripture, but we must also plant it in the soil of our own spiritual life, and present our people with the plants which come from it. Doctrines are well taught when our inner life confirms them, and promises are fitly discoursed upon when we can testify that we have tried and proved them. As precepts can never be powerfully enforced unless they are carefully practised by the preacher, so high ideals of spiritual life are likely to remain mere dreams, unless the person who proposes them has himself realized them. It is never wise to stretch your arm beyond your sleeve : we must teach that which we know, and no more. Experience gives assurance and authority, and such preaching is, through the Spirit of God, very frequently attended with an unction from the Holy One, such as we do not find in the mere professor who describes what he has never seen, and talks of matter with which he has no acquaintance. The best education for the Christian ministry is a deep experience of divine truth in the heart and life. Truth without the experience of it is without dew; and very little refreshment arises from it to those to whom it comes. Truth, which we have made our own by experience, will be to our hearers like food prepared for their use, roasted in the fire, or baked in the oven : apart from this it will be raw and hard, and the hearer will not be able to digest it, and will lose the nutriment which it is intended to convey.

Oh, that I may help some of my brethren so to preach as to win souls for Jesus ! Warm, personal testimony is greatly useful in this direction ; and, therefore, I trust that, by adding his own hearty witness to the truths which I have here outlined, many a believer may speak successfully for the Lord. I commend my humble labours to him whom I desire to serve by them. Without the Holy Spirit there is nothing here but a valley of dry bones ; but if the breath shall come from the four winds, every line will become instinct with life.

Your brother in Christ Jesus,

C. H. Spurgeon

CONTENTS.

CCXXX. Col. iii. 11.—CHRIST IS ALL 300

CCXXXI. 1 Thess. ii. 13, 14.—A HAPPY MINISTER'S MEETING 303

CCXXXII. 2 Thess. iii. 13.—WEARINESS IN WELL-DOING... 306

CCXXXIII. 1 Tim. i. 15.—THE FAITHFUL SAYING... ... 309

CCXXXIV. 1 Tim. i. 16.—PAUL'S CONVERSION A PATTERN 312

CCXXXV. 2 Tim. i. 12.—OUR GOSPEL 315

CCXXXVI. 2 Tim. i. 18.—MERCY IN THE DAY OF JUDGMENT 318

CCXXXVII. 2 Tim. ii. 9.—THE WORD OF GOD UNBOUND... 321

CCXXXVIII. Titus ii. 10.—GOSPEL JEWELLERY 324

CCXXXIX. Heb. iv. 12.—THE SWORD OF THE LORD ... 327

CCXL. Heb. iv. 16.—BOLDNESS AT THE THRONE ... 330

CCXLI. Heb. v. 2.—COMPASSION ON THE IGNORANT ... 333

CCXLII. Heb. v. 8.—THE EDUCATION OF SONS OF GOD 336

CCXLIII. Heb. x. 9.—THE FIRST AND THE SECOND ... 339

CCXLIV. Heb. xii. 13.—LAME SHEEP 342

CCXLV. Heb. xii. 25.—HEAR! HEAR! 345

CCXLVI. Heb. xiii. 5.—NEVER, NO NEVER, NO NEVER... 348

CCXLVII. James i. 12.—THE TRIED MAN THE BLESSED MAN 351

CCXLVIII. James iv. 6.—MORE AND MORE 354

CCXLIX. 1 Peter i. 9.—SALVATION AS IT IS NOW RECEIVED 357

CCL. 1 Peter iv. 18.—IF SO—WHAT THEN?... ... 359

CCLI. 1 Peter v. 1.—A WITNESS AND A PARTAKER ... 362

CCLII. 2 Peter ii. 9.—THE LORD'S KNOWLEDGE OUR SAFEGUARD 364

CCLIII. 1 John iii. 2.—BY-AND-BY 366

CCLIV. 1 John iii. 3.—PURIFICATION BY HOPE ... 369

CCLV. 1 John iii. 14.—LIFE PROVED BY LOVE ... 372

CCLVI. 1 John iii. 20, 21.—THE LOWER COURTS ... 375

CCLVII. 1 John v. 4.—VICTORIOUS FAITH 378

CCLVIII. 3 John 2.—SOUL-HEALTH 381

CCLIX. Jude 24, 25.—JUDE'S DOXOLOGY 384

CCLX. Rev. i. 7.—THE COMING WITH CLOUDS ... 386

CCLXI. Rev. xi. 19.—THE ARK OF HIS COVENANT ... 389

CCLXII. Rev. xvi. 8, 9.—THE REPENTANCE WHICH GLORIFIES GOD 392

CCLXIII. Rev. xix. 9.—THE MARRIAGE SUPPER OF THE LAMB 395

CCLXIV. Rev. xix. 9.—THE SCRIPTURES DIVINELY TRUE 398

CXCVI

Romans ii. 4 —"Or despisest thou the riches of his goodness and forbearance and longsuffering; not knowing that the goodness of God leadeth thee to repentance?"

It is an instance of divine condescension that the Lord reasons with men, and asks this question, and others like it. Is. i. 5, lv. 2 ; Jer. iii. 4 ; Ezek. xxxiii. 11.

God not only acts kindly to sinners, but when they misuse his kindness he labours to set them right. Is. i. 18 ; Hosea xi. 8.

It is a sad thing that any who have seen God's judgments on others, and have escaped themselves, should draw from this special mercy a reason for adding sin to sin. Jer. iii. 8.

From the Lord's earnest question let us learn wisdom.

I. LET US HONOUR THE LORD'S GOODNESS AND FORBEARANCE.
A reverent sense of it will be a sure safeguard against despising it.

   1. It is manifested to us in a threefold form—
      Goodness which has borne with past sin. Ps. lxxviii. 38.
      Forbearance which bears with us in the present. Ps. ciii. 10.
      Longsuffering which, in the future as in the past and the present, is prepared to bear with the guilty. Luke xiii. 7-9.

   2. It is manifested in great abundance : "riches of his goodness."
      Riches of mercies bestowed, temporal and spiritual. Ps. lxviii. 19.
      Riches of kindness seen in gracious deliverance, measured by evils averted which might have befallen us, such as sickness, poverty, insanity, death, and hell. Ps. lxxxvi. 13.
      Riches of grace promised and provided for all needs.

   3. It is manifested in its excellence by four considerations—
      The person who shows it. It is "the goodness *of God*" who is omniscient to see sin, just to hate it, powerful to punish it, yet patient towards the sinner. Ps. cxlv. 8.

The being who receives it. It is dealt out to man, a guilty, insignificant, base, provoking, ungrateful being. Gen. vi. 6.

The conduct to which it is a reply. It is love's response to sin. Often God forbears, though sins are many, wanton, aggravated, daring, repeated, etc. Mal. iii. 6.

The boons which it brings. Life, daily bread, health, gospel, Holy Spirit, new birth, hope of heaven, etc. Ps. lxviii. 19.

4. It has been in a measure manifested to you. " Despisest *thou* ? "

II. LET US CONSIDER HOW IT MAY BE DESPISED.

1. By allowing it to remain unnoticed : ungratefully passing it over.

2. By claiming it as our due, and talking as if God were bound to bear with us.

3. By opposing its design, and refusing to repent. Prov. i. 24, 25.

4. By perverting it into a reason for hardness of heart, presumption, infidelity, and further sin. Zeph. i. 12 ; Eccl. viii. 11.

5. By urging it as an apology for procrastination. 2 Pet. iii. 3, 4.

III. LET US FEEL THE FORCE OF ITS LEADINGS.

The forbearance of God should lead us to repentance.

For we should argue thus :—

1. He is not hard and unloving, or he would not have spared us.

2. His great patience deserves recognition at our hands. We are bound to respond to it in a generous spirit.

3. To go on to offend would be cruel to him, and disgraceful to ourselves. Nothing can be baser than to make forbearance a reason for provocation.

4. It is evident from his forbearance that he will rejoice to accept us if we will turn to him. He spares that he may save.

5. He has dealt with each one personally, and by this means he is able to put it, as in the text, " God leadeth *thee* to repentance." He calls us individually to himself. Let each one personally remember his own experience of sparing mercies.

6. The means are so gentle, let us yield to them cheerfully. Those who might refuse to be driven should consent to be drawn.

O sinner, each gift of *goodness* draws thee to Jesus !
Forbearance would fain weep thee to Jesus !
Longsuffering waits and woos thee to Jesus !
Wilt thou not turn from sin and return unto thy God, or "despisest thou the riches of his goodness ? "

ARGUMENTS

Here is a select variety of admirable words, where the critics tell us that the first word signifies the infinite goodness and generosity of the Divine nature, whereby he is inclined to do good to his creatures, to pity and relieve. The second expresses his offers of mercy upon repentance, and the notices and warnings sinners have to amend. The third is his bearing the manners of bold sinners, waiting long for their reformation, and from year to year deferring to give the final stroke of vengeance. In what an apt opposition do *riches* of Divine *goodness,* and *treasures* of *wrath* to come, stand to one another !—*Anthony Blackwall.*

The forbearance and longsuffering of God towards sinners is truly astonishing. He was longer destroying Jericho than in creating the world.—*Benjamin Beddome.*

According to the proverb of the Jews, " Michael flies but with one wing, and Gabriel with two"; God is quick in sending angels of peace, and they fly apace; but the messengers of wrath come slowly : God is more hasty to glorify his servants than to condemn the wicked.—
Jeremy Taylor.

It is observable that the Roman magistrates, when they gave sentence upon any one to be scourged, a bundle of rods tied hard with many knots was laid before them. The reason was this : that whilst the beadle, or flagellifer, was untying the knots, which he was to do in a certain order, and not in any other hasty or sudden way, the magistrate might see the deportment and carriage of the delinquent, whether he were sorry for his fault, and showed any hope of amendment, that then he might recall his sentence, or mitigate the punishment; otherwise he was to be corrected the more severely. Thus God in the punishment of sinners, how patient is he ! how loath to strike ! how slow to anger if there be but any hopes of recovery ! How many knots doth he untie ! How many rubs doth he make in his way to justice ! He doth not try us by martial law, but pleads the case with us, " Why will ye die, O house of Israel?" And all this to see whether the poor sinner will throw himself down at his feet, whether he will come in and make his peace, and be saved.— *Thomas Fuller.*

To sin against law is daring, but to sin against love is dastardly. To rebel against justice is inexcusable, but to fight against mercy is abominable. He who can sting the hand which nourishes him is nothing less than a viper. When a dog bites his own master, and bites him when he is feeding him and fondling him, no one will wonder if his owner becomes his executioner.

203

CXCVII

Romans iv. 24 —"Jesus our Lord."

It is the part of faith to accept great contrasts, if laid down in the Word, and to make them a part of her daily speech.

This name, Lord, is a great contrast to incarnation and humiliation.

In the manger, in poverty, shame, and death, Jesus was still Lord.

These strange conditions for "our Lord" to be found in are no difficulties to that faith which is the fruit of the Spirit.

For she sees in the death of Jesus a choice reason for his being our Lord. Phil. ii. 7–11. "Wherefore God hath highly exalted him."

She delights in that Lordship as the fruit of resurrection; but there could have been no resurrection without death. Acts ii. 32–36.

She hears the voice of Jehovah behind all the opposition endured by Jesus proclaiming him Lord of all. Pss. ii.; cx.

It never happens that our faith in Jesus for salvation makes us less reverently behold in him the Lord of all. He is "Jesus" and also "our Lord." "Born a child, and yet a King." "My Beloved," and yet "My Lord and my God."

Our simple trust in him, our familiar love to him, our bold approaches to him in prayer, our near and dear communion with him, and, most of all, our marriage union with him, still leave him "our Lord."

I. HIS TENDER CONDESCENSIONS ENDEAR THE TITLE. "Jesus our Lord" is a very sweet name to a believer's heart.

  1. We claim to render it to him specially as man, "who was delivered for our offences, and was raised again for our justification": verse 25. As Jesus of Nazareth he is Lord.

  2. We acknowledge him as Lord the more fully and unreservedly, because he loved us, and gave himself for us.

  3. In all the privileges accorded to us in him he is Lord :—

In our salvation, we have "received Christ Jesus the Lord" Col. ii. 6.

In entering the church we find him the head of the body, to whom all are subject. Eph. v. 23.

In our life-work he is Lord. "We live unto the Lord": Rom. xiv. 8. We glorify God in his name. Eph. v. 20.

In resurrection he is the firstborn from the dead. Col. i. 18.

At the Advent his appearing will be the chief glory. Titus ii. 13.

In eternal glory he is worshipped for ever. Rev. v. 12, 13.

4. In our dearest fellowship at the table he is "Jesus our Lord."

It is the Lord's table, the Lord's supper, the cup of the Lord, the body and blood of the Lord ; and our object is to show the Lord's death. 1 Cor. xi. 20, 26, 27, 29.

II. OUR LOVING HEARTS READ THE TITLE WITH PECULIAR EMPHASIS.

1. We yield it to him only. Moses is a servant, but Jesus alone is Lord. "One is your Master": Matt. xxiii. 8, 10.

2. To him most willingly. Ours is delighted homage.

3. To him unreservedly. We wish our obedience to be perfect.

4. To him in all matters of law-making and truth-teaching. He is Master and Lord : his word decides practice and doctrine.

5. To him in all matters of administration in the church, and in providence. "It is the Lord, let him do what seemeth him good": 1 Sam. iii. 18.

6. To him trustfully, feeling that he will act a Lord's part right well. No king can be so wise, good, great as he. Job i. 21.

7. To him for ever. He reigns in the church without successor. Now, as in the first days, we call him Master and Lord. Heb. vii. 3.

III. WE FIND MUCH SWEETNESS IN THE WORD "OUR."

1. It makes us remember our personal interest in the Lord.

Each believer uses this title in the singular, and calls him from his heart, " My Lord."
David wrote, " Jehovah said unto my Lord."
Elizabeth spoke of "The mother of my Lord."
Magdalene said, "They have taken away my Lord."
Thomas said, "My Lord and my God."
Paul wrote, "The knowledge of Christ Jesus my Lord," etc.

2. It brings a host of brethren before our minds ; for it is in union with them that we say "our Lord"; and so it makes us remember each other. Eph. iii. 14, 15.

3. It fosters unity, and creates a holy clanship, as we all rally around our "one Lord." Saints of all ages are one in this.

4. His example as Lord fosters practical love. Remember the foot-washing and his words on that occasion. John xiii. 14.

5. Our zeal to make him Lord forbids all self-exaltation. "Be not ye called Rabbi: for one is your Master, even Christ. Neither be ye called masters," etc.: Matt. xxiii. 8, 10.

6. His position as Lord reminds us of the confidence of the church

in doing his work. "All power is given unto me in heaven and in earth. Go ye, therefore, and teach," etc: Matt. xxviii. 18, 19. "The Lord working with them": Mark xvi. 20.

7. Our common joy in Jesus as our Lord becomes an evidence of grace, and thus of union with each other. 1 Cor. xii. 3.

Let us worship Jesus as our Lord and God.
Let us imitate him, copying our Lord's humility and love.
Let us serve him, obeying his every command.

Gems

It ought to be the great care of every one of us to follow the Lord fully. We must in a course of obedience to God's will, and service to his honour, follow him universally, without dividing; uprightly, without dissembling; cheerfully, without disputing; and constantly, without declining: and this is following him fully.—*Matthew Henry.*

A disciple of Christ is one that gives up himself to be wholly at Christ's disposing; to learn what he teaches, to believe what he reveals, to do what he commands, to avoid what he forbids, to suffer what is inflicted by him or for him, in expectation of that reward which he hath promised. Such a one is a disciple of Christ, and he, and none else, is a Christian.—*David Clarkson.*

It was thought a wondrous act of condescension when King George III. visited the tent of the dying gipsy woman in Windsor forest, and entered into religious conversation with her. What shall we think of him, who, though he was the King of glory, came down to us, and took our sins and sorrows upon himself, that he might bring us into fellowship with himself for ever?

A little child hearing others speak of the Lord Jesus asked, "Father, was it *our* Jesus?" In the same sweet simplicity of faith let us speak of "Jesus *our* Lord."

Some years ago, an aged minister, who had long and lovingly known Christ, was on his death-bed. Memory had gone. In relation to those he loved best it was a perfect blank. But some one whispered in his ear, "Brother, do you know Jesus Christ?" With a voice of rapture he exclaimed,

> "Jesus, my Lord! I know his name;
> His name is all my trust;
> Nor will he put my hope to shame,
> Nor let my soul be lost."

CXCVIII

Romans bi. 11, 12 —"**Likewise reckon ye also yourselves to be dead indeed unto sin, but alive unto God through Jesus Christ our Lord.**"

"**Let not sin therefore reign in your mortal body, that ye should obey it in the lusts thereof.**"

How intimately the believer's duties are interwoven with his privileges ! Because he is alive unto God he is to renounce sin, since that corrupt thing belongs to his estate of death.

How intimately both his duties and his privileges are bound up with Christ Jesus his Lord !

How thoughtful ought we to be upon these matters ; *reckoning* what is right and fit ; and carrying out that reckoning to its practical issues.

We have in our text,—

I. A GREAT FACT TO BE RECKONED UPON. "Likewise reckon ye also yourselves to be dead indeed unto sin, but alive unto God through Jesus Christ our Lord."

1. We are dead with Christ to sin by having borne the punishment in him. In Christ we have endured the death penalty, and are regarded as dead by the law (verses 6 and 7).

2. We are risen with him into a justified condition, and have reached a new life (verse 8).

3. We can no more come under sin again than he can (verse 9).

4. We are therefore for ever dead to its guilt and reigning power : "Sin shall not have dominion over you" (verses 12—14).

This reckoning is based on truth, or we should not be exhorted to it.

To reckon yourself to be dead to sin, so that you boast that you do not sin at all, would be a reckoning based on falsehood, and would be exceedingly mischievous. "There is no man that sinneth not." 1 Kings viii. 46 ; 1 John i. 8. None are so provoking to God as sinners who boast their own fancied perfection.

The reckoning that we do not sin must either go upon the Antinomian theory, that sin in the believer is no sin, which is a shocking notion,

Or else our conscience must tell us that we do sin in many ways ; in omission or con mission, in transgression or short-coming, in temper or in spirit. James iii. 2 ; Ecc. vii. 20 ; Rom. iii. 23.

207

To reckon yourself dead to sin in the scriptural sense is full of benefit both to heart and life.   Be a ready reckoner in this fashion.

II. A GREAT LESSON TO BE PUT IN PRACTICE. " Let not sin therefore reign in your mortal body, that ye should obey it in the lusts thereof."

1. Sin has great power ; it is in you, and will strive to reign.

It remains as an outlaw, hiding away in your nature.

It remains as a plotter, planning your overthrow.

It remains as an enemy, warring against the law of your mind.

It remains as a tyrant, worrying and oppressing the true life.

2. Its field of battle is the body.

Its wants, hunger, thirst, cold, &c., may become occasions of sin, by leading to murmuring, envy, covetousness, robbery, etc.

Its appetites may crave excessive indulgence, and unless continually curbed, will easily lead to evil.

Its pains and infirmities, through engendering impatience and other faults, may produce sin.

Its pleasures, also, can readily become incitements to sin.

Its influence upon the mind and spirit may drag our noble nature down to the grovelling materialism of earth.

3. The body is *mortal*, and we shall be completely delivered from sin when set free from our present material frame, if indeed grace reigns within.   Till then we shall find sin lurking in one member or another of "this vile body."

4. Meanwhile we must not let it reign.

If it reigned over us it would be our god.   It would prove us to be under death, and not alive unto God.

It would cause us unbounded pain and injury if it ruled only for a moment.

Sin is within us, aiming at dominion ; and this knowledge, together with the fact that we are nevertheless alive unto God, should—

Help our peace; for we perceive that men may be truly the Lord's, even though sin struggles within them.

Aid our caution ; for our divine life is well worth preserving, and needs to be guarded with constant care.

Draw us to use the means of grace, since in these the Lord meets with us and refreshes our new life.

Let us come to the table of communion and to all other ordinances, as alive unto God ; and in that manner let us feed on Christ.

In the fourth century, when the Christian faith was preached in its power in Egypt, a young brother sought out the great Macarius. "Father," said he, "what is the meaning of being dead and buried with Christ?"

"My son," answered Macarius, "you remember our dear brother who died, and was buried a short time since? Go now to his grave, and tell him all the unkind things that you ever heard of him, and that we are glad he is dead, and thankful to be rid of him, for he was such a worry to us, and caused so much discomfort in the church. Go, my son, and say that, and hear what he will answer."

The young man was surprised, and doubted whether he really understood; but Macarius only said, "Do as I bid you, my son, and come and tell me what our departed brother says."

The young man did as he was commanded, and returned.

"Well, and what did our brother say?" asked Macarius.

"Say, father!" he exclaimed; "how could he say anything? He is dead."

"Go now again, my son, and repeat every kind and flattering thing you have ever heard of him; tell him how much we miss him; how great a saint he was; what noble work he did; how the whole church depended upon him; and come again and tell me what he says."

The young man began to see the lesson Macarius would teach him. He went again to the grave, and addressed many flattering things to the dead man, and then returned to Macarius.

"He answers *nothing*, father; he is dead and buried."

"You know now, my son," said the old father, "what it is to be dead with Christ. Praise and blame equally are nothing to him who is really dead and buried with Christ."—*Anon.*

Though the lowest believer be above the power of sin, yet the highest believer is not above the presence of sin. Sin never ruins but where it reigns. It is not *destroying* where it is *disturbing*. The more evil it receives from us, the less evil it does to us.— *William Secker.*

Sin may rebel, but it shall never reign, in a saint. It fareth with sin in the regenerate as with those beasts that Daniel speaks of, " that had their dominion taken away, yet their lives were prolonged for a season and a time."—*Thomas Brooks.*

Men must not suffer a single sin to survive. If Saul had destroyed all the Amalekites, no Amalekite would have lived to destroy him.
David Roland.

CXCIX

𝕽𝔬𝔪. 𝔳𝔦𝔦𝔦. 17 —" 𝕬𝔫𝔡 𝔦𝔣 𝔠𝔥𝔦𝔩𝔡𝔯𝔢𝔫, 𝔱𝔥𝔢𝔫 𝔥𝔢𝔦𝔯𝔰 ; 𝔥𝔢𝔦𝔯𝔰 𝔬𝔣 𝔊𝔬𝔡, 𝔞𝔫𝔡 𝔧𝔬𝔦𝔫𝔱-𝔥𝔢𝔦𝔯𝔰 𝔴𝔦𝔱𝔥 𝕮𝔥𝔯𝔦𝔰𝔱 ; 𝔦𝔣 𝔰𝔬 𝔟𝔢 𝔱𝔥𝔞𝔱 𝔴𝔢 𝔰𝔲𝔣𝔣𝔢𝔯 𝔴𝔦𝔱𝔥 𝔥𝔦𝔪, 𝔱𝔥𝔞𝔱 𝔴𝔢 𝔪𝔞𝔶 𝔟𝔢 𝔞𝔩𝔰𝔬 𝔤𝔩𝔬𝔯𝔦𝔣𝔦𝔢𝔡 𝔱𝔬𝔤𝔢𝔱𝔥𝔢𝔯."

This chapter is like the garden of Eden, which had in it all manner of delights. If one were shut up to preach only from the eighth of Romans he would have a subject which might last a life-time. Every line of the chapter serves for a text. It is an inexhaustible mine. Paul sets before us a golden ladder, and from every step he climbs to something yet higher : from sonship he rises to heirship, and from heirship to joint-heirship with the Lord Jesus.

I. THE GROUND OF HEIRSHIP. "If children, then heirs."

1. It does not follow from ordinary creation. It is not written—if creatures, then heirs.

2. Neither is it found in natural descent. It is not written—if children of Abraham, then heirs. Rom. ix. 7—13.

3. Nor can it come by meritorious service. It is not written—if servants, then heirs. Gal. iv. 30.

4. Nor by ceremonial observances. It is not written—if circumcised or baptized, then heirs. Rom. iv. 9—12.

Our being regenerated or born again unto God by his Holy Spirit is our one ground of heirship.

Let us enquire—

Have we been born again ? John iii. 3.

Have we the spirit of adoption ? Gal. iv. 6.

Are we fashioned in the likeness of God ? Col. iii. 10.

Have we believed on Jesus ? John i. 12.

II. THE UNIVERSALITY OF THE HEIRSHIP. "Children, then heirs."

1. The principle of priority as to time cannot enter into this question. The elder and the younger in the divine family are equally heirs.

2. The love of God is the same to them all.

3. They are all blessed under the same promise. Heb. vi. 17.

4. They are all equally related to that great First-born Son through whom their heirship comes to them. He is the first-born among many brethren.

5. The inheritance is large enough for them all.

They are not all prophets, preachers, apostles, or even well-instructed and eminent saints; they are not all rich and influential ; they are not all strong and useful ; but they are all heirs.

Let us, then, all live as such, and rejoice in our portion.

III. The inheritance which is the subject of heirship. " Heirs of God."

Our inheritance is divinely great. We are—

Heirs of all things. " He that overcometh shall inherit all things:" Rev. xxi. 7. "All things are yours :" 2 Cor. iii. 21.

Heirs of salvation. Heb. i. 14.

Heirs of eternal life. Tit. iii. 7.

Heirs of promise. Heb. vi. 17.

Heirs of the grace of life. 1 Pet. iii. 7.

Heirs of righteousness. Heb. xi. 7.

Heirs of the kingdom. James ii. 5.

Whereas we are said to be " heirs of God," it must mean that we are—

1. Heirs of all that God possesses.

2. Heirs of all that God is. Of his love; for God is love. Hence heirs of all possible good ; for God is good.

3. Heirs of God himself. What an infinite portion !

4. Heirs of all that Jesus has and is, as God and man.

IV. The partnership of the claimants to heirship. " And joint-heirs with Christ."

1. This is the test of our heirship. We are not heirs except with Christ, through Christ, and in Christ.

2. This sweetens it all. Fellowship with Jesus is our best portion.

3. This shows the greatness of the inheritance. Worthy of Jesus. Such an inheritance as the Father gives to the Well-beloved.

4. This ensures it to us ; for Jesus will not lose it, and his title-deed and ours are one and indivisible.

5. This reveals and endears his love. That he should become a partner with us in all things is love unbounded.

His taking us into union with himself secures our inheritance.

His prayer for us attains it.

His going into heaven before us prepares it.

His coming again will bring us the full enjoyment of it.

6. This joint heirship binds us faster to Jesus, since we are nothing, and have nothing apart from him.

Let us joyfully accept the present suffering with Christ, for it is part of the heritage.

Let us believe in the glorification which is sure to follow in due time, and let us anticipate it with immediate rejoicing.

How God treats men. " He pardons them and receives them into his house, he makes them all children, and all his children are his heirs, and all his heirs are princes, and all his princes are *crowned."—John Pulsford.*

As a dead man cannot inherit an estate, no more can a dead soul inherit the kingdom of God.—*Salter.*

It is not easy to imagine a more cautious, lawyer-like record than the following entry in a MS. book written by the celebrated Lord Eldon : " I was born, *I believe,* on the 4th June, 1751." We may suppose that this hesitating statement refers to the date, and not to the fact, of his birth. Many, however, are just as uncertain about their spiritual birth. It is a grand thing to be able to say, " We know that we have passed from death unto life," even though we may not be able to put a date to it.

As justification is union and communion with Christ in his righteousness ; and sanctification is union and communion with Christ in his holiness, or his holy character and nature ; so, by parity of reasoning, adoption must be held to be union and communion with Christ in his Sonship ; surely the highest and best union and communion of the three.—*Dr. Candlish.*

Inheritance.—What is it ? The pay of a soldier is not inheritance ; neither are the fees of a lawyer, nor of a physician ; nor the gains of trade ; nor the wages of labour. The rewards of toil or skill, these are earned by the hands that receive them. What is inherited, on the other hand, may be the property of a new-born babe ; and so the coronet, won long ago by the stout arm of valour, and first blazoned on a battered shield, now stands above the cradle of a wailing infant.—*Dr. Guthrie.*

The question lies in that first word "*if.*" Can you cast out all uncertainty from that matter by proving your sonship ? " *Then*"—ah ! then, no doubt remains as to your heirship. No man need question that heaven will be his if he is the Lord's. The inheritance is—to be glorified together with Christ. What more could a child desire than to inherit as much as his eldest brother ? If we are as favoured as Jesus, what more can we be?

CC

Romans x. 16 —"But they have not all obeyed the gospel. For Esaias saith, Lord, who hath believed our report?"

Man is the same disobedient creature under all dispensations. We bemoan his rejection of the gospel, and so did Isaiah, who spoke in the name of the whole company of the prophets.

It is one of the greatest proofs of the depravity of man's heart that he will no more obey the gospel than the law, but disobeys his God, whether he speaks to him in love or in law.

Men will sooner be lost than trust their God.

When any receive the gospel it is a work of grace—"the arm of the Lord is revealed"; but when they refuse it, it is their own sin—"they have not obeyed the gospel."

I. THE GOSPEL COMES TO MEN WITH THE FORCE OF A COMMAND.

It is not optional to men to accept or refuse it at pleasure. "God now commandeth all men every where to repent": Acts xvii. 30. He also commands them to repent and believe the gospel. Mark i. 15.

To refuse to believe is to incur great sin. John xvi. 8.

There is a death penalty attached to disobedience. Mark xvi. 16.

It is so put—

1. To secure the honour of God. It is not the offer of an equal to an equal, but of the great God to a condemned sinner.

2. To embolden the proclaimer of it. The minister now speaks boldly with his Master's authority.

3. To remind man of his obligations. Repentance and faith are natural duties from which the gospel does not exonerate a man, although it blesses him by bestowing them upon him.

4. To encourage the humble seeker. He must be at full liberty to believe in Jesus, since he is commanded to do so, and threatened if he does not do so.

5. To suggest to men the urgent duty of seeing to their soul's welfare. Suicide, whether of the body or of the soul, is always a great crime. To neglect the great salvation is a grave offence.

The gospel is set forth as a feast, to which men are bound to come, under penalty of the King's displeasure. Matt. xxii. 1—7.

The prodigal was right in returning to his father; and if he was right in doing so, so would each one of us be in doing the same.

213

II. What, then, are the claims of the gospel to obedience?

1. The authority of the sender. Whatever God commands, man is under bonds to do.
2. The motive of the sender. Love shines in the gospel command, and no man should slight infinite love. To refuse to obey the gospel of salvation is an insult to divine love.
3. The great gift of the sender: he has given us his only begotten Son. To refuse Jesus is a high affront to measureless love.
4. The reasonableness of the demand of the sender. Should not men believe their God, and trust their Saviour?
5. The earnestness of the sender. His whole heart is in the gospel. Note the high position which the scheme of salvation occupies in the esteem of God. Shall we not obey an appeal put before us with such energy of compassion?

Ask your own consciences whether you do right to refuse or neglect the gospel of the grace of God.

Ask those who are now saved what they think of their long unbelief.

Do not incur a world of regrets in after years by long delays.

Do not jeopardize your souls by refusing the gospel.

III. What is the obedience required by the gospel?

Not mere hearing, crediting, liking, professing, or proclaiming; but a hearty obedience to its command. It claims,

1. Faith in the Lord Jesus Christ.
2. Renunciation of self-righteousness, and confession of guilt.
3. Repentance and practical quittance of sin.
4. Discipleship under the Lord Jesus; and this means obedience both to his teaching and his example.
5. Public confession of his name, in his own way, namely, by baptism.

If you refuse to obey the gospel—

Your hearts will harden to a deeper unbelief.

Others will obtain the blessing which you refuse; and this will deepen your own condemnation. Rom. x. 19.

You will die in your sins, with your blood on your own heads.

Enforcements

A powerful argument to prove the enmity of man's heart against God is the unsuccessfulness of the gospel; which can be resolvable into nothing else but such an enmity. The design of the gospel is to bring us into a union with the Son of God, and to believe on him whom the Father hath sent. Christ seeks to gather in souls to God, but they will not be gathered. This is matter of fearful consideration, that when God is calling after men by his own Son, there be so few that will come to him. How few there are that say, "Give me Christ, or I am lost! None can reconcile me to God, but Christ"! You are daily besought, in Christ's stead, to be reconciled, but in vain! What does this signify, but obstinate, invincible enmity.?—*John Howe.*

"All God's biddings are enablings," says an old writer.

Obedience is faith incarnate.

To disobey the gospel is far worse than to break the law. For disobedience to the law there is a remedy in the gospel, but for disobedience to the gospel no remedy can be found. "There remaineth no more sacrifice for sins."

It is reported of the old kings of Peru, that they were wont to use a tassel, or fringe, made of red wool, which they wore upon their heads, and when they sent any governor to rule as viceroy in any part of their country, they delivered unto him one of the threads of their tassel, and, for one of those simple threads, he was as much obeyed as if he had been the king himself—yea, it hath so happened that the king hath sent a governor only with this thread to slay men and women of a whole province, without any further commission ; for of such power and authority was the king's tassel with them, that they willingly submitted thereunto, even at the sight of one thread of it. Now, it is to be hoped that, if one thread shall be so forcible to draw heathen obedience, there will be no need of cart-ropes to haul on that which is Christian. Exemplary was that obedience of the Romans which was said to have come abroad to all men. And certainly gospel obedience is a grace of much worth, and of great force upon the whole man ; for when it is once wrought in the heart, it worketh a conformity to all God's will. Be it for life or death, one word from God will command the whole soul as soon as obedience hath found admittance into the heart.—*Spencer*; *Things New and Old.*

Romans xii. 15 —" Rejoice with them that do rejoice."

It is supposed that some are rejoicing, and this is a happy supposition : you are invited to sympathize with them, and this is a happy
duty.

Sympathy is a duty of our common humanity, but far more of our
regenerated manhood. Those who are one in the higher life should
show their holy unity by true fellow-feeling.

Joyful sympathy is doubly due when the joy is spiritual and eternal.

I invite you to this joy because of those who have lately been
brought to Jesus, and are now to be added to the church. The occasion
is joyous ; let the joy spread all around.

I. Rejoice with the converts.

1. Some delivered from lives of grievous sin. All saved from that
which would have ruined them eternally, but certain of them
from faults which injure men in society.

2. Some of them rescued from agonizing fear and deep despair.
Could you have seen them under conviction you would indeed
rejoice to behold them free and happy.

3. Some of them have been brought into great peace and joy. The
blissful experience of their first love should charm us into
sympathetic delight.

4. Some of them are aged. These are called at the eleventh hour.
Rejoice that they are saved from imminent peril.

5. Some of them are young, with years of happy service before them.

6. Each case is special. In some we think of what they would have
been, and in others of what they will be.

There is great gladness in these new-born ones, and shall we be
indifferent ? Let us welcome them with hearty joy.

II. Rejoice with their friends.

1. Some have prayed long for them, and now their prayers are heard.

2. Some have been very anxious, have seen much to mourn over in
the past, and feared much of evil in the future.

3. Some are relatives with a peculiar interest in these saved ones,
Parents, children, brothers, etc.

4. Some are expecting, and in certain cases already receiving, much
comfort from these newly-saved ones. They have already
brightened the family circle, and made heavy hearts glad.

Holy parents have no greater joy than to see their children walking in the truth. Do we not share their joy?

III. Rejoice with those who brought them to Jesus.

The spiritual parents of these converts are glad.

The Pastor, Evangelist, Missionary, Author.

The Parent, elder sister, or other loving relation.

The Teacher in the Sabbath School or Bible Class.

The Friend who wrote or spoke to them of Jesus.

What a joy belongs to those who by personal effort win souls! Endeavour to win the same joy for yourself, and meanwhile be glad that others have it.

IV. Rejoice with the Holy Spirit.

1. He sees his strivings successful.
2. He sees his instructions accepted.
3. He sees his quickening power operating in new life.
4. He sees the renewed mind yielding to his divine guidance.
5. He sees the heart comforted by his grace.

Let us rejoice in the love of the Spirit.

V. Rejoice with the angels.

They have noted the repentance of the returning sinner.

They will henceforth joyfully guard the footsteps of the pilgrim.

They expect his life-long perseverance, or their joy would be premature. He is and will be for ever their fellow-servant.

They look one day to bear him home to glory.

The evil angel makes us groan; should not the joy of good angels make us sing in harmony with their delight?

VI. Rejoice with the Lord Jesus.

1. His joy is proportioned to the ruin from which he has saved his redeemed ones.
2. His joy is proportioned to the cost of their redemption.
3. His joy is proportioned to the love which he bears to them.
4. His joy is proportioned to their future happiness, and to the glory which their salvation will bring to him.

Do you find it hard to rejoice with these newly baptized believers? Let me urge you to do so, for —

You have your own sorrows, and this communion of joy will prevent brooding too much over them.

217

You will renew the love of your espousals by communion with these young ones.

It will comfort you for your own erring ones if you rejoice with the *friends* of converts.

It will forbid envy if you rejoice with *workers* who are successful.

It will elevate your spirit if you endeavour to rejoice with the Holy Spirit and the angels.

It will fit you to partake in a like success if you rejoice with Jesus, the Sinner's Friend.

SYMPATHETICS.

About three hundred years after the time of the Apostles, Caius Marius Victorius, an old pagan, was converted from his impiety and brought over to the Christian faith ; and when the people of God heard this, there was a wonderful rejoicing, and shouting, and leaping for gladness, and psalms were sung in every church, while the people joyously said one to another, "Caius Marius Victorius is become a Christian ! Caius Marius Victorius is become a Christian !"

Mr. Haslam, telling the story of his conversion, says : "I do not remember all I said, but I felt a wonderful light and joy coming into my soul. Whether it was something in my words, or my manner, or my look, I know not ; but all of a sudden a local preacher, who happened to be in the congregation, stood up, and putting up his arms, shouted out in Cornish manner, 'The parson is converted! the parson is converted! Hallelujah !' And in another moment his voice was lost in the shouts and praises of three or four hundred of the congregation. Instead of rebuking this extraordinary 'brawling,' as I should have done in a former time, I joined in the outburst of praise ; and to make it more orderly, I gave out the Doxology—'Praise God from whom all blessings flow'—which the people sung with heart and voice, over and over again."

An ungodly youth accompanied his parents to hear a certain minister. The subject of the discourse was the heavenly state. On returning home, the young man expressed his admiration of the preacher's talents ; "But," said he, turning to his mother, "I was surprised that you and my father were in tears." "Ah, my son !" replied the anxious mother, "I did weep, not because I feared my own personal interest in the subject, or that of your father ; but I wept for fear that you, my beloved child, would be for ever banished from the blessedness of heaven." "I supposed," said the father, turning to his wife, "that those were your reflections, the same concern for our dear son made me weep also." These tender remarks found their way to the young man's heart, and led him to repentance.—*Arvine.*

CCII

Romans xb. 4.—"For whatsoever things were written aforetime were written for our learning, that we through patience and comfort of the scriptures might have hope."

This is the text from which old Hugh Latimer was wont to preach continually in his latter days. Certainly it gave him plenty of sea room.

The apostle declares that the Old Testament Scriptures are meant to teach New Testament believers.

Things written aforetime were written for our time.

The Old Testament is not outworn ; apostles learned from it.

Nor has its authority ceased ; it still teaches with certainty.

Nor has its divine power departed; for it works the graces of the Spirit in those who receive it: patience, comfort, hope.

In this verse the Holy Ghost sets his seal upon the Old Testament, and for ever enters his protest against all undervaluing of that sacred volume.

The Holy Scriptures produce and ripen the noblest graces.

Let us carefully consider—

I. THE PATIENCE OF THE SCRIPTURES.

1. Such as they inculcate.

   Patience under every appointment of the divine will.
   Patience under human persecution and satanic opposition.
   Patience under brotherly burdens. Gal. vi. 2.
   Patience in waiting for divine promises to be fulfilled.

2. Such as they exhibit in examples.

   Job under divers afflictions triumphantly patient.
   Abraham, Isaac and Jacob patiently waiting as sojourners with God, embracing the covenant promise in a strange land.
   Joseph patiently forgiving the unkindness of his brethren, and bearing the false accusation of his master.
   David in many trials and under many reproaches, patiently waiting for the crown, and refusing to injure his persecutor.
   Our Saviour patient under all the many forms of trial.

3. Such as they produce by their influence.

   By calling us to the holiness which involves trial.
   By revealing the design of God in our tribulations, and so sustaining the soul in steadfast resolve.
   By declaring to us promises as to the future which make us cheerfully endure present griefs.

II. The comfort of the scriptures.

   1. Such as they inculcate.

      They bid us rise above fear. Ps. xlvi. 1—3.

      They urge us to think little of all transient things.

      They command us to find our joy in God.

      They stimulate us to rejoice under tribulations, because they make us like the prophets of old.

   2. Such as they exhibit.

      Enoch walking with God.

      Abraham finding God his shield and exceeding great reward.

      David strengthening himself in God.

      Hezekiah spreading his letter before the Lord.

Many other cases are recorded, and these stimulate our courage.

   3. Such as they produce.

      The Holy Spirit as the Comforter uses them to that end.

      Their own character adapts them to that end.

      They comfort us by their gentleness, certainty, fulness, graciousness, adaptation, personality, etc.

      Our joyous experience is the best testimony to the consoling power of the Holy Scriptures.

III. The hope of the scriptures.

      Scripture is intended to work in us a good hope.

      A people with a hope will purify themselves, and will in many other ways rise to a high and noble character.

By the hope of the Scriptures we understand—

   1. Such a hope as they hold forth.

      The hope of salvation. 1 Thess. v. 8.

      "The blessed hope, and the appearing of our Lord": Titus ii. 13.

      The hope of the resurrection of the dead. Acts xxiii. 6.

      The hope of glory. Col. i. 27.

This is a good hope, a lively hope, the hope set before us in the gospel.

   2. Such a hope as they exhibit in the lives of saints. A whole martyrology will be found in Heb. xi.

   3. Such a hope as they produce.

      We see what God has done for his people, and therefore hope.

      We believe the promises through the Word, and therefore hope.

      We enjoy present blessing, and therefore hope.

Let us hold constant fellowship with the God of patience and consolation, who is also the God of hope; and let us rise from stage to stage of joy as the order of the words suggests.

How much important matter do we find condensed in this single verse! What a light and glory does it throw on the Word of God! It has been well noted, that we have here *its authority*, as it is a written word; *its antiquity*, as it was written aforetime; *its utility*, as it is written for our learning. We may also infer from what immediately follows, *its Divine origin;* for, if by means of the Holy Scriptures, and the accompanying lively power of the Holy Spirit (Isaiah lix. 21), God imparts to our soul patience, and comfort, and hope, it is because he is himself, as the apostle here expressly teaches, *the God of patience and comfort,* and *the God of hope* (verse 13). He is the fountain of these gifts and graces, which by the channel of his inspired Word flow down into our hearts and lives, to strengthen them for his service. Nor must we fail to notice the gracious method of their communication, their regular development within us, as we find this to be the order of their course— 1, *patience;* 2, *comfort;* 3, *hope.* From a calm sense of inward peace and comfort we are led by the same Spirit to feel a blessed, and, it may be, a joyous hope. But, in order to this, there must always be in us the ground-work of *patience,* in our suffering or doing the will of God.

James Ford.

Oliver Cromwell once read aloud Phil. iv. 11—13, and then remarked, "There, in the day when my poor child died, this Scripture did go nigh to save my life."

When George Peabody was staying at Sir Charles Reed's house, he saw the youngest child bringing to his father a large Bible for family prayers. Mr. Peabody said, "Ah! my boy, you carry the Bible now; but the time is coming when you will find that *the Bible must carry you.*"

"Speak to me now in Scripture language alone," said a dying Christian. "I can trust the words of God; but when they are the words of man, it costs me an effort to think whether I may trust them."—*G. S. Bowes.*

As an instance of the patience, comfort and hope, which come from the gospel, note the following from *Dr. Payson:*—Christians might avoid much trouble if they would believe that God is able to make them happy without anything else. God has been depriving me of one blessing after another; but as every one was removed, he has come in and filled up its place; and now, when I am a cripple, and not able to move, I am happier than ever I was in my life before, or ever expected to be. If I had believed this twenty years ago, I might have been spared much anxiety.

CCIII

1 **Cor. vi. 19, 20** —"And ye are not your own, for ye are bought with a price: therefore glorify God in your body, and in your spirit, which are God's."

With what ardour does the apostle pursue sin to destroy it !

He is not so prudish as to let sin alone, but cries out, in plainest language, " Flee fornication." The shame is not in the rebuke, but in the sin which calls for it.

He chases this foul wickedness with arguments. See verse 18.

He drags it into the light of the Spirit of God. " What ? Know ye not that your body is the temple of the Holy Ghost ? " Verse 19.

He slays it at the cross. " Ye are bought with a price."

Let us consider this last argument, that we may find therein death for our sins.

I. A BLESSED FACT. " Ye are bought with a price."

" Ye are bought." This is that idea of Redemption which modern heretics dare to style *mercantile*. The mercantile redemption is the Scriptural one ; for the expression, " bought with a price," is a double declaration of that idea.

Redemption is a greater source of obligation than creation or preservation. Hence it is a well-spring of holiness.

"With a price." This indicates the greatness of the cost. The Father gave the Son. The Son gave himself ; his happiness, his glory, his repose, his body, his soul, his life.

Measure the price by the bloody sweat, the desertion, the betrayal, the scourging, the cross, the heart-break.

Our body and spirit are both bought with the body and spirit of Jesus.

1. This is either a fact or not. " Ye are bought," or ye are un- redeemed. Terrible alternative.

2. If a fact, it is *the* fact of your life. A wonder of wonders.

3. It will remain to you eternally the grandest of all facts. If true at all, it will never cease to be true, and it will never be outdone in importance by any other event.

4. It should therefore operate powerfully upon us both now and ever.

II. A PLAIN CONSEQUENCE. " Ye are not your own."

NEGATIVE. It is clear that if bought, ye are *not* your own.

1. This involves privilege.

You are not your own provider : sheep are fed by their shepherd.
You are not your own guide : ships are steered by their pilot.
You are not your own father : children loved by parents.

2. This also involves responsibility.

We are not our own to injure. Neither body nor soul.

Not our own to waste, in idleness, amusement, or speculation.

Not our own to exercise caprice, and follow our own prejudices, depraved affections, wayward wills, or irregular appetites.

Not our own to lend our service to another master.

Not our own to serve self. Self is a dethroned tyrant. Jesus is a blessed husband, and we are his.

POSITIVE. "Your body and your spirit, which are God's."

We are altogether God's. Body and spirit include the whole man.

We are always God's. The price once paid, we are for ever his.

We rejoice that we know we are God's, for thus

We have a beloved owner.

We pursue an honoured service.

We fill a blessed position. We are in Christ's keeping.

III. A PRACTICAL CONCLUSION. "Glorify God in your body, and in your spirit, which are God's."

Glorify God *in your body*

By cleanliness, chastity, temperance, industry, cheerfulness, self-denial, patience, etc.

Glorify God—

In a suffering body by patience unto death.

In a working body by holy diligence.

In a worshipping body by bowing in prayer.

In a well-governed body by self-denial.

In an obedient body by doing the Lord's will with delight.

Glorify God *in your spirit*

By holiness, faith, zeal, love, heavenliness, cheerfulness, fervour, humility, expectancy, etc.

Remember, O redeemed one, that—

1. You will be closely watched by Christ's enemies.

2. You will be expected to be more gracious than others ; and rightly so, since you claim to be Christ's own.

3. If you are not holy, the sacred name of your Redeemer, your Proprietor, and your Indweller will be compromised.

4. But if you live a redeemed life, your God will be honoured.

Let the world see what Redemption can do.
Let the world see what sort of men " God's Own " are.

PIECES OF MONEY

But why should so vast a price be required ? Is man worth the cost ?
A man may be bought in parts of the world for the value of an ox. It
was not man simply, but man in a certain relation, that had to be
redeemed. See one who has been all his days a drunken, idle, worthless fellow. All appropriate to him the epithet " worthless "—worth
nothing. But that man commits a crime for which he is sentenced to
be hanged, or to be imprisoned for life. Go and try to buy him now.
Redeem him and make him your servant. Let the richest man in
Cambridge offer every shilling he possesses for that worthless man, and
his offer would be wholly vain. Why? Because now there is not only
the man to be considered, but the law. It needs a very great price
to redeem one man from the curse of the law of England ; but Christ
came to redeem all men from the curse of the Divine law.— *William
Robinson.*

Does not **justice** demand the dedication of yourself to your Lord ?
God has not only procured a title for you, but a title to you : and unless
you devote yourself to his service, you rob him of his right. What a
man has bought, he deems his own ; and especially when the purchase
has been costly. And has not God bought you with a price of infinite
value ? And would you rob him of a servant from his family ; of a
vessel from his sanctuary? To take what belongs to a man is robbery,
but to take what belongs to God is sacrilege.— *William Jay.*

The Lord Jesus is everything in redemption, for he is both the Buyer
and the price.

A silly child when he plays at selling would like to take the price and
keep the article too ; but everybody knows that this cannot be. If you
keep the goods you cannot have the price, and if you accept the price
the goods are no longer yours. You may have either the one or the
other, but not both. So you may be your own, if you wish ; but then
the redemption price is not yours. If you accept the ransom, then the
thing redeemed is no longer yours, but belongs to him who bought it.
If I am redeemed, I am Christ's. If I am resolved to be my own, I
must renounce my Redeemer, and die unransomed.

1 𝔊𝔬𝔯. 𝔵𝔦. 24 — "𝔄𝔫𝔡 𝔴𝔥𝔢𝔫 𝔥𝔢 𝔥𝔞𝔡 𝔤𝔦𝔳𝔢𝔫 𝔱𝔥𝔞𝔫𝔨𝔰, 𝔥𝔢 𝔟𝔯𝔞𝔨𝔢 𝔦𝔱, 𝔞𝔫𝔡 𝔰𝔞𝔦𝔡, 𝔗𝔞𝔨𝔢, 𝔢𝔞𝔱: 𝔱𝔥𝔦𝔰 𝔦𝔰 𝔪𝔶 𝔟𝔬𝔡𝔶, 𝔴𝔥𝔦𝔠𝔥 𝔦𝔰 𝔟𝔯𝔬𝔨𝔢𝔫 𝔣𝔬𝔯 𝔶𝔬𝔲: 𝔱𝔥𝔦𝔰 𝔡𝔬 𝔦𝔫 𝔯𝔢𝔪𝔢𝔪𝔟𝔯𝔞𝔫𝔠𝔢 𝔬𝔣 𝔪𝔢."

Men have made evil use of this most blessed ordinance.

Yet they have no excuse from any obscurity of Scripture.

Nothing is said of a sacrifice or an altar, but everything is plain.

The Supper, as we find it in Holy Scripture, is a service of remembrance, testimony, and communion, and nothing more.

No pompous ceremony is arranged for. Not even a posture is prescribed; but merely the providing of bread and the juice of the vine; taking, breaking, eating, drinking, and no more.

The spiritual action is specially prescribed; the remembrance of our Lord must be there, or we fail to keep the feast.

I. OTHER MEMORIES WILL COME, BUT MUST NOT CROWD OUT THE ONE MEMORY.

The following remembrances may be natural, allowable, and profitable, but they must be kept in a secondary place :—

1. Of ourselves when we were strangers and foreigners.

2. Of our former onlooking and wishing to be at the table.

3. Of our first time of coming, and the grace received since then.

4. Of the dear departed who once were with us at the table.

5. Of beloved ones who cannot be with us at this time because they are kept at home by sickness.

6. Of many present with us, and what grace has done in their cases We may think of their needs and of their holy lives, etc.

7. Of the apostates who have proved their falseness, like Judas.

However these memories may press upon us, we must mainly remember *him* for whose honour the feast is ordained.

II. THE ORDINANCE IS HELPFUL TO THAT ONE SACRED MEMORY.

1. Set forth, the signs display the person of our Lord as really man, substantial flesh and blood.

2. Placed on the table, their presence betokens our Lord's dear familiarity with us, and our nearness to him.

3. Broken and poured forth, they show his sufferings.

4. Separated, bread apart from wine, the flesh divided from the blood, they declare his death for us.

5. Eating, we symbolize the life-sustaining power of Jesus and our reception of him into our innermost selves.

6. Remaining when the Supper is ended, the fragments suggest that there is yet more bread and wine for other feasts ; and, even so, our Lord is all-sufficient for all time.

Every particle of the ordinance points at Jesus, and we must therein behold the Lamb of God.

III. THAT SACRED MEMORY IS IN ITSELF MOST NEEDFUL FOR US.

It is needful to remember our crucified Lord, for—

1. It is the continual sustenance of faith.

2. It is the stimulus of love.

3. It is the fountain of hope.

4. It is a recall, from the world, from self, from controversy, from labour, from our fellows—to our Lord.

5. It is the *réveille*, the up-and-away. It is the prelude of the marriage supper, and makes us long for "the bridal feast above."

Above all things, it behoves us to keep the name of our Lord engraven on our hearts.

IV. THIS SYMBOLIC FESTIVAL IS HIGHLY BENEFICIAL IN REFRESHING OUR MEMORIES, AND IN OTHER WAYS.

1. We are yet in the body, and materialism is a most real and potent force ; we need that there be a set sign and form to incarnate the spiritual and make it vivid to the mind.

Moreover, as the Lord actually took upon him our flesh and blood, and as he means to save even the material part of us, he gives us this link with materialism, lest we spirit things away as well as spiritualize them.

2. Jesus, who knew our forgetfulness, appointed this festival of love ; and we may be sure he will bless it to the end designed.

3. Experience has ofttimes proved its eminent value.

4. While reviving the memories of the saints, it has also been sealed by the Holy Spirit ; for he has very frequently used it to arouse and convince the spectators of our solemn feast.

To observe the Supper is binding on all believers.

It is binding to the extent of " oft."

Only as it assists *remembrance* can it be useful. Seek grace lovingly to remember your Lord.

It is common enough in human history to meet with periodical celebrations, anniversaries of the day of their birth, or of their death, held in honour of those who have greatly distinguished themselves by their virtues, their genius, or their high services to their country or to mankind. But where except here do we read of any one in his own lifetime originating and appointing the method by which he was to be remembered, himself presiding at the first celebration of the rite, and laying an injunction upon all his followers regularly to meet for its observance? Who among all those who have been the greatest ornaments of our race, the greatest benefactors of humanity, would ever have risked his reputation, his prospect of being remembered by the ages that were to come, by exhibiting such an eager and premature desire to preserve and perpetuate the remembrance of his name, his character, his deeds? They have left it to others after them to devise the means for doing so; neither vain enough, nor bold enough, nor foolish enough to be themselves the framers of those means. Who, then, is he who ventures to do what none else ever did? Who is this, who, ere he dies, by his own act and deed sets up the memorial institution by which his death is to be shown forth? Surely he must be one who knows and feels that he has claims to be remembered such as none other ever had— claims of such a kind that, in pressing them in such a way upon the notice of his followers, he has no fear whatever of what he does being attributed to any other, any lesser motive than the purest, deepest, most unselfish love! Does not Jesus Christ in the very act of instituting in his own lifetime this memorial rite, step at once above the level of ordinary humanity, and assert for himself a position toward mankind utterly and absolutely unique?—*Dr. Hanna.*

Miss Edgeworth, in one of her tales, relates an anecdote of a Spanish artist, who was employed to depict the "Last Supper." It was his object to throw all the sublimity of his art into the figure and countenance of the Master; but he put on the table in the foreground some chased cups, the workmanship of which was exceedingly beautiful, and when his friends came to see the picture on the easel, every one said, "What beautiful cups they are!" "Ah!" said he, "I have made a mistake, these cups divert the eyes of the spectator from the Master, to whom I wished to direct the attention of the observer"; and he took his brush and rubbed them from the canvas, that the strength and vigour of the chief object might be seen as it should.—*G. S. Bowes.*

He that remembers not Christ's death, so as to endeavour to be like him, forgets the end of his redemption, and dishonours the cross, on which his satisfaction was wrought.—*Anthony Horneck.*

CCV

1 Cor. xi. 28 —"But let a man examine himself, and so let him eat of that bread, and drink of that cup."

The Lord's Supper is not for all men, but only for those who are able spiritually to discern the Lord's body.

It is not meant for the conversion of sinners, but for the edification of disciples.

Hence the need of examination, lest we intrude ourselves where we have no right to be.

I. THE OBJECT OF THE EXAMINATION.

 1. That the communicant may eat and drink. "Examine, and so let him eat." He is not to examine in order to justify his stopping away.

 2. That he may know that the responsibility rests with himself. The examination is not by priest or minister : he examines *himself*.

 3. That he may communicate solemnly, and not come to the table carelessly, and as a matter of course. He is to make heart-searching enquiry, and so approach the table with self-humiliation.

 4. That he may come to the table intelligently, knowing to what he comes, and why, and wherefore.

 5. That he may do so with appreciative confidence and joy. After examination he will know his right to come, and feel at ease.

Many good results would follow if this examination were universally practised. "A man" in this text means "any man," and "every man."

The examination should be as frequent as the eating of the bread. No man has reached a point at which he is beyond the need of further self-searching.

II. THE MATTER OF THE EXAMINATION.

 Points of examination may be suggested by the following thoughts :—

 1. It is a feast.

  Have I life ? The dead sit not at banquets.

  Have I appetite ? Else how can I eat ?

  Have I a friendship toward the Lord who is the Host ?

  Have I put on the wedding garment ?

 2. Jesus bids us show forth his death.

228

Have I faith in his death ?
Do I live by his death ?

3. Jesus bids us do this by eating bread.
   Is this eating a symbol of a fact, or is it a mere mockery?
   Is Jesus really and truly the food of my soul?

4. Jesus bids each believer do this in union with others.
   Am I truly one of his people, and one with them ?
   Am I dwelling in love with them all ?

5. This cup is the New Covenant in Christ's blood.
   Am I in covenant with God in Christ Jesus ?
   Do I rest in that covenant for all my hopes ?

6. Jesus calls his people to remember him in this Supper.
   Can I remember Christ ? Or am I attempting a vain thing ?
   Do I know him ?   How else can I remember him ?
   Are my past dealings with him such as I wish to remember ?
   Is he so loved by me that I wish to bear him in my memory?

Our profession, experience, conduct, hopes, and designs should all
pass the test of this self-examination.

III. THE DUTY AFTER EXAMINATION.

1. To eat of the bread.
   Not to neglect communion, or postpone it, or go away trembling
      from the table ; but to partake reverently.

2. To drink of the cup.
   This is specially commanded.   Hence we cannot go to Popish
      mass, where there is no cup.

3. To eat and drink so as to discern the Lord's body.   Having the
      mind awake to see Jesus symbolized in this ordinance.

4. To give thanks unto the Lord for so great a privilege.   Twice did
      our Lord give thanks during the Supper, and at the close he
      sang.   It is not a funeral, but a festival.

Ye who have come to this table heedlessly, repent of your wicked
intrusion, and keep away till ye can come aright.

Ye who have never come at all, remember, if you are not fit for the
communion below, you are not fit for heaven above.

All of you, bethink yourselves of Jesus, and having examined yourselves to your humbling, behold him to your consolation.

OBSERVATIONS

The three questions which Philip Henry advised people to put to

229

themselves in self-examination before the sacrament were, What am I? What have I done? and, What do I want?—*John Whitecross.*

It is every man's duty solemnly and seriously to examine himself about his interest in Christ, his habitual grace, his actual right and fitness for the Lord's Supper, before his approach to it. It is not said as to the first time of our partaking, but **as** to every time, "*so* let him eat." Now, the second and third time, as well as before, we are so to eat. Great preparations are necessary for great duties. The particle *so* bars men from coming without this previous work of examination. Let a man come only in such a manner; if he neglects this self-examination, let him not venture upon this great mystery. Thus, Ps. xxvi. 6, "I will wash my hands in innocency, so will I compass thy altar, O Lord," alluding to the ancient custom of testifying the purity of their souls by the cleansing of their hands, or to the washings used before sacrifices. If we take the gloss of Ambrose, it will read—I will with a purity of heart embrace the Messiah, signified both by the altar and sacrifice. "*So* will I compass thy altar"; without such an inward purification, I dare not presume upon an approach unto it.

Stephen Charnock.

The duty required for preventing the sin and danger of unworthy communicating is the great and necessary duty of self-examination. It is a metaphor taken from goldsmiths, who try the truth of their gold by the touchstone, the purity of their gold by the fire, and the weight of it by the scale. We have here, 1. The person examining: "Let a man examine." 2. The person examined; it is "himself"; he is to call himself to the bar of conscience, and to put questions to himself. (1) Concerning his state, whether he has a right to come or not. (2) His sins and shortcomings. (3) His wants and necessities. (4) His ends and designs; whether it be to obey the charge of his dying Saviour, to show forth his death, renew and seal his covenant with God, get nearness and communion with him, nourishment to his soul, and supply to his wants. And (5) concerning his graces and qualifications, particularly as to knowledge, faith, repentance, fear, love, thankfulness, holy desires, and new obedience.—*John Willison.*

CCVI

1 Cor. xv. 6 —"Some are fallen asleep."

Yes, the companions of Jesus died one by one.

Consider the great value of such men and of all good men to the church, and the loss caused by their removal.

Yet no word of lamentation is used. It is not said that they have perished, or passed into the land of shades, but that "they are fallen asleep."

The spirit is with Jesus in glory: the body rests till his appearing.

"Fallen asleep" suggests a very different idea from that which distressed the minds of the heathen when they thought of death.

I. THE FIGURE HERE USED.

1. An act of the most natural kind: "fallen asleep."
   It is the fit ending of a weary day.
   It is not painful, but the end of pain.
   It is so desirable that, if denied, we should pray for it.
   It is most sweet when the place of our sleep is Jesus.

2. A state of which rest is the main ingredient.

3. A position of safety from a thousand dangers, such as beset the pilgrim, the worker, the warrior.

4. A condition by no means destructive.
   Neither sleep nor death destroys existence, nor even injures it.
   Neither sleep nor death should be viewed as an evil.

5. A posture full of hope.
   We shall awake from this sleep.
   We shall awake without difficulty.
   We shall arise greatly refreshed.

II. THE THOUGHTS AROUSED BY THAT FIGURE.

1. How did we treat those who are now asleep?
   Did we value their living presence, work, and testimony?
   Ought we not to be more kind to those who are yet alive?

2. How can we make up for the loss caused by their sleep?
   Should we not fill their vacant places?
   Should we not profit by their examples?

3. How fit that we also should be prepared to fall asleep!
   Is our house in order?
   Is our heart in order?
   Is our Christian work in order?

4. How much better that the faithful should fall asleep than that the wicked should die in their sins !

5. How patiently should we bear up under the labours and sufferings of the day, since there remaineth a rest for the people of God !

III. THE HOPES CONFIRMED BY THAT FIGURE.

   1. The sleepers are yet ours, even as those in the house who are asleep are numbered with the rest of the inhabitants.
     They have the same life in them which dwells in us.
     They are part of the same family. "We are seven."
     They make up one church. "One church above, beneath."

   2. The sleepers will yet awake.
     Their Father's voice will arouse them.
     They shall be awake indeed : full of health and energy.
     They shall have new clothes to dress in.
     They shall not again fall asleep.

   3. The sleepers and ourselves will enjoy sweet fellowship.
     Sleep does not destroy the love of brothers and sisters now.
     We shall arise as one unbroken family, saved in the Lord.

Let us not hopelessly sorrow over those asleep.
Let us not ourselves sleep till bed-time comes.
Let us not fear to sleep in such good company.

NIGHT THOUGHTS

A pious Scotch minister being asked by a friend during his last illness whether he thought himself dying, answered : " Really, friend, I care not whether I am or not ; for if I die, I shall be with God ; if I live, he will be with me."—*Arvine.*

God's finger touched him, and he slept.—*Tennyson.*

S. T. Coleridge speaking of a dear friend's death, said, " It is recovery, and *not death.* Blessed are they that sleep in the Lord ; his life is hidden in Christ. In his Redeemer's life it is hidden and in his glory will it be disclosed. Physiologists hold that it is during sleep chiefly that we grow ; what may we not hope of such a sleep in such a bosom ? "

There must be life in Christ before death can become sleep in him. " Louis, the beloved, sleeps in the Lord," said the priest who announced the death of Louis the Fifteenth. " If," was *Thomas Carlyle's* stern comment, " if such a mass of laziness and lust sleeps in the Lord, who, think you, sleeps elsewhere ? "

CCVII

2 **Cor. i. 3, 4** — "**Blessed be God, even the Father of our Lord Jesus Christ, the Father of mercies, and the God of all comfort;**

"**Who comforteth us in all our tribulation, that we may be able to comfort them which are in any trouble, by the comfort wherewith we ourselves are comforted of God.**"

The apostle began with invoking the blessing of God.   Verse 1.

He then went on to bless God.

He was much tried, but he was in a grateful and cheerful humour, for he wrote of most comfortable things.

Here we have—

I. THE COMFORTABLE OCCUPATION. Blessing God. "Blessed be God."

If a man under affliction blesses the Lord—

1. It argues that his heart is not vanquished,
   So as to gratify Satan by murmuring, or
   So as to kill his own soul with despair.

2. It prophesies that God will send to him speedy deliverances to call forth new praises. It is natural to lend more to a man when the interest on what he has is duly paid.
   Never did man bless God but sooner or later God blessed him.

3. It profits the believer above measure.
   It takes the mind off from present trouble.
   It lifts the heart to heavenly thoughts and considerations.
   It gives a taste of heaven, for heaven largely consists in adoring and blessing God.
   It destroys distress by bringing God upon the scene.

4. It is the Lord's due in whatsoever state we may be.

II. THE COMFORTABLE TITLES.

1. A name of affinity, "The Father of our Lord Jesus Christ."
2. A name of gratitude, "The Father of mercies."
3. A name of hope, "The God of all comfort."
4. A name of discrimination, "Who comforteth *us*." The Lord has a special care for those who trust in him.

233

III. THE COMFORTABLE FACT. "The God of all comfort comforteth us in all our tribulation."

1. God personally condescends to comfort the saints.
2. God habitually does this. He has always been near to comfort us in all past time, never once leaving us alone.
3. God effectually does this. He has always been able to comfort us in all tribulation. No trial has baffled his skill.
4. God everlastingly does this, he will comfort us to the end, for he is "the God of all comfort," and he cannot change.

Should we not be always happy since God always comforts us?

IV. THE COMFORTABLE DESIGN. "That we may be able to comfort."

1. To make us comforters of others. The Lord aims at this: the Holy Ghost, the Comforter, trains us up to be comforters. There is great need for this holy service in this sin-smitten world.
2. To make us comforters on a large scale. "To comfort them which are in any trouble." We are to be conversant with all kinds of grief, and ready to sympathize with all sufferers.
3. To make us experts in consolation—"able to comfort"; because of our own experience of divine comfort.
4. To make us willing and sympathetic, so that we may through personal experience instinctively care for the state of others.

Let us now unite in special thanksgiving to the God of all comfort.

Let us drink in comfort from the word of the Lord, and be ourselves happy in Christ Jesus.

Let us be on the watch to minister consolation to all tried ones.

COMFORTABLE WORDS

Music is sweetest near or over rivers, where the echo thereof is best rebounded by the water. Praise for pensiveness, thanks for tears, and blessing God over the floods of affliction, make the most melodious music in the ear of heaven.—*Thomas Fuller.*

> Many an Alleluia
>   That rings through the Father's home,
> Sobbed out its first rehearsal
>   In the shades of a darkened room.

When we try to comfort one another, let it be God's comfort that we give.—*T. T. Lynch.*

We have no more religion than what we have in times of trial.

Andrew Fuller.

Away over in India a poor native woman—like Naomi—"was left of her two sons." She did not, perhaps, know enough to think about God at all in her grief; but she would take no comfort. To everything that could be said she had one answer: "I had but two, and they are both gone."

Day after day she pined and fretted, going listlessly about, her life "empty" of all but a blank despair. One morning, as she wandered here and there among the people of the mission, one of them again remonstrated; but the poor thing gave her old reply: "I had but two, and they are both gone." "Look," said the worker, turning, and pointing towards a group near by, where a white lady of the mission stood directing some dusky natives; "Do you see *her*?" The woman looked, and saw a sweet, pale face; patient, gentle, glad, as clear as a sky washed blue with storms, but wearing that unmistakable look which tells that storms have been. "Yes," she said, "I see her." "Well," said the other, "she has lost her sons, too!"

The poor native mother gazed for a minute, spell-bound; then she sprang towards her. "Oh, lady"! she cried, "did you have two sons? and are they both gone?"

And now the white mother on her part turned and looked. "Yes," she said, "I had two."

"And are they both gone?"

"Both."

"But they were all I had," cried the other, "and they are both gone!"

"And mine are both gone," said the white lady, clasping the hands of her poor sister in sorrow. "But Jesus took them; and they are with Jesus, and Jesus is with me. And by-and-by I shall have them again."

From that hour the native woman sat at her white sister's feet, followed her about, hung on her words, and from her would take comfort —"the comfort wherewith she herself was comforted of God."—*From* "*What Aileth Thee?*"

He would put off a meditated journey, rather than leave a poor parishioner who required his services; and from his knowledge of human nature, he was able, and in a remarkable manner, to throw himself into the circumstances of those who needed his help. No sympathy was like his.—*Chambers, on George Crabbe.*

CCVIII

2 Cor. i. 10 —"Who delivered us from so great a death, and doth deliver: in whom we trust that he will yet deliver us."

Grammarians have here a lesson in the tenses; and Christians may profitably join in the exercise.

We may consider the past, present, and future, each one by itself.

We may also view them in their relation to each other.

Our text points out the delivering mercy of God as at all times working out the safety of his people. The case of Paul did not stand alone: hence he uses the plural : "who delivered *us*"; "*we* trust."

We shall take the words out of the apostle's mouth and apply them to our own cases.

I. THE TEXT SUGGESTS THREE TRAINS OF THOUGHT.

   1. Memory tells of deliverances in the past—

     From violent death. In Paul's case, "so great a death" may mean death by fierce mobs, or by the emperor.

     From our death in sin : "So great a death " indeed.

     From fierce despair when under conviction.

     From total overthrow when tempted by Satan.

     From faintness under daily tribulation.

     From destruction by slander and the like.

The Lord has most graciously delivered us hitherto. Let us express our gratitude.

   2. Observation calls attention to present deliverance.

     By the good hand of the Lord, we are at this time preserved—

     From unseen dangers to life.

     From the subtle assaults of Satan.

     From the rampant errors of the times.

     From inbred sin and natural corruption.

     From the sentence of death within, and from the greater danger of self-trust. See the preceding verse.

     Our present standing is wholly due to the grace of God, and, trusting in that grace, we may indulge a happy confidence.

   3. Expectation looks out of the window upon the future.

     Faith rests alone in God, "in whom we trust," and through him she looks for future deliverance—

     From all future common trials.

From coming losses and afflictions, and from sicknesses, which
may be coming upon us.

From the infirmities and wants of age.

From the peculiar glooms of death.

This expectation makes us march on with cheerfulness.

II. THE TEXT SUPPLIES THREE LINES OF ARGUMENT.

That the Lord will preserve us to the end is most sure. We can
say of him, " In whom we trust that he will yet deliver us."

1. From the Lord's beginning to deliver we argue that he will yet
deliver, for

There was no reason in us for his beginning to love us. If his
love arises out of his own nature it will continue.

He has obtained no fresh knowledge. He foreknew all our
misbehaviours : hence there is no reason for casting us off.

The reason which moved him at first is operating now, and none
better can be required.

2. From the Lord's continuing to deliver we argue that he will yet
deliver ; for

His deliverances have been so many ;

They have displayed such wisdom and power ;

They have come to us when we have been so unworthy ;

They have continued in such an unbroken line ;

That we feel sure he will never leave nor forsake us.

3. From the Lord himself—" In whom we trust " : we argue that he
will yet deliver ; for

He is as loving and strong now as aforetime.

He will be the same in the future.

His purpose never changes, and it is to his glory to complete
what he has begun. Verily, " he will yet deliver us."

III. THE TEXT IS OPEN TO THREE INFERENCES.

1. We infer that we shall always be so in danger as to need to be
delivered : wherefore we are not high-minded, but fear.

2. We infer our constant need of God's own interposition. He
alone has met our case in the past, and he only can meet it in
the future : wherefore we would ever abide near our Lord.

3. We infer that our whole life should be filled with the praise of God,
who, for past, present, and future, is our Deliverer.

FOR THE TIMES.

First, God hath a time, as for all things, so for our deliverance.
Secondly, God's time is the best time. He is the best discerner of

237

opportunities. Thirdly, this shall be when he hath wrought his work upon our souls, specially when he hath made us to trust in him. As here, when Paul had learned to trust in God, then he delivered him.

Richard Sibbes.

The Roman noblemen could give no greater proof of their confidence in their city and army, than when they bought the land on which their Carthaginian enemies were encamped around the city. And we can give no greater proof of our confidence in God, than by trusting him in the land which our enemies, darkness and sickness and trouble, seem to possess, and acting as if God were their master, and mightier than they all. This is but to act upon the truth.

There is an ante-war incident which illustrates the power for despair which lies in forgetfulness of God, and the hope which leaps up when God is fully believed in. A dark cloud hung over the interests of the African race in our land. There seemed no way of deliverance. Frederick Douglas, at a crowded meeting, depicted the terrible condition. Everything was against his people. One political party had gone down on its knees to slavery; the other proposed not to abolish it anywhere, but only to restrict it. The Supreme Court had given judgment against black men as such. He drew a picture of his race writhing under the lash of the overseer, and trampled upon by brutal and lascivious men. As he went on with his despairing words, a great horror of darkness seemed to settle down upon the audience. The orator even uttered the cry for blood. There was no other relief. And then he showed that there was no relief even in that. Everything, every influence, every event was gathering, not for good, but for evil, about the doomed race. It seemed as if they were fated to destruction. Just at the instant when the cloud was most heavy over the audience, there slowly rose, in the front seat, an old black woman. Her name, " Sojourner Truth." She had given it to herself. Far and wide she was known as an African prophetess. Every eye was on her. The orator paused. Reaching out towards him her long bony finger, as every eye followed her pointing, she cried out, " *Frederick, is God dead?* " It was a lightning-flash upon that darkness. The cloud began to break, and faith and hope and patience returned with the idea of a personal and ever-living God.

Sword and Trowel, 1887.

Who murmurs that in these dark days
His lot is cast?
God's hand within the shadow lays
The stones whereon his gates of praise
Shall rise at last.—*J. G. Whittier.*

CCIX

2 Cor. i. 20 —"For all the promises of God in him are yea, and in him Amen, unto the glory of God by us."

Paul had altered his mind about visiting Corinth.

He had done this from the best of reasons.

The prejudices of certain Corinthians made them misconstrue his conduct, and speak of him as one whose word was not to be relied on.

He asserted that he did not use lightness, and that his mind was not of the "yea and nay" order, even upon so small a matter as a journey to Corinth at a certain date.

This led him to say that his preaching "was not yea and nay."

This further brought out the declaration that the promises of God are not "yea and nay."

Thus a trivial circumstance and an ungenerous remark led to the utterance of a most precious truth. This has often been the case.

From these words let us be led carefully to consider—

I. THE DIGNITY OF THE PROMISES. They are "the promises *of God.*"

1. They were each one made by him according to the purpose of his own will.

2. They are links between his decrees and his acts ; being the voice of the decree, and the herald of the act.

3. They display the qualities of him who uttered them. They are true, immutable, powerful, eternal, etc.

4. They remain in union with God. After the lapse of ages, they are still *his* promises as much as when he first uttered them.

5. They are guaranteed by the character of God who spoke them.

6. They will glorify him as he works out their fulfilment.

II. THE RANGE OF THE PROMISES : "*All* the promises."

It will be instructive to note the breadth of the promises by observing that—

1. They are found both in the Old and New Testaments ; from Genesis to Revelation, running through centuries of time.

2. They are of both sorts—conditional and unconditional : promises to certain works, and promises of an absolute order.

3. They are of all kinds of things—bodily and spiritual, personal and general, eternal and temporal.

239

4. They contain blessings to varied characters, such as—
   The Penitent: Lev. xxvi. 40-42; Isa. lv. 7, lvii. 15; Jer. iii. 12, 13.
   The Believing : John iii. 16, 18, vi. 47 ; Acts xvi. 31 ; 1 Pet. ii. 6.
   The Serving : Ps. xxxvii. 3, ix. 40 ; Prov. iii. 9, 10 ; Acts x. 35.
   The Praying : Isa. xlv. 11 ; Lam. iii. 25 ; Matt. vi. 6 ; Ps. cxlv. 18.
   The Obeying : Ex. xix. 5 ; Ps. cxix. 1-3 ; Isa. i. 19.
   The Suffering : Matt. v. 10-12 ; Rom. viii. 17 ; 1 Pet. iv. 12-14.
5. They bring us the richest boons : pardon, justification, sanctification, instruction, preservation, etc.

What a marvellous wealth lies in promises—" all the promises" !

III. THE STABILITY OF THE PROMISES : " All the promises *in him are yea, and in him Amen.*"

A Greek word " Yea," and a Hebrew word " Amen," are used to mark certainty, both to Gentile and Jew.

1. They are established beyond all doubt as being assuredly the mind and purpose of the eternal God.
2. They are confirmed beyond all alteration. The Lord hath said " Amen," and so must it be for ever.
3. Their stability is in Christ Jesus beyond all hazard ; for he is—
   The witness of the promise of God,
   The surety of the covenant,
   The sum and substance of all the promises,
   The fulfilment of the promises, by his actual incarnation, his atoning death, his living plea, his ascension power, etc.
   The security and guarantee of the promises, since all power is in his hand to fulfil them.

IV. THE RESULT OF THE PROMISES : " The glory of God by us."

By us, his ministers and his believing people, the God of the promises is made glorious.

1. We glorify his condescending love in making the promise.
2. We glorify his power as we see him keeping the promise.
3. We glorify him by our faith, which honours his veracity, by expecting the boons which he has promised.
4. We glorify him in our experience which proves the promise true.

Let us confidently rest in his sure word.

Let us plead the special promise appiicable to the hour now passing.

GATHERINGS

A speaker at the Fulton Street prayer-meeting said, " I count all cheques as cash when I am making up my money and striking a balance;" and so, when we feel that we have not much of this world's goods, we can at least take hold of God's promises, for they are just so many drafts at sight upon divine mercy, and we may count them among our possessions. Then we shall feel rich, and the soul is rich who trusts God's word and takes his promises as something for present use.

In the streets of ancient Pompeii there still remain the three stepping-stones, placed here and there, by which men crossed over the street when the water was high. The promises are such stepping-stones on which " the wayfaring man " may place his footstep and be enabled the better to cross some stream of trouble or doubt, or, perhaps, with more ease and safety to escape the mire of some Slough of Despond.

Promises are like the clothes we wear; if there is life in the body they warm us, but not otherwise. When there is living faith the promise will afford warm comfort, but on a dead, unbelieving heart it lies cold and ineffectual. It has no more effect than pouring a cordial down the throat of a corpse.— *William Gurnell.*

If thou lean upon the promises of God themselves, and not upon Jesus Christ in them, all will come to nothing. . . . Whence is it that so many souls bring a promise to the throne of grace, and carry so little away from it? They lean upon the promises without leaning on Christ in the promise.—*Faithful Teate.*

" By us " as *ministers*—publishing, explaining, applying them. A promise is often like a box of ointment, very precious; but the fragrance does not fill the room till the preacher breaks it. Or it is like the water that was near Hagar, which she saw not, till the angel of the Lord opens our eyes and shows us the well. " By us " as *believers* realizing the excellency and efficacy of them in our character and conduct. It is when these promises are reduced to experience—when they are seen cleansing us from all filthiness of flesh and spirit, making us partakers of the divine nature, leading us to walk worthy of the vocation wherewith we are called, filling us with kindness and benevolence, supporting us cheerfully under all our trials—it is then they glorify God " by us."

William Jay.

CCX

2 Cor. vii. 1 — "Having therefore these promises, dearly beloved, let us cleanse ourselves from all filthiness of the flesh and spirit, perfecting holiness in the fear of God."

Kindling with strong emotion, constrained by the love of Christ, and animated by the fellowship of all spiritual blessings, the apostle here strikes out an exhortation, in which he appeals to the noblest passions of the children of God, to their possession of divine lineage, a present endowment, and their expectation of an exalted destiny. These he uses as incentives to holiness of life.

To stir up in us this godly ambition he sets before us the Christian in various lights—

I. As POSSESSED OF MOST GLORIOUS PRIVILEGES. "Having these promises." Not promises in reversion merely, but in actual possession, received, embraced, enjoyed.

The promises referred to are mentioned in the previous chapter.

1. Divine indwelling : "I will dwell in them." (Chap. vi. 16.)
2. Divine manifestation : "I will walk in them."
3. Divine covenanting : "I will be their God, and they shall be my people."
4. Divine acceptance : "I will receive you." (Chap. vi. 17.)
5. Divine adoption : "I will be a Father unto you, and ye shall be my sons and daughters, saith the Lord Almighty." (Chap. vi. 18.)

These promises are already fulfilled in our experience.

II. As LABOURING TO BE RID OF OBNOXIOUS EVILS. "Let us cleanse ourselves." The matter has in it—

1. Personality : "Let us cleanse *ourselves*."
2. Activity : we must continue vigorously to cleanse both body and mind.
3. Universality : "From all filthiness."
4. Thoroughness : "Of the flesh and spirit."

If God dwells in us, let us make the house clean for so pure a God.

Has the Lord entered into covenant with us that we should be his people? Does not this involve a call upon us to live as becometh godliness?

Are we his children ? Let us not grieve our Father, but imitate him as dear children.

III. AS AIMING AT A MOST EXALTED POSITION. "Perfecting holiness."
  1. We must set before us perfect holiness as a thing to be reached.
  2. We must blame ourselves if we fall short of it.
  3. We must continue in any degree of holiness which we have reached.
  4. We must agonize after the perfecting of our character.

IV. AS PROMPTED BY THE MOST SACRED OF MOTIVES. " Perfecting holiness *in the fear of God.*"
  1. The fear of God casts out the fear of man, and thus saves us from one prolific cause of sin.
  2. The fear of God casts out the love of sin, and with the root the fruit is sure to go.
  3. The fear of God works in and through love to him, and this is a great factor of holiness.
  4. The fear of God is the root of faith, worship, obedience, and so it produces all manner of holy service.

See how promises supply arguments for precepts.
See how precepts naturally grow out of promises.

OUTPOURINGS

"*Cleanse ourselves.*" It is the Lord that is the sanctifier of his people, he purges away their dross and tin. He pours clean water, according to his promises, yet doth he call us to cleanse ourselves ; having such promises, let us cleanse ourselves. He puts a new life into us, and causes us to act, and excites us to excite it, and call it up to act in the progress of sanctification. Men are strangely inclined to a perverse construction of things : tell them that we are to act and work, and give diligence, then they would fancy a doing in their own strength, and be their own saviours. Again, tell them that God works all our works in us, and for us, then they would take the ease of doing nothing : if they cannot have the praise of doing all, they will sit still with folded hands, and use no diligence at all. But this is the corrupt logic of the flesh ; its base sophistry. The apostle reasons just contrary, Phil. ii. 13 : "It is God that worketh in us both to will and to do." Therefore, would a carnal heart say, we need not work, or at least, may work very carelessly. But he infers, " Therefore let us work out our salvation with fear and trembling," *i. e.*, in the more humble obedience to God, and dependence on him, not obstructing the influences of his grace, and, by sloth and negligence, provoking him to withdraw or abate it. Certainly many in whom there is truth of grace, are kept low in the growth of it by their own slothfulness, sitting still, and not bestirring themselves, and exercising the proper actions of that spiritual life, by which it is entertained and advanced.—*Archbishop Leighton.*

> Virtue, for ever frail, as fair, below,
> Her tender nature suffers in the crowd,
> Nor touches on the world without a stain :
> The world's infectious ; few bring back at eve,
> Immaculate, the manners of the morn—
> Something we thought, is blotted ; we resolved,
> Is shaken ; we renounc'd, returns again.
>
> *Edward Young.*

"Let us *go on* to perfection" (Heb. vi. 1) should rather be rendered, "Let us be *carried* on." . . . . If we are unable to *go on*, we are surely able to be *carried* on to perfection.—*Charles Stanford.*

The promises, as they have a quickening, so they have a purging power ; and that upon sound reasoning. Doth God promise that he will be my Father, and I shall be his son ? and doth he promise me life everlasting ? and doth that estate require purity ? and no unclean thing shall come there ? Certainly, these promises being apprehended by faith, as they have a quickening power to comfort, so they purge with holiness. We may not think to carry our filthiness to heaven. Doth the swearer think to carry his blasphemies thither ? Filthy persons and liars are banished thence, there is "no unclean thing." He that hath these promises purgeth himself, and "perfecteth holiness in the fear of God." "He that hath this hope purifieth himself, as he is pure": 1 John iii. 3.—*Richard Sibbes.*

A spiritual mind has something of the nature of the sensitive plant: a holy shrinking from the touch of evil.—*Richard Cecil.*

CCXI

2 Cor. vii. 10 —"For godly sorrow worketh repentance to salvation not to be repented of: but the sorrow of the world worketh death."

Time was when inner experience was considered to be everything, and experimental preaching was the order of the day.

Now it is apt to be too much slighted.

Introspection was formerly pushed to the extreme of morbid self-searching ; yet it ought not now to be utterly abandoned.

A correct diagnosis of disease is not everything, but yet it is valuable.

A sense of poverty cannot by itself enrich, but it may stimulate.

Sinners were unwisely influenced by certain ministries to look to their own feelings, many began to seek comfort from their own misery.

Now it is " only believe." And rightly so : but we must discriminate. *There must be sorrow for sin working repentance.*

Upon this point we must—

I. REMOVE CERTAIN ERRONEOUS IDEAS WITH REGARD TO REPENTANCE AND SORROW FOR SIN.

Among popular delusions we must mention the suppositions—

1. That mere sorrow of mind in reference to sin is repentance.

2. That there can be repentance without sorrow for sin.

3. That we must reach a certain point of wretchedness and horror, or else we are not truly penitent.

4. That repentance happens to us once, and is then over.

5. That repentance is a most unhappy feeling.

6. That repentance must be mixed with unbelief, and embittered by the fear that mercy will be unable to meet our wretched case.

II. DISTINGUISH BETWEEN THE TWO SORROWS MENTIONED IN THE TEXT.

1. The godly sorrow which worketh repentance to salvation is—

Sorrow for sin as committed against God.

Sorrow for sin arising out of an entire change of mind.

Sorrow for sin which joyfully accepts salvation by grace.

Sorrow for sin leading to future obedience.

Sorrow for sin which leads to perpetual perseverance in the ways of God. The ways of sin are forsaken because abhorred.

This kind of repentance is never repented of.

2. The sorrow of the world is
    Caused by shame at being found out;
    Is attended by hard thoughts of God;
    Leads to vexation and sullenness;
    Incites to hardening of heart;
    Lands the soul in despair.
    Works death of the worst kind.

This needs to be repented of, for it is in itself sinful and terribly prolific of more sin.

III. INDULGE OURSELVES IN GODLY SORROW FOR SIN.

Come, let us be filled with a wholesome grief that we

1. Have broken a law, pure and perfect.
2. Have disobeyed a gospel, divine and gracious.
3. Have grieved a God, good and glorious.
4. Have slighted Jesus, whose love is tender and boundless.
5. Have been ungrateful, though loved, elected, redeemed, forgiven, justified, and soon to be glorified.
6. Have been so foolish as to lose the joyous fellowship of the Spirit the raptures of communion with Jesus.

Let us confess all this, lie low at Jesus' feet, wash his feet with tears, and love, yea, love ourselves away.

FOR DISCRIMINATION

A cognate text in Rom. ii. 2, 4, will help us here. These two allied but distinct intimations may be placed in parallel lines, and treated like an equation; thus—

"The goodness of God leadeth thee to repentance."

"Godly sorrow worketh repentance."

We learn, as the result of the comparison, that the goodness of God leads to repentance by the way of godly sorrow. The series of cause and effect runs thus: goodness of God; godly sorrow; repentance.

Do not mistake; a fear of hell is not sorrow for sin: it may be nothing more than a regret that God is holy.

So hard is a heart long accustomed to evil, that nothing can melt it but goodness; and no goodness but God's; and no goodness of his but the greatest. Thanks be to God for his unspeakable gift. "Looking unto Jesus" is the grand specific for producing godly sorrow in a human heart. It was a hard heart that quivered under the beams of his loving eye on the threshold of Pilate's judgment hall. When Jesus looked on Peter, Peter went out and wept. Emmanuel's love has lost none of its melting power; the hardest hearts laid fairly open to it must ere long flow down. God's goodness, embodied in Christ crucified, becomes, under the ministry of the Spirit, the cause of godly sorrow in believing men.— *William Arnot.*

> The mind that broods o'er guilty woes,
>   Is like the scorpion girt by fire ;
> In circle narrowing as it glows,
> The flames around their captive close,
> Till inly searched by thousand throes,
>   And maddening in her ire,
> One sad and sole relief she knows,
> The sting she nourished for her foes,
> Whose venom never yet was vain,
> Gives but one pang and cures all pain,
> And darts into her desperate brain ;
> So do the dark in soul expire,
> Or live like scorpion girt by fire.
> So writhes the mind Remorse has riven,
> Unfit for earth, undoomed for heaven,
> Darkness above, despair beneath,
> Around it flame, within it Death.—*Byron.*

Once a mother told her pastor that she was troubled about her daughter, who was going to join the church. "She has not conviction enough," was the complaint ; "and yet I have talked to her about her sins over and over again, setting them all in order before her till both of us were in tears ; oh, what can I do more ? " Then he gave her in her own hands a Bible, and he read aloud to her slowly Isaiah vi. 1-5. She saw, without any word of his, that the prophet became intelligent as the sight of God flashed upon him, and grew penitent at the moment when the seraphim cried " Holy." Then he turned to Job xlii. 5, 6. She saw in silence that the patriarch repented, not when his exasperating friends pelted him with accusations, but when his eyes were opened to see God. She went away quietly to talk, with a wondering and awe-struck heart, about the *holiness of Jehovah;* thus her child melted into contrition before the vision, and wept.—*C. S. Robinson.*

Sin, repentance, and pardon are like to the three vernal months of the year, March, April, and May. Sin comes in like March, blustering, stormy, and full of bold violence. Repentance succeeds like April, showering, weeping, and full of tears. Pardon follows like May, springing, singing, full of joys and flowers. Our eyes must be full of *April,* with the sorrow of repentance ; and then our hearts shall be full of *May,* with the true joy of forgiveness.—*Thomas Adams.*

247

CCXII

Gal. i. 16 —"Immediately I conferred not with flesh and blood."

The conversion of Paul is a memorable proof of the truth of Christianity. A consideration of it has been the means of the conversion of many thoughtful persons.

His case is a noble instance of the gospel's power over men of mark, men of learning, men of zealous mind, and men of energetic character.

Paul, being converted, took an independent course.

Being taught of God,

> He did not consult those who were already believers, lest he should seem to have received his religion at second-hand.
>
> He did not consult his relatives, who would have advised caution.
>
> He did not consult his own interests, which all lay in the opposite direction. These he counted loss for Christ.
>
> He did not consult his own safety, but risked life itself for Jesus.

In this independent course he was justified, and should be imitated.

I. FAITH NEEDS NO WARRANT BUT THE WILL OF GOD.

1. Good men in all ages have acted upon this conviction.

> Noah, Abraham, Jacob, Moses, Samson, David, Elijah, Daniel, the three who were cast into the furnace, etc.

2. To ask more is virtually to renounce the Lord as our Commander and Guide, and to lift man into his place.

3. To hesitate from self-interest is openly to defy the Lord.

4. To submit the claims of duty to the judgment of the flesh is diametrically opposed to the character and claims of the Lord Jesus, who gave himself to us, and expects us to give ourselves to him without question or reserve.

5. To delay duty until we have held such consultation almost always ends in not doing the right thing at all. Too often it is sought after that an excuse may be found for avoiding an unpleasant duty.

II. THE PRINCIPLE HAS A WIDE RANGE OF APPLICATION.

1. To known duties.

> In forsaking sin we are not to consult society.
>
> In upright dealing we are not to consult the custom of trade.
>
> In consecration to Christ we are not to follow the lower standard so common among our fellow Christians.

248

In service we are not to consult personal liking, ease, honour, prospect of advancement, or remuneration.

2. To needful sacrifices.   We are not to shrink from—
Losses of situation through honesty or holiness.
Losses in trade through religion.
Losses of friendships and kindly feeling through faithfulness.
Losses of position and worldly honour through inability to lie, bribe, cringe, flatter, compromise, conceal, or change.

We had better not confer with flesh and blood ; for—
Good men may be self-indulgent, and so consult their own flesh.
Bad men may practically be consulted by our fearing that they will ridicule us, and by our acting on that fear.
Our own flesh and blood may be consulted by unduly considering wife, husband, brother, child, friend, etc.

3. To special service.   We are not to be held back from this by—
Considerations of personal weakness.
Considerations of want of visible means.
Considerations of how others will interpret our actions.

Consult not even your brethren here ; for—
Good men may not have your faith.
They cannot judge your call.
They cannot remove your responsibility.

4. To an open avowal of Christ.   We must not be deterred from it by—
The wishes of others, who think themselves involved in our act.
The dread of contempt from those who deride godliness.
The fear of not holding on, and of thus disgracing religion.
Reluctance to give up the world, and a secret clinging to its ways.
This is a very perilous vice.   " Remember Lot's wife."

III. THE PRINCIPLE COMMENDS ITSELF TO OUR BEST JUDGMENT.

It is justified by—

1. The judgment which we exercise upon others.
We blame them if they have no mind of their own.
We applaud them if they are bravely faithful.

2. The judgment of an enlightened conscience.

3. The judgment of a dying bed.

4. The judgment of an eternal world.

Let us be in such communion with God that we need not confer with flesh and blood.

Let us not wait for second thoughts, but at once carry out convictions of duty, and obey calls for help, or impulses of love.

An Indian missionary says that the Hindoos do not act on their own convictions, but according to their own phrase, " I do as ten men do." Let the maxim of the Christian be, " I do as my God would have me do."

" Sir," said the Duke of Wellington to an officer of engineers, who urged the impossibility of executing the directions he had received, " I did not ask your opinion, I gave you my orders, and I expect them to be obeyed." Such should be the obedience of every follower of Jesus. The words which he has spoken are our law. We are not permitted to oppose thereto our judgments or fancies. Even if death were in the way, it is—

> " Not ours to reason why—
> Ours but to dare and die " ;

and, at our Master's bidding, advance through flood or flame.—" *Feathers for Arrows.*"

But this is a hard lesson to learn. I read some time ago of a German captain who found this out. He was drilling a company of volunteers. The parade ground was a field by the seaside. The men were going through their exercises very nicely, but the captain thought he would give them a lesson about obeying orders. They were marching up and down in the line of the water at some distance from it. He concluded to give them an order to march directly towards the water, and see how far they would go. The men are marching along. " Halt, company," says the captain. In a moment they halt. " Right face " is the next word, and instantly they wheel round. " *Forwart martch,*" is then the order. At once they begin to march directly towards the water : on they go, nearer and nearer to it. Soon they reach the edge of the water. Then there is a sudden halt. " Vat for you stop? I no say, Halt," cried the captain. " Why, captain, here is the water," said one of the men. " Vell, vot of it," cried he, greatly excited, " Vater is nothing ; fire is nothing ; everything is nothing. Ven I say, Forwart martch, then you must forwart martch." The captain was right ; the first duty of a soldier is to learn to obey.—*Dr. Richard Newton.*

What God calls a man to do he will carry him through. I would undertake to govern half-a-dozen worlds if God called me to do it ; but if he did not call me to do it, I would not undertake to govern half-a-dozen sheep.—*Dr. Payson.*

CCXIII

Gal. iii. 23 —" But before faith came, we were kept under the law, shut up unto the faith which should afterwards be revealed."

Here we have a condensed history of the world before the gospel was fully revealed by the coming of our Lord Jesus.

The history of each saved soul is a miniature likeness of the story of the ages. God acts upon the same principles both with the race and with individuals.

I. THE UNHAPPY PERIOD : " Before faith came."
  1. We had no idea of faith by nature. It would never occur to the human mind that we could be saved by believing in Jesus.
  2. When we heard of faith as the way of salvation we did not understand it. We could not persuade ourselves that the words used by the preacher had their common and usual meaning.
  3. We saw faith in others, and wondered at its results ; but we could not exercise it for ourselves.
  4. We could not reach to faith, even when we began to see its necessity, admitted its efficacy, and desired to exercise it.
      The reason of this inability was moral, not mental :
      We were proud, and did not care to renounce self-righteousness.
      We could not grasp the notion of salvation by faith, because it was contrary to the usual run of our opinions.
      We were bewildered, because faith is a spiritual act, and we are not spiritual.
  5. We were without the Spirit of God, and therefore incapable.

We do not wish to go back to the state in which we were "before faith came," for it was one of darkness, misery, impotence, hopelessness, sinful rebellion, self-conceit, and condemnation.

II. THE CUSTODY WE WERE IN : " Kept under the law, shut up."
  1. We were always within the sphere of law. In fact, there is no getting out of it. As all the world was only one prison for a man who offended Cæsar, so is the whole universe no better than a prison for a sinner.
  2. We were always kicking against the bounds of the law, sinning, and pining because we could not sin more.

251

3. We dared not overleap it altogether, and defy its power. Thus, in the case of many of us, it checked us, and held us captive with its irksome forbiddings and commandings.
4. We could not find rest. The law awakened conscience, and fear and shame attend such an awakening.
5. We could not discover a hope; for, indeed, there is none to discover while we abide under the law.
6. We could not even fall into the stupor of despair; for the law excited life, though it forbade hope.

Among the considerations which held us in bondage were these :
The spirituality of the law, touching thoughts, motives, desires.
The need of perfect obedience, making one sin fatal to all hope of salvation by works.
The requirement that each act of obedience should be perfect.
The necessity that perfect obedience should be continual throughout the whole of life.

III. THE REVELATION WHICH SET US FREE : "The faith which should afterwards be revealed." The only thing which could bring us out of prison was faith. Faith came, and then we understood—

1. What was to be believed.
Salvation by another.
Salvation of a most blessed sort, gloriously sure, and complete.
Salvation by a most glorious person.

2. What it was to believe.
We saw that it was "trust," implicit and sincere.
We saw that it was ceasing from self, and obeying Christ.

3. Why we believed.
We were shut up to this one way of salvation.
We were shut out of every other.
We were compelled to accept free grace, or perish.

Our duty is to show men how the way of human merit is closed.
We must shut them up to simple faith only, and show them that the way of faith is available.

To ARREST ATTENTION

The Law and the Gospel are two keys. The law is the key that shutteth up all men under condemnation, and the gospel is the key which opens the door and lets them out.— *William Tyndale.*

"Shut up unto the faith." To let you more effectually into the meaning of this expression, it may be right to state that in the preceding clause,

252

"kept under the law," the term, *kept*, is, in the original Greek, derived from a word which signifies a sentinel. The mode of conception is altogether military. The law is made to act the part of a sentry, guarding every avenue but one, and that one leads those who are compelled to take it to the faith of the gospel. They are shut up to this faith as their only alternative—like an enemy driven by the superior tactics of an opposing general, to take up the only position in which they can maintain themselves, or fly to the only town in which they can find a refuge or a security. This seems to have been a favourite style of argument with Paul, and the way in which he often carried on an intellectual warfare with the enemies of his Master's cause. It forms the basis of that masterly and decisive train of reasoning which we have in his epistle to the Romans. By the operation of skilful tactics, he (if we may be allowed the expression) manœuvred them, and shut them up to the faith of the gospel. It gave prodigious effect to his argument, when he reasoned with them, as he often does, upon their own principles, and turned them into instruments of conviction against themselves. With the Jews he reasoned as a Jew. He made use of the Jewish law as a sentinel to shut them out of every other refuge, and to shut them up to the refuge laid before them in the gospel. He led them to Christ by a schoolmaster whom they could not refuse ; and the lesson of this schoolmaster, though a very decisive, was a very short one—" Cursed be he that continueth not in all the words of the law to do them." But in point of fact, they had not done them. To them, then, belonged the curse of the violated law. The awful severity of its sanctions was upon them. They found the faith and the free offer of the gospel to be the only avenue open to receive them. They were shut up unto this avenue ; and the law, by concluding them all to be under sin, left them no other outlet but the free act of grace and of mercy laid before us in the New Testament.—*Dr. Chalmers.*

The law was meant to prepare men for Christ, by showing them that there is no other way of salvation except through him. It had two especial ends : the first was to bring the people who lived under it into a consciousness of the deadly dominion of sin, to shut them up, as it were, into a prison-house out of which only one door of escape should be visible, namely, the door of faith in Jesus ; the second intention was to fence about and guard the chosen race to whom the law was given—to keep them as a peculiar people separate from all the world, so that at the proper time the gospel of Christ might spring forth and go out from them as the joy and comfort of the whole human race.—*T. G. Rooke.*

CCXIV

Gal. v. 7 —"Ye did run well ; who did hinder you that ye should not obey the truth ? "

Never censure indiscriminately ; admit and praise that which is good, that you may the more effectually rebuke the evil.   Paul did not hesitate to praise the Galatians, and say, "Ye did run well."

, It is a source of much pleasure to see saints running well.   To do this they must run in the right road, straight forward, perseveringly, at the top of their pace, with their eye on Christ, &c.

It is a great grief when such are hindered, or put off the road.

The way is the truth, and the running is obedience : men are hindered when they cease to obey the truth.

It may be helpful to try and find out who has hindered us in our race.

I. WE SHALL USE THE TEXT IN REFERENCE TO HINDERED BELIEVERS.
1. You are evidently hindered.
>You are not so loving and zealous as you were.
>You are quitting the old faith for new notions.
>You are losing your first joy and peace.
>You are not now leaving the world and self behind.
>You are not now abiding all the day with your Lord.

2. Who has hindered you ?
>Did I do it ?   Pray, then, for your minister.
>Did your fellow-members do it ?   You ought to have been proof against them : they could not have intended it.   Pray for them.
>Did the world do it ?   Why so much in it ?
>Did the devil do it ?   Resist him.
>Did you not do it yourself?   This is highly probable.
>>Did you not overload yourself with worldly care ?
>>Did you not indulge carnal ease ?
>>Did you not by pride become self-satisfied ?
>>Did you not neglect prayer, Bible reading, the public means of grace, the Lord's Table, &c. ?
>Mend your ways, and do not hinder your own soul.
>Did not false teachers do it, as in the case of the Galatians ?
>If so, quit them at once, and listen only to the gospel of Christ.

3. You must look to it, and mend your pace.
>Your loss has been already great.   You might by this time have been far on upon the road

Your natural tendency will be to slacken still more.
Your danger is great of being overtaken by error and sin.
Your death would come of ceasing to obey the truth.
Your wisdom is to cry for help, that you may run aright.

II. WE SHALL USE THE TEXT IN REFERENCE TO DELAYING SINNERS

1. You have sometimes been set a-running.
   God has blessed his word to your arousing.
   God has not yet given you up ; this is evident.
   God's way of salvation still lies open before you.
2. What has hindered you ?
   Self-righteousness and trust in yourself ?
   Carelessness, procrastination, and neglect ?
   Love of self-indulgence, or the secret practice of pleasurable sins ?
   Frivolous, sceptical, or wicked companions ?
   Unbelief and mistrust of God's mercy ?
3. The worst evils will come of being hindered.
   Those who will not obey truth will become the dupes of lies.
   Truth not obeyed is disobeyed, and so sin is multiplied.
   Truth disregarded becomes an accuser, and its witness secures
   our condemnation.

God have mercy on *hinderers*. We must rebuke them.
God have mercy on the *hindered*. We would arouse them.

SPURS

Cecil says that some adopt the Indian maxim, that it is better to walk
than to run, and better to stand than to walk, and better to sit than to
stand, and better to lie than to sit. Such is not the teaching of the
gospel. It is a good thing to be walking in the ways of God, but it is
better to be running—making real and visible progress, day by day
advancing in experience and attainments. David likens the sun to a
strong man rejoicing to run a race ; not dreading it and shrinking back
from it, but delighting in the opportunity of putting forth all his
powers. Who so runs, runs well.—*The Christian.*

The Christian race is by no means easy. We are sore let and
hindered in running "the race that is set before us," because of—(1.)
Our sinful nature still remaining in the holiest saints. (2.) Some easily-
besetting sin (Heb. xii. 1). (3.) The entanglements of the world, like
heavy and close-fitting garments, impeding the racer's speed. (4.) Our
weakness and infirmity, soon tired and exhausted, when the race is long,
or the road is rough.—"*In Prospect of Sunday," by G. S. Bowes.*

Some are too busy, they run about too much to run well ; some run too fast at the outset ; they run themselves out of breath.—*T. T. Lynch.*

Henry Ward Beecher, in a sermon on this text, describes one of the hindrances to Christian progress thus : " We have fallen off immensely on the side of religious culture—earnest, prolonged, habitual, domestic, religious culture, conducted by the reading of God's Word, and by prayer, and its family influences. And this tendency is still further augmented by the increase of religious books, of tracts, of biographies and histories, of commentaries, which tend to envelop and hide the Word of God from our minds. In other words, these things, which are called ' helps,' have been increased to such a degree, and have come to occupy so much of our attention, that when we have read our helps, we have no time left to read the things to be helped ; and the Bible is covered down and lost under its ' helps.' "

It is possible that *fellow-professors* may hinder. We are often obliged to accommodate our pace to that of our fellow-travellers. If they are laggards we are very likely to be so too. We are apt to sleep as do others. We are stimulated or depressed, urged on or held back, by those with whom we are associated in Christian fellowship. There is still greater reason to fear that in many cases *worldly friends and companions* are the hinderers. Indeed, they can be nothing else. None can help us in the race but those who are themselves running it : all others must hinder. Let a Christian form an intimate friendship with an ungodly person, and from that moment all progress is stayed ; he must go back; for when his companion is going in the opposite direction, how can he walk with him except by turning his back upon the path which he has formerly trodden ?—*P.*

A sailor remarks—" Sailing from Cuba, we thought we had gained sixty miles one day in our course ; but at the next observation we found we had lost more than thirty. It was an under-current. The ship had been going forward by the wind, but going back by the current." So a man's course in religion may often seem to be right and progressive, but the under-current of his besetting sins is driving him the very contrary way to what he thinks.—*Cheever.*

256

CCXV

Gal. b. 11 —"*Then is the offence of the cross ceased.*"

Paul intends here to declare that the offence of the cross never has ceased, and never can cease. To suppose it to have ceased is folly.

The religion of Jesus is most peaceful, mild and benevolent.

Yet its history shows it to have been assailed with bitterest hate all along. It is clearly offensive to the unregenerate mind.

There is no reason to believe that it is one jot more palatable to the world than it used to be. The world and the gospel are both unchanged.

I. WHEREIN LIES THE OFFENCE OF THE CROSS?

   1. Its doctrine of atonement offends man's pride.

   2. Its simple teaching offends man's wisdom, and artificial taste.

   3. Its being a remedy for man's ruin offends his fancied power to save himself.

   4. Its addressing all as sinners offends the dignity of Pharisees.

   5. Its coming as a revelation offends "modern thought."

   6. Its lofty holiness offends man's love of sin.

II. HOW IS THIS OFFENCE SHOWN ?

   1. Frequently by the actual persecution of believers.

   2 More often by slandering believers, and sneering at them as old-fashioned, foolish, weak-minded, morose, self-conceited, etc.

   3. Often by omitting to preach the cross. Many nowadays preach a Christless, bloodless gospel.

   4. Or by importing new meanings into orthodox terms.

   5. Or by mixing the truth of Christ with errors.

   6. Or by openly denying the Deity of him who died on the cross, and the substitutionary character of his sufferings.

Indeed, there are a thousand ways of showing that the cross offends us in one respect or another.

III. WHAT THEN ?

   1. Herein is folly, that men are offended
      With that which God ordains ;
      With that which must win the day ;
      With the only thing which can save them ;
      With that which is full of wisdom and beauty.

2. Herein is grace,

> That we who once were offended by the cross, now find it to be
> The one hope of our hearts,
> The great delight of our souls.
> The joyful boast of our tongues.

3. Herein is heart-searching.

> Perhaps we are secretly offended at the cross.
> Perhaps we give no offence to haters of the cross.   Many professed
> Christians never cause offence to the most godless.
> Is this because they bear no testimony to the cross?
> Is this because they are not crucified to the world?
> Is this because there is no real trust in the cross, and no true
> knowledge of Christ?

Let us not follow those preachers who are not friends to the cross.

Let us have no fellowship with those who have no fellowship with Christ.

Preachers who have caught the spirit of the age are of the world, and the world loves its own; but we must disown them.

Let us not be distressed by the offence of the cross, even when it comes upon us with bitterest scorn.

Let us look for it and accept it as a token that we are in the right.

ANNOTATIONS

There is a want in the human mind which nothing but the Atonement can satisfy, though it may be a stumbling-block to the Jew, and foolishness to the Greek.   In the words of Henry Rogers : " It is adapted to human nature, as a bitter medicine may be to a patient.   Those who have taken it, tried its efficacy, and recovered spiritual health, gladly proclaim its value.   But to those who have not, and will not try it, it is an unpalatable potion still."

I open an ancient book, written in opposition to Christianity by Arnobius, and I read : " Our gods are not displeased with you Christians for worshipping the Almighty God; but you maintain the deity of one who was put to death on the cross, you believe him to be yet alive, and you adore him with daily supplications."   Men showed me at Rome, in the Kircherian Museum, a square foot of the plaster of a wall of a palace not many years ago uncovered on the Palatine hill.   On the poor clay was traced a cross bearing a human figure with a brute's head.   The figure was nailed to the cross, and before it a soldier was represented kneeling, and extending his hands in the Greek posture of devotion. Underneath all was scratched in rude lettering in Greek, "*Alexamenos adores his God.*" That representation of the central thought of Christianity was made in a jeering moment by some rude soldier in the days of Caracalla ; but it blazes there now in Rome, the most majestic monument of its age in the world.—*Joseph Cook.*

If any part of the truth which I am bound to communicate be concealed, this is sinful artifice. The Jesuits in China, in order to remove the offence of the cross, declared that it was a falsehood invented by the Jews that Christ was crucified ; but they were expelled from the empire, and this was designed, perhaps, to be held up as a warning to all missionaries that no good end is to be answered by artifice.

Richard Cecil.

The cross is the strength of a minister. I, for one, would not be without it for the world. I should feel like a soldier without weapons, like an artist without his pencil, like a pilot without his compass, like a labourer without his tools. Let others, if they will, preach the law and morality. Let others hold forth the terrors of hell and the joys of heaven. Let others drench their congregations with teachings about the sacraments and the church. Give me the cross of Christ. This is the only lever which has ever turned the world upside down hitherto, and made men forsake their sins. And if this will not do it, nothing will. A man may begin preaching with a perfect knowledge of Latin, Greek, and Hebrew ; but he will do little or no good among his hearers unless he knows something of the cross. Never was there a minister who did much for the conversion of souls who did not dwell much on Christ crucified. Luther, Rutherford, Whitefield, M'Cheyne, were all most eminent preachers of the cross. This is the preaching that the Holy Ghost delights to bless. He loves to honour those who honour the cross.—*J. C. Ryle.*

> My thoughts once prompt round hurtful things to twine,
> What are they now, when two dread deaths are near?
> The one impends, the other shakes his spear.
> Painting and sculpture's aid in vain I crave :
> My one sole refuge is that love Divine,
> Which from the cross stretched forth its arms to save.
> *Last lines written by Michael Angelo, when over eighty*

CCXVI

Gal. vi. 2, 5 —"Bear ye one another's burdens, and so fulfil the law of Christ.

"For every man shall bear his own burden."

Galatians apparently fond of the law and its burdens : at least, they appeared to be ready to load themselves with ceremonies, and so fulfil the law of Moses.

Paul would have them think of other burdens, by the bearing of which they would fulfil the law of Christ.

We are not under law, but under love.

But love is also law in the best sense. The law of Christ is love.

Love is the fulfilling of the law. " Bear ye one another's burdens, and so fulfil the law of Christ."

Lest this principle should be presumed upon, he mentions the principle of individual responsibility. " Every man shall bear his own burden."

I. COMMUNITY. " Bear ye one another's burdens."

  1. Negatively.

    It tacitly forbids certain modes of action.

      We are not to burden others. Some take a liberty to do so from this very text, as if it said, " Let others bear your burdens," which is just the reverse of what it urges.

      We are not to spy out others' burdens, and report thereon.

      We are not to despise them for having such loads to bear.

      We are not to act as if all things existed for ourselves, and we were to bend all to our own purposes.

      We are not to go through the world oblivious of the sorrows of others. We may not shut our eyes to the woes of mankind.

  2. Positively.

    We are to share the burdens of others.

      By compassion bear with their former sins. Verse 1.

      By patience bear with their infirmities, and even with their conceit. Verse 3.

      By sympathy bear their sorrows. Verses 2, 3.

      By assistance bear their wants. Verses 6, 10.

      By communion, in love and comfort, bear their struggles.

      By prayer and practical help bear the burden of their labours, and thus lighten it. Verse 6.

  3. Specially : We ought to consider—

      The erring brother. Referred to in verse 1 as " overtaken in a fault." We must tenderly restore him.

The provoking brother, who thinks himself to be something. See verse 3. Bear with him : his mistake will bring him many a burden before he has done with it.

The brother who is peculiarly trying is to be borne with to seventy times seven, even to the measure of the law of Christ

The greatly tried. is to have our greatest sympathy.

The minister of Christ should be released from temporal burdens, that he may give himself wholly to the burden of the Lord.

II. IMMUNITY. "For every man shall bear his own burden."

We shall not bear all the burdens of others.

We are not so bound to each other that we are partakers in wilful transgression, or negligence, or rebellion.

1. Each must bear his own sin if he persists in it.

2. Each must bear his own shame, which results from his sin.

3. Each must bear his own responsibility in his own sphere.

4. Each must bear his own judgment at the last.

III. PERSONALITY. "Every man . . . his own burden."

True godliness is a personal affair, and we cannot cast off our individuality : therefore, let us ask for grace to look well to ourselves in the following matters :—

1. Personal religion. The new birth, repentance, faith, love, holiness, fellowship with God, etc., are all personal.

2. Personal self-examination. We cannot leave the question of our soul's condition to the judgment of others.

3. Personal service. We have to do what no one else can do.

4. Personal responsibility. Obligations cannot be transferred.

5. Personal effort. Nothing can be a substitute for this.

6. Personal sorrow. "The heart knoweth its own bitterness."

7. Personal comfort. We need the Comforter for ourselves, and we must personally look up to the Lord for his operations.

All this belongs to the Christian, and we may judge ourselves by it.

So bear your own burden as not to forget others.

So live as not to come under the guilt of other men's sins.

So help others as not to destroy their self-reliance.

PITHY BREVITIES

An old anecdote of the great Napoleon records that, while walking along a country road attended by some of his officers, he encountered a peasant heavily laden with faggots for fuel. The peasant was about to be jostled aside, as a matter of course, by his social superiors, when the Emperor, laying his hand on the arm of the foremost member of his escort, arrested the whole party, and gave the labouring man the use of the road, with the remark, " Messieurs, respect the burden."

Let him who expects one class in society to prosper to the highest degree, while others are in distress, try whether one side of his face can smile while the other is pinched.—*Thomas Fuller.*

There is a proverb, but none of Solomon's, " Every man for himself, and God for us all." But where every man is for himself, the devil will have all.—*William Secker.*

" Every man shall bear his own burden "; this is the law of necessity. " Bear ye one another's burdens "; this is the law of Christ. Let a man lighten his own load by sharing his neighbour's burden.—*T. T. Lynch.*

There is a gateway at the entrance of a narrow passage in London, over which is written, " No burdens allowed to pass through." " And yet we do pass constantly with ours," said one friend to another, as they turned up this passage out of a more frequented and broader thorough-fare. They carried no visible burdens, but they were like many who, although they have no outward pack upon their shoulders, often stoop inwardly beneath the pressure of a heavy load upon the heart. The worst burdens are those which never meet the eye.

Bishop Burnet, in his charges to the clergy of his diocese, used to be extremely vehement in his declamations against pluralities. In his first visitation to Salisbury, he urged the authority of St. Bernard, who being consulted by one of his followers, whether he might accept of two benefices, replied, "And how will you be able to serve them both ? " " I intend," answered the priest, " to officiate in one of them by a deputy." " Will your deputy suffer eternal punishment for you, too ? " asked the saint. " Believe me, you may serve your cure by proxy, but you must suffer the penalty in person." This anecdote made such an impression on Mr. Kelsey, a pious and wealthy clergyman then present, that he immediately resigned the rectory of Bernerton, in Berkshire, worth two hundred a year, which he then held with another of great value.—*Whitecross.*

With many personal service in the cause of humanity is commuted for a money payment. But we are to be soldiers in the campaign against evil, and not merely to pay the war-tax.—" *Ecce Homo.*"

CCXVII

Gal. vi. 7 —" Be not deceived ; God is not mocked : for whatsoever a man soweth, that shall he also reap."

Both Luther and Calvin confine these words to the support of the ministers of the Word, and certainly therein they have weighty meaning.
Churches that starve ministers will be starved themselves.
But we prefer to take the words as expressing a general principle.

I. GOD IS NOT TO BE TRIFLED WITH.

1. Either by the notion that there will be no rewards and punishmen's.
2. Or by the idea that a bare profession will suffice to save us.
3. Or by the fancy that we shall escape in the crowd.
4. Or by the superstitious supposition that certain rites will set all straight at last, whatever our lives may be.
5. Or by a reliance upon an orthodox creed, a supposed conversion, a presumptuous faith, and a little almsgiving.

II. THE LAWS OF HIS GOVERNMENT CANNOT BE SET ASIDE.

1. It is so in nature.   Law is inexorable.   Gravitation crushes the man who opposes it.
2. It is so in providence.   Evil results surely follow social wrong.
3. Conscience tells us it must be so.   Sin must be punished.
4. The Word of God is very clear upon this point.
5. To alter laws would disarrange the universe, and remove the foundation of the hopes of the righteous.

III. EVIL SOWING WILL BRING EVIL REAPING.

1. This is seen in the present result of certain sins.
    Sins of lust bring disease into the bodily frame.
    Sins of idolatry have led men to cruel and degrading practices.
    Sins of temper have caused murders, wars, strifes, and misery.
    Sins of appetite, especially drunkenness, cause want, misery, delirium, etc.
2. This is seen in the mind becoming more and more corrupt, and less able to see the evil of sin, or to resist temptation.
3. This is seen when the man becomes evidently obnoxious to God and man, so as to need restraint, and invite punishment.

4. This is seen when the sinner becomes himself disappointed in the result of his conduct. His malice eats his heart; his greed devours his soul; his infidelity destroys his comfort; his raging passions agitate his spirit.

5. This is seen when the impenitent is confirmed in evil, and eternally punished with remorse. Hell will be the harvest of a man's own sin. Conscience is the worm which gnaws him.

IV. GOOD SOWING WILL BRING GOOD REAPING.

The rule holds good both ways.

Let us, therefore, enquire as to this good sowing:

1. In what power is it to be done?

2. In what manner and spirit shall we set about it?

3. What are its seeds?

Towards God, we sow in the Spirit, faith, and obedience.

Towards men, love, truth, justice, kindness, forbearance.

Towards self, control of appetite, purity, etc.

4. What is the reaping of the Spirit?

Life everlasting dwelling within us and abiding there for ever.

Let us sow good seed always.

Let us sow it plentifully, that we may reap in proportion.

Let us begin to sow it at once.

SEEDS

They that would mock God mock themselves much more.—*John Trapp.*

It is not an open question at all whether I shall sow or not to-day; the only question to be decided is: Shall I sow good seed or bad? Every man always is sowing for his own harvest in eternity either tares or wheat. According as a man soweth, so shall he also reap; he that sows the wind of vanity shall reap the whirlwind of wrath. Suppose a man should collect a quantity of small gravel and dye it carefully, so that it should resemble wheat, and sow it in his fields in spring, expecting that he would reap a crop of wheat like his neighbour's in harvest. The man is mad; he is a fool to think that by his silly trick he can evade the laws of nature, and mock nature's God. Yet equally foolish is the conduct, and far heavier the punishment, of the man who sows wickedness now, and expects to reap safety at last. Sin is not only profitless and disastrous; it is eminently a deceitful work. Men do not of set purpose cast themselves away: sin cheats a sinner out of his soul.

But sowing righteousness is never, and nowhere, lost labour. Eveiy act done by God's grace, and at his bidding, is living and fruitful. It may appear to go out of sight, like seed beneath the furrow ; but it will rise again. Sow on, Christians ! Sight will not follow the seed far ; but when sight fails, sow in faith, and you will reap in joy soon.— *William Arnot.*

" Whatsoever a man soweth that shall he also reap," etc. — No blight, nor mildew, nor scorching sun, nor rain deluge, can turn that harvest into failure.

Cast forth thy act, thy word, into the ever-living, ever-working universe : it is a seed-grain that cannot die : unnoticed to-day, it will be found flourishing as a Banyan grove (perhaps, alas ! as a Hemlock forest) after a thousand years.— *Thomas Carlyle.*

So it is with all temptations and lusts. They are ever scattering seeds — as weeds do. What a power there is in seeds ! How long-lived they are !—as we see in the mummies of Egypt, where they may have lain for thousands of years in darkness, but now come forth to grow. What contrivances they have to continue and to propagate themselves . They have wings, and they fly for miles. They may float over wide oceans, and rest themselves in foreign countries. They have hooks and attach themselves to objects. Often they are taken up by birds, which transport them to distant places. As it is with the seeds of weeds, so it is with every evil propensity and habit. It propagates itself and spreads over the whole soul, and goes down from generation to generation.

Dr. James McCosh.

Doth any think he shall lose by his charity ? No worldling, when he sows his seed, thinks he shall lose his seed ; he hopes for increase at harvest. Darest thou trust the ground, and not God ? Sure, God is a better paymaster than the earth ; grace doth give a larger recompense than nature. Below, thou mayest receive forty grains for one ; but in heaven (by the promise of Christ) a hundred-fold : a measure heapen, and shaken, and thrust together, and yet running over. " Blessed is he that considereth the poor " ; there is the seeding : " The Lord shall deliver him in the time of trouble " (Ps. xli. 1) ; there is the harvest. Is that all ? No ; Matt. xxv. 35 : " Ye fed me when I was hungry, and gave me drink when thirsty "—comforted me in misery ; there is the sowing. *Venite, beati.* " Come, ye blessed of my Father, inherit the kingdom prepared for you " ; there is the harvest.— *Thomas Adams.*

CCXVIII

Gal. vi. 14 —"But God forbid that I should glory, save in the cross of our Lord Jesus Christ, by whom the world is crucified unto me, and I unto the world."

Paul vigorously rebuked those who went aside from the doctrine of the Cross. Verses 12, 13.

When we rebuke others, we must take care to go right ourselves; hence he says, "God forbid that I should glory, save in the cross."

Our own resolute adherence to truth, when practically carried out, is a very powerful argument against opponents.

Paul rises to warmth when he thinks of the opponents of the cross. He no sooner touches the subject than he glows and burns.

Yet he has his reasons, and states them clearly and forcibly in the latter words of the text.

Here are three crucifixions :—

I. CHRIST CRUCIFIED : " The cross of our Lord Jesus Christ."

He mentions the atoning death of Jesus in the plainest and most obnoxious terms. The cross was shameful as the gallows tree.

Yet with the clearest contrast as to the person enduring it; for to him he gives his full honours in the glorious title—" our Lord Jesus Christ."

He refers to the doctrine of free justification and full atonement by the death of Jesus upon the cross.

In this he gloried so as to glory in nothing else, for he viewed it—

1. As a display of the divine character. "God was in Christ ": 2 Cor. v 19.

2. As the manifestation of the love of the Saviour. John xv. 13.

3. As the putting away of sin by atonement. Heb. ix. 26.

4. As the breathing of hope, peace, and joy to the desponding soul.

5. As the great means of touching hearts and changing lives.

6. As depriving death of terror, seeing Jesus died.

7. As ensuring heaven to all believers.

In any one of these points of view the cross is a pillar of light, flaming with unutterable glory.

II. THE WORLD CRUCIFIED : " The world is crucified unto me."

As the result of seeing all things in the light of the Cross, he saw the world to be like a felon executed upon a cross.

1. Its character condemned. John xii. 31.

266

2. Its judgment contemned. Who cares for the opinion of a gibbeted felon?

3. Its teachings despised. What authority can it have?

4. Its pleasures, honours, treasures, rejected.

5. Its pursuits, maxims, and spirit cast out.

6. Its threatenings and blandishments made nothing of.

7. Itself soon to pass away, its glory and its fashion fading.

III. THE BELIEVER CRUCIFIED : "And I unto the world."

To the world Paul was no better than a man crucified.

If faithful, a Christian may expect to be treated as only fit to be put to a shameful death.

He will probably find—

1. Himself at first bullied, threatened, and ridiculed.

2. His name and honour held in small repute because of his association with the godly poor.

3. His actions and motives misrepresented.

4. Himself despised as a sort of madman, or of doubtful intellect.

5. His teaching described as exploded, dying out, &c.

6. His ways and habits reckoned to be Puritanic and hypocritical.

7. Himself given up as irreclaimable, and therefore dead to society.

Let us glory in the cross, because it gibbets the world's glory, and honour, and power.

Let us glory in the cross when men take from us all other glory.

MEMORANDA

It is a subject of rejoicing and glorying that we have *such* a Saviour. The world looked upon him with contempt; and the cross was a stumbling-block to the Jew, and folly to the Greek. But to the Christian that cross is the subject of glorying. It is so because—(1) of the love of him who suffered there ; (2) of the purity and holiness of his character, for the innocent died there for the guilty ; (3) of the honour there put on the law of God by his dying to maintain it unsullied ; (4) of the reconciliation there made for sin, accomplishing what could be done by no other oblation, and by no power of man ; (5) of the pardon there procured for the guilty ; (6) of the fact that through it we become dead to the world, and are made alive unto God ; (7) of the support and consolation which go from that cross to sustain us in trial ; and (8) of the fact that it procured for us admission into heaven, a title to the world of glory. All is glory around the cross. It was a glorious

Saviour who died ; it was glorious love that led him to die ; it was a glorious object to redeem a world ; and it is unspeakable glory to which he will raise lost and ruined sinners by his death. Oh, who would not glory in such a Saviour !—*Albert Barnes.*

If you have not yet found out that Christ crucified is the foundation of the whole volume, you have hitherto read your Bible to very little profit. Your religion is a heaven without a sun, an arch without a key-stone, a compass without a needle, a clock without spring or weights, a lamp without oil. It will not comfort you ; it will not deliver your soul from hell.—*J. C. Ryle.*

Do not be satisfied with so many others only to know the cross in its power to atone. The glory of the cross is, that it was not only to Jesus the path to life, but that each moment it can become to us the power that destroys sin and death, and keeps us in the power of the eternal life. Learn from your Saviour the holy art of using it for this. Faith in the power of the cross and its victory will day by day make dead the deeds of the body, the lusts of the flesh. This faith will teach you to count the cross, with its continual death to self, all your glory. Because you regard the cross not as one who is still on the way to crucifixion, with the prospect of a painful death, but as one to whom the crucifixion is past, who already lives in Christ, and now only bears the cross as the blessed instrument through which the body of sin is done away (Rom. vi. 6, R. V.). The banner under which complete victory over sin and the world is to be won is the cross.—*Andrew Murray.*

When Ignatius, pastor of the church at Antioch, was condemned by the emperor Trajan to suffer death at Rome, he was apprehensive that the Christians there, out of their great affection for him, might endeavour to prevent his martyrdom ; and therefore wrote a letter from Smyrna to the Roman Christians, which he sent on before him, wherein he earnestly besought them to take no measures for the continuance of his life ; and, amongst other things, said, "I long for death," adding as a reason why he was desirous of thus testifying his love to Christ, "My love is crucified."

Love makes the cross easy, amiable, admirable, delicious.
Brethren, the cross of Christ is your crown, the reproach of Christ your riches ; the shame of Christ your glory.—*Joseph Alleine, written from " The Common Prison."*

CCXIX

Eph. i. 13, 14 —" That holy Spirit of promise, which is the earnest of our inheritance."

Heaven is ours by inheritance. It is not purchased by merit, nor won by strength, but obtained by birthright.

Of this inheritance we have a foretaste here below ; and that foretaste is of the nature of a pledge or earnest, guaranteeing our coming to full possession.

An earnest is of the same nature as the ultimate blessing of which it is an earnest. A pledge is returned, but an earnest is retained as part of the thing promised.

Great enjoyment attends the possession of the earnest of our inheritance when rightly understood.

I. THE HOLY SPIRIT IS HIMSELF THE EARNEST OF THE HEAVENLY INHERITANCE.

He is not only the pledge but the foretaste of everlasting bliss.

1. His entrance into the soul brings with it that same life which enters heaven, namely, the eternal life.

2. His abiding in us consecrates us to the same purpose to which we shall be devoted throughout eternity, namely, the service of the Lord our God.

3. His work in us creates that same holiness which is essential to the enjoyment of heaven.

4. His influence over us brings us that same communion with God which we shall enjoy for ever in heaven.

5. His being ours is as much as heaven being ours, if not more ; for if we possess the God of heaven we possess heaven, and more.

The possession of the Spirit is the dawn of glory.

II. THE HOLY SPIRIT BRINGS TO US MANY THINGS WHICH ARE BLESSED FORETASTES OF THE HEAVENLY INHERITANCE.

1. Rest. This is a leading idea of heaven, and we have rest at this moment in Jesus Christ. Heb. iv. 3.

2. Delight in service. We serve the Lord with gladness even now.

3. Joy over repenting sinners. This we can now attain

4. Communion with saints. How sweet even in this imperfect state !

5. Enlarged knowledge of God and of all divine things. Here also we know in part the same things which are known above.

269

6. Victory over sin, Satan, and the world.

7. Security in Christ Jesus.

8. Nearness to our Beloved.

By these windows we look into the things which God has prepared for them that love him. "He hath revealed them unto us by his Spirit."

III. THERE IS A VERY DARK CONTRAST TO THIS BRIGHT THEME.
There are "evident tokens of perdition," pledges of woe.
There are also earnests and foretastes of the eternal state of misery.

Ungodly men may pretty clearly guess what sin will bring them to when it has ripened. Let them learn from—

1. The fruit of some sins in this life : shame, rags, disease, etc.

2. Their fear of death, alarm at the thought of it.

3. Their frequent unrest and foreboding. " They flee when no man pursueth "; they are "tossed to and fro as the locust."

4. Their disappointments in their companions ; their mutual quarrels and hates. What will it be to be shut up with such persons for ever?

5. Their distaste for good things, inability to pray, etc., all earnests of the impossibility of their joining saints and angels in heaven.

Oh to be filled by the Spirit, so as to find heaven begun below !

STRIKING EXTRACTS

There is great resemblance betwixt an earnest and the indwelling of the Spirit with the graces which he works in us. 1st. The earnest is part of the whole sum, which is on a certain account to be paid at the time appointed ; so the Spirit we have, and his grace, are the beginning of that glorious being which we shall ultimately receive—the same for substance, though differing in degree. 2nd. An earnest is but little in comparison of the whole. Twenty shillings is earnest sufficient to make sure of a hundred pounds ; thus, all the grace we have is but a small thing in comparison of the fulness we look for, even as the first-fruits were in comparison of the full harvest. 3rd. An earnest doth assure him that receiveth it of the honest meaning of him with whom he contracteth ; so the Spirit and grace which we receive from God do assure us of his settled purpose of bringing us to eternal glory.—*Paul Bayne.*

Christians ! God is nearer to us than our nearest friend ; nearer to us than Christ himself would be, if we *only* felt the touch of his hand and the sweep of his vesture ; for he takes up his abode *within* us. Plato seemed to have a glimpse of this glorious truth when he said, " God is more inward to us than we are to ourselves." What was to him a beautiful speculation, is to us an inspiring reality; for we are the "temples of the Holy Ghost."—*Dr. Charles Stanford.*

As soon as we have set out on our journey to go home, our home, by foretastes, comes to meet us. The peace of our home embraces us; the Spirit, like a dove, rests upon our hearts; the glory of our home allures us; and angel-servants from our home bear us company and help us on our road. Oh, what a sweet home ours must be, that can send us such pledges of its sweetness while we are yet a great way off!—*John Pulsford.*

"*The earnest.*" The Greek word is *arrhâbôn.* It is Hebrew (at least, Shemitic) by derivation; the identical Hebrew word appearing in Gen. xxxviii. By derivation it has to do with *exchange,* and so first means a *pledge:* but usage brought it to the kindred meaning of an *earnest.* It was used for the bridegroom's betrothal-gifts to the bride, a case exactly in point here. In ecclesiastical Latin it appears usually in the shortened form, *arra.* It survives in the French *arrhes,* the money paid to strike a bargain. *Arrhâbôn* occurs elsewhere in the New Testament: 2 Cor. i. 22; v. 5. There, as here, it denotes the gifts of the Holy Spirit given to the saints, as the part payment of the coming "weight of glory," the inmost essence of which is the complete attainment (1 John iii. 2) of that likeness to the Lord which the Spirit begins and develops here (2 Cor. iii. 18). A kindred expression is, "*The first-fruits* of the Spirit" (Rom. viii. 23).—"*Cambridge Bible for Schools and Families." A work which we commend to all ministers.*

CCXX

Eph. iii. 15 —"**Of whom the whole family in heaven and earth is named.**"

Many are the weights which drag us toward earth, and the cords which bind us to it.

Among these last our families are not the least.

We need an upward impulse. Oh that we may find it in the text!

There is a blessed connection between saints below and saints above.

Oh to feel that we are one family!

I. LET US UNDERSTAND THE LANGUAGE OF THE TEXT.

    1. The *keyword* is '*family.*"

        A building sets forth the unity of the builder's design.

        A flock, unity of the shepherd's possession.

        The title of citizen implies unity of privilege.

        The idea of an army displays unity of object and pursuit.

Here we have something closer and more instructive still: "family.'

        The same Father, and thus unity of relationship.

        The same life, and so unity of nature.

        The same mutual love growing out of nature and relations.

        The same desires, interests, joys, and cares.

        The same home for abode, security, and enjoyment.

        The same inheritance to be soon possessed.

    2. The *link-word* is "*whole.*" "Whole family in heaven and earth."

There is but one family, and it is a whole.

        On earth we find a portion of the family —

            Sinning and repenting: not yet made perfect.

            Suffering and despised: strangers and foreigners among men.

            Dying and groaning, because yet in the body.

        In heaven we find another part of the family—

            Serving and rejoicing. Sinless and free from all infirmity.

            Honouring God, and honoured by him.

            Free from sighing, and engrossed in singing.

The militant and the triumphant are one undivided family.

    3. The *crowning word* is "*named.*"

We are named after the first-born, even Jesus Christ.

Thus are we all acknowledged to be as truly sons as the Lord Jesus; for the same name is named on us.

Thus is he greatly honoured among us. His name is glorified by each one who truly bears it.

Thus are we greatly honoured in him by bearing so august a name,

Thus are we taught whom to imitate. We must justify the name. Thus are we forcibly reminded of his great love to us, his great gift to us, his union with us, and his value of us.

II. LET US CATCH THE SPIRIT OF THE TEXT.

Let us now endeavour to feel and display a family feeling.

1. As members of one family let us enjoy the things we have in common. We all have —

The same occupations. It is our meat and drink to serve she Lord, to bless the brotherhood, and win souls.

The same delights ; communion, assurance, expectation, &c.

The same love from the Father.

The same justification and acceptance with our God.

The same rights to the throne of grace, angelic ministration, divine provision, spiritual illumination, &c.

The same anticipations. Growth in grace, perseverance to the end, and glory at the end.

2. As members of one family, let us be familiar with each other.

3. As members of one family, let us practically help each other.

4. As members of one family, let us lay aside all dividing names, aims, feelings, ambitions, and beliefs.

5. As members of one family, let us strive for the honour and kingdom of our Father who is in heaven.

Let us seek out the lost members of the family.

Let us cherish the forgotten members of the family.

Let us strive for the peace and unity of the family.

CHOICE WORDS

The Scripture knows but two places for the receipt of all believers, either heaven or earth. So when the apostle will tell us where all they were who were gathered under Christ as their Head and Redeemer, he rangeth them in these orders, "things in heaven, and things in earth." (Eph. i. 10); the apostle forgot limbo there, and purgatory here. As the Scripture doth know but two sorts of saints, so but two places, heaven for the triumphant, earth for the militant.—*Paul Bayne.*

"The *whole* family in heaven and earth," not the two families, nor the divided family, but the whole family in heaven and earth. It appears, at first sight, as if we were very effectually divided by the hand of *death.* Can it be that we are one family when some of us labour on, and others sleep beneath the greensward ? There was a great truth in the sentence

which Wordsworth put into the mouth of the little child, when she said,
"O master, we are seven."

> " But they are dead : those two are dead '
> Their spirits are in heaven ! "
> 'Twas throwing words away ; for still
> The little maid would have her will,
> And said : " Nay, we are seven."

Should we not thus speak of the divine family? for death assuredly
has no separating power in the household of God.—*C. H. S.*

" When I was a boy," says one, " I thought of heaven as a great shining
city, with vast walls and domes and spires, and with nobody in it except
white tenuous angels, who were strangers to me. By-and-by my little
brother died ; and I thought of a great city with walls and domes and
spires, and a flock of cold unknown angels, and one little fellow that I was
acquainted with, he was the only one I knew in that time. Then another
brother died, and there were two that I knew. Then my acquaintances
began to die, and the flock continually grew. But it was not till I had
sent one of my little children to his Grandparent—God —that I began
to think I had got a little in myself. A second went, a third went, a
fourth went ; and by that time I had so many acquaintances in heaven
that I did not see any more walls and domes and spires. I began to
think of the residents of the celestial city. And now there have so many
of my acquaintance gone there, that it sometimes seems to me that I
know more in heaven than I do on earth."—*Handbook of Illustration.*

Stein, a great German statesman, head of the Prussian government in
1807, wrote in 1812 to Count Münster :— " I am sorry your excellency
suspects a Prussian in me, and betrays a Hanoverian in yourself I have
but one Fatherland, and that is Germany ; and as under the old con-
stitution I belonged to Germany alone, and not to any part of Germany,
so to Germany alone, and not to any part of it, I am devoted with my
whole heart."

Thomas Brooks mentions a woman who lived near Lewes, in Sussex,
who was ill, and therefore was visited by one of her neighbours, who to
cheer her, told her that if she died she would go to heaven, and be with
God, and Jesus Christ, and the saints and angels. To this the sick
woman in all simplicity replied, " Ah, mistress, I have no relations there !
Nay, not so much as a gossip, or acquaintance ; and as I know nobody, I
had a great deal sooner stop with you and the other neighbours, than go
and live among strangers." It is to be feared that if a good many were
to speak their thoughts they would say much the same.

CCXXI

Eph. iii. 16, 17, 18, 19 —"That he would grant you, according to the riches of his glory, to be strengthened with might by his Spirit in the inner man;

"That Christ may dwell in your hearts by faith; that ye, being rooted and grounded in love,

"May be able to comprehend with all saints what is the breadth, and length, and depth, and height;

"And to know the love of Christ, which passeth knowledge, that ye might be filled with all the fulness of God."

The ability to comprehend and measure described in our text was the subject of the apostle's prayer, and therefore we may be quite sure that it is a most desirable attainment.

Observe how he prays, and how wisely he arranges his petitions.

He would have us measure the immeasurable, but he would first have us made fit to do so.

We shall make our chief point the fourfold measurement, but we shall note that which comes before, and that which follows after.

I. THE PREVIOUS TRAINING REQUIRED FOR THIS MEASUREMENT.

1. He would have their spiritual faculties vigorous.

"Your inner man": understanding, faith, hope, love, all need power from a divine source.

"Strengthened," made vigorous, active, healthy, capacious.

"With might": no low degree of force will suffice.

"By his Spirit." The power required is spiritual, holy, heavenly, divine, actually imparted by the Holy Ghost.

2. He would have the subject always before them. "That Christ may dwell in your heart by faith."

"In your heart." Love must learn to measure Christ's love. It is revealed to the heart rather than to the head.

"By faith." A carnal man measures by sight, a saint by faith.

"May dwell." He must be ever near, that we may learn to measure him. Communion is the basis of this knowledge.

3. He would have them exercised in the art of measurement. "That ye, being rooted and grounded in love," &c.

We must love him ourselves if we would measure Christ's love.

We must, by experience of his love, be confirmed in our own love to him, or we cannot measure his love.

275

We must also have a vital grip of Christ. We must be rooted as a tree, which takes many a hold upon the soil.

We must settle down on his love as our foundation, on which we are grounded, as a building.

We must also show fixedness, certainty, and perseverance in our character, belief, and aim; for thus only shall we learn.

II. THE MENSURATION ITSELF.

This implies a sense of the reality of the matter.

It includes a coming near to the object of our study.

It indicates an intimate study, and a careful survey.

It necessitates a view from all sides of the subject.

The order of the measurement is the usual order of our own growth in grace. Breadth and length before depth and height.

1. *The breadth.* Immense.

Comprehending all nations. "Preach the gospel to every creature."

Covering hosts of iniquities. " All manner of sin."

Compassing all needs, cares, &c.

Conferring boundless boons for this life and worlds to come.

It were well to sail across this river and survey its broad surface.

2. *The length.* Eternal.

We wonder that God should love us at all. Let us meditate upon—

Eternal love in the fountain. Election and the covenant.

Ceaseless love in the flow. Redemption, calling, perseverance.

Endless love in endurance. Longsuffering, forgiveness, faithfulness, patience, immutability.

Boundless love, in length exceeding our length of sin, suffering, backsliding, age, or temptation.

3. *The depth.* Incomprehensible.

Stoop of divine love, condescending to consider us, to commune with us, to receive us in love, to bear with our faults, and to take us up from our low estate.

Stoop of love personified in Christ.

He stoops, and becomes incarnate; endures our sorrows, bears our sins; and suffers our shame and death.

Where is the measure for all this?

Our weakness, meanness, sinfulness, despair, make one factor of the measurement.

His glory, holiness, greatness, Deity, make up the other.

4. *The height.* Infinite.

As developed in present privilege, as one with Jesus.

As to be revealed in future glory.

As never to be fully comprehended throughout the ages.

276

III. THE PRACTICAL RESULT OF THIS MENSURATION. "That ye might
    be filled with all the fulness of God."
Here are words full of mystery, worthy to be pondered.
    Be *filled*. What great things man can hold !
    Filled *with God*. What exaltation !
    Filled *with the fulness* of God. What must this be ?
    Filled *with all the fulness of God*. What more can be imagined ?

This love and this fulness will lead to the imitation of Christ's love.
Our love to him will be broad, long, deep, high.

INSERTIONS

In the gospel history we find that Christ had a fourfold entertainment
amongst the sons of men ; some received him into house, not into heart, as
Simon the Pharisee, who gave him no kiss, nor water to his feet ; some
into heart, but not into house, as Nicodemus, and others ; some neither
into heart nor house, as the graceless, swinish Gergesenes ; some both into
house and heart, as Lazarus, Mary, Martha. And thus let all good Christians do ; endeavour that Christ may dwell in their hearts by faith, that their
bodies may be fit temples of his Holy Spirit, that now in this life, whilst
Christ stands at the door of their hearts, knocking for admission, they will
lift up the latch of their souls, and let him in ; for if ever they expect to
enter into the gates of the city of God hereafter, they must open their
hearts, the gates of their own city, to him here in this world.—*John Spencer.*

> Faith makes man's heart,
>   That dark, low, ruin'd thing,
> By its rare art,
>   A palace for a king.
> Higher than proud Babel's tower by many a story ·
> By faith Christ dwells in us, the hope of glory.—*F. Tate.*

The more we know the more are we conscious of our ignorance of that
which is unknown, or, as Dr. Chalmers used to put it in his class—bor-
rowing an illustration from his favourite mathematics—" The wider the
diameter of light, the greater is the circumference of darkness." The more
a man knows, he comes at more points into contact with the unknown.

> 'Tis hard to find God ; but to comprehend
> Him as he is, is labour without end.—*Robert Herrick.*

A gentleman passing a church with Daniel Webster, asked him, " How
can you reconcile the doctrine of the Trinity with reason ? " The statesman replied by asking, " Do you understand the arithmetic of heaven ? '

CCXXII

Eph. iv. 15, 16 —"**The head, even Christ:**
"**From whom the whole body fitly joined together and compacted by that which every joint supplieth, according to the effectual working in the measure of every part, maketh increase of the body unto the edifying of itself in love.**"

The words are as "compacted" as the body itself.

We shall not attempt full or even accurate exposition of the original, but dwell on the figure of the English text, undoubtedly a Scriptural one, and full of profitable instruction.

Four subjects are brought before us in the text.

I. OUR UNION TO CHRIST : " The Head, even Christ."

   1. Essential to life.   Severed from him we are dead.

   2. Essential to growth.   We grow up into him who is the head.

   3. Essential to perfection.   What should we be without a head ?

   4. Essential to every member.   The strongest needs union to the head as much as the weakest.

II. OUR INDIVIDUALITY : " Every joint " ; " every part."

Each one must mind his own office.

   1. We must each one personally see to his own vital *union* with the body, and chiefly with the head.

   2. We must be careful to find and keep our fit *position* in the body.

   3. We must be careful of our personal *health*, for the sake of the whole body ; for one ailing member injures the whole.

   4. We must be careful of our *growth*, for the sake of the whole body.

The most careful self-watch will not be a selfish measure, but a sanitary duty involved by our relationship to the rest.

III. OUR RELATIONSHIP TO EACH OTHER : " Joined together " ; " that which every joint supplieth."

   1. We should in desire and spirit be fitted to work with others.   We are to have joints.   How could there be a body without them ?

   2. We should supply the joint-oil of love when so doing ; indeed, each one must yield his own peculiar influence to the rest.

278

3. We should aid the compactness of the whole by our own solidity, and healthy firmness in our place.

4. We should perform our service for all. We should guard, guide, support, nourish, and comfort the rest of the members, as our function may be.

IV. Our compact unity as a church : " The body edifying itself in love."

1. There is but one body of Christ, even as he is the one Head.

2. It is an actual, living union. Not a mere professed unity, but a body quickened by "the effectual working" of God's Spirit in every part.

3. It is a growing corporation. It increases by mutual edification. Not by being puffed up, but by being built up. It grows as the result of its own life, sustained by suitable food.

4. It is an immortal body. Because the Head lives, the body must live also.

Are we in the body of Christ?

Are we not concerned to see it made perfect?

Are we ministering the supply which the body may fairly expect from us as members?

To fit in

There is great fitness in the figure of the head and the members. The head is—(1.) The highest part of the body, the most exalted. (2.) The most sensitive part, the seat of nerve and sensation, of pleasure and pain. (3.) The most honourable part, the glory of man, the part of man's body that receives the blessing, wears the crown, and is anointed with the oil of joy and of consecration. (4.) The most exposed part, especially assailed in battle, and liable to be injured, and where injury would be most dangerous. (5.) The most expressive part, the seat of expression, whether in the smile of approval, the frown of displeasure, the tear of sympathy, the look of love.—*G. S. Bowes.*

Every one knows that it would be far better to lose our feet than our head. Adam had feet to stand with, but we have lost them by his disobedience : yet, glory be to God, we have found a Head, in whom we abide eternally secure, a Head which we shall never lose.—"*Feathers for Arrows.*"

The moment I make of myself and Christ two, I am all wrong. But when I see that we are one, all is rest and peace.—*Luther.*

279

What a happy condition the Church and members of Christ are in!
(1.) Interested in the same love as the Head. (2) Under the same
decree of election with the Head. (3) Allied to the same relations,
interested in the same riches, and assured by membership of the same
life and immortality in the world to come: "Because I live, ye shall
live also."—*Benjamin Keach.*

Of all the symbols which set forth Christ's church, I prefer this.
Bringing out, as well as any other, our relationship to Christ, and better
than any other our relationship to each other, it teaches us lessons of
love, and charity, and tender sympathy. When bill-hook or pruning-
knife lops a branch from the tree, the stem bends; it seems for a while
to drop some tears, but they are soon dried up; and the other boughs
suffer no pain, show no sympathy—their leaves dancing merrily in the
wind over the poor dead branch that lies withering below. But a
tender sympathy pervades the body and its members. Touch my
finger roughly, and the whole body feels it; wound this foot, and
thrilling through my frame, the pang shoots upward to the head; let
the heart, or even a tooth, ache, and all the system suffers disorder.
With what care is a diseased member touched! What anxious efforts do
we make to save a limb! With what slow reluctance does a patient, after
long months or years of suffering, consent to the last remedy, the
surgeon's knife! Many holy lessons of love, charity, and sympathy,
our Lord teaches by this figure.—*Dr. Guthrie.*

We must work in concert. Stress is laid on this in Scripture, as may
be seen from such expressions as these:—"If two of you shall agree,"
"Fellow-helpers to the truth," "With one mind striving together for the
faith of the gospel." It is as with the human hand. Take one of the
fingers, the forefinger, for example; it can do many things by itself
separately. I lay it on my pulse, to know how my heart beats; I turn
over the leaf of a book with it; I use it to point a stranger the way; I
place it on my lips to signify silence; I single out the individual to whom
I would say, "*Thou art the man*"; I shake it in warning or remonstrance.
But the hand can do, not five times as much as a single finger, not fifty
times as much, not five hundred times as much, but five thousand times—
and more. So with Christian churches; there must not merely be individual effort, but combined and united effort, on the New Testament
principle, "As every man hath received the gift, even so let him minister."
Dr. Culross.

280

CCXXIII

Eph. iv. 20, 21 —" But ye have not so learned Christ,
" If so be that ye have heard him, and have been taught
by him, as the truth is in Jesus."

The distinction between the Christian and others. " But ye."

There must be this separation as long as the world is "the world."

The means of this distinction is our discipleship : we have learned Christ, and learned him in a different way from that which satisfies many who profess to know him.

We have not so learned Christ as to be able to profess his name, and yet practise lasciviousness.

We are converted into learners, and are under the tutelage of the Holy Spirit. How we learn is a test question. Some have learned Christ, and yet are not saved, and others have not *so* learned him, but are truly his disciples.

I. OUR LESSON. "Learned Christ."

This learning Christ is—

Much more than learning doctrine, precept, or ceremony.

Much more than knowing about Christ, or learning from Christ.

It includes several forms of knowledge.

1. To know him as a personal Christ.
2. To know his nature, and to treat him accordingly.
3. To know his offices, and how to use them.
4. To know his finished work for God and for us.
5. To know his influence over men, and to test it.
6. To know by learning Christ the way to live like him.

II. HOW WE HAVE <u>NOT</u> LEARNED IT.

1. So as to remain as we were before. Unchanged, and yet at peace.
2. So as to excuse sin because of his atonement.
3. So as to feel a freedom to sin because of pardon.
4. So as even to commit sin in Christ's name.
5. So as to reckon that we cannot conquer sin, and so sit down under the dominion of some constitutional temptation.
6. So as to profess reverence for his name and character, and then think little of the truth which he reveals.

III. How we have learned it.

We know the truth, and know it in its best light—

1. As directly taught by his own self, and by his own Spirit.
2. As distinctly embodied in his life and character.
3. As it relates to him and honours him.
4. Consequently as it is in him. Truth is in Jesus, indeed and of a truth, for in him everything is real.
5. Consequently as it works a total change in us, and makes us like to him in whom truth is embodied.

See, then, that we not only learn of Jesus, but we learn Jesus.

It is not enough to hear him and to be taught by him ; we want to know himself.

Knowing him, we know the truth ; for it is in him.

THOUGHTS

Instead of "*if so be that,*" many very competent scholars propose to render the original "inasmuch as," or, "since ye have heard," &c.; for the apostle is not referring to a supposed case, but stating a fact, as verse 20 proves.— *W. O'Neill.*

He exhorts not to an outward reformation of their converse only, but to that truth and sincerity of sanctification, which the doctrine and power of grace in Christ teacheth and worketh in all true Christians : "If so be," saith he, "ye have learned the truth as it is in Jesus." Which doeth not, as other doctrines of philosophers, &c., teach you to put off the evils of your outward converse only, and to put on a new conversation over an old nature, as a sheep-skin over a wolfish nature ; he that doth no more falls short of that truth of grace which Christ requires ; but it teacheth principally to put off the old man, as the cause of all the evils in the outward converse ; and that is his meaning, when he saith, "As concerning the outward converse put off the old man," without which it is impossible to reform the converse.— *Thomas Goodwin.*

An illustration of the foregoing remarks is found in Lord Chesterfield, who trained his only son, not to abandon vice, but to be a gentleman in the practice of it.

Some persons, instead of "putting off the old man," dress him up in a new shape.— *St. Bernard.*

Unsanctified wisdom is the devil's greatest tool.

A handful of good life is worth a bushel of learning.

282

CCXXIV

Eph. b. 11 —"And habe no fellowship with the unfruitful works of darkness, but rather reprobe them."

Directions how to live while here below are very needful.

We constantly come into contact with ungodly men: this is unavoidable; but here we are taught to avoid such communion with them as would make us partakers in their evil deeds.

Three truths are incidentally mentioned: evil works are sterile, they are works of darkness, and they deserve reproof.

We must have *no* fellowship with them; neither at any time, nor in any manner, nor in any degree.

I. WHAT IS FORBIDDEN? "Fellowship with works of darkness."

This fellowship may be produced in several ways:

1. By personally committing the sins so.described, or by joining with others in bringing them about.

2. By teaching wrong doing, either by plain word or by just inference.

3. By constraining, commanding, or tempting: by threat, request, persuasion, inducement, compulsion, bribery, or influence.

4. By provoking, through exciting anger, emulation, or discouragement.

5. By neglecting to rebuke: especially by parents and masters misusing their office and allowing known evils in the family.

6. By counselling, and advising, or by guiding by example.

7. By consenting, agreeing, and co-operating. By smiling at an evil attempt, and, in the end, partaking in the spoil. Those who join with churches in error come under this head.

8. By conniving at sin: tolerating, concealing, and making light of it.

9. By commending, countenancing, defending, and excusing the wrong already done; and contending against those who would expose, denounce, and punish it.

II. WHAT IS COMMANDED? "Reprove them."

"Reprove" in the original is a word of large meaning.

1. Rebuke. Declare the wrong of it, and show your hatred thereof.

2. Convict. As the Holy Spirit reproves the world of sin, so aim at proving the world guilty by your holy life and bold witness.

3. Convert. This is to be your continual aim with those about you. You are so to reprove as to win men from ways of evil.

Oh that we had more of honest and loving reproof of all evil!

III. WHY IT IS COMMANDED TO ME?

It is specially my duty to be clear of other men's sins.

1. As an imitator of God and a dear child.   Verse 1.
2. As one who is an inheritor of the kingdom of God.   Verses 5, 6.
3. As one who has come out of darkness into marvellous light in the Lord.   Verse 8
4. As one who bears fruit, even the fruit of the Spirit, which is in all goodness, righteousness and truth.   Verse 9.
5. As one who would not be associated with that which is either shameful or foolish.   Verses 12, 15.

If our fellowship is with God, we must quit the ways of darkness.

IV. WHAT MAY COME OF OBEDIENCE TO THE COMMAND.

Even if we could see no good result, yet our duty would be plain enough; but much benefit may result.

1. We shall be clear of complicity with deeds of darkness.
2. We shall be honoured in the consciences of the ungodly.
3. We may thus win them to repentance and eternal life.
4. We shall glorify God by our separated walk and by the godly perseverance with which we adhere to it.
5. We may thus establish others in holy nonconformity to the world.

Let us use the text as a warning to worldly professors.
Let us take it as a directory in our conversation with the ungodly.

EXAMPLES

A member of his congregation was in the habit of going to the theatre. Mr. Hill went to him and said, "This will never do—a member of my church in the habit of attending the theatre!" Mr. So-and-so replied that it surely must be a mistake, as he was not in the habit of going there, although it was true he did go now and then *for a treat.* "Oh!" said Rowland Hill, "then you are a worse hypocrite than ever, sir. Suppose any one spread the report that I ate carrion, and I answered, 'Well, there is no wrong in that; I don't eat carrion every day in the week, but I have a dish now and then *for a treat!*' Why, you would say, 'What a nasty, foul, and filthy appetite Rowland Hill has, to have to go to carrion for a treat!' Religion is the Christian's truest treat, Christ is his enjoyment."—*Charlesworth's Life of Rowland Hill.*

On one occasion, travelling in the Portsmouth mail, Andrew Fuller was much annoyed by the profane conversation of two young men who sat opposite. After a time, one of them, observing his gravity, accosted him with an air of impertinence, inquiring, in rude and indelicate language, whether on his arrival at Portsmouth he should not indulge himself in a manner evidently corresponding with their own intentions. Mr. Fuller, lowering his ample brows, and looking the inquirer full in the face, replied in measured tones : " Sir, I am a man that fears God." Scarcely a word was uttered during the remainder of the journey.

Memoir of Andrew Fuller.

Matthew Wilks once rode by coach with a young nobleman and a female passenger. The nobleman entered upon an improper conversation with the coachman and the woman. At a favourable opportunity Mr. Wilks attracted his attention, and said, " My lord, maintain your rank ! " The reproof was felt and acted upon. Let the Christian ever maintain his rank.

A distinguished Christian lady was recently spending a few weeks in a hotel at Long Branch, and an attempt was made to induce her to attend a dance, in order that the affair might have the prestige bestowed by her presence, as she stood high in society. She declined all the importunities of her friends, and finally an honourable senator tried to persuade her to attend, saying, " Miss B., this is quite a harmless affair, and we want to have the exceptional honour of your presence." " Senator," said the lady, " I cannot do it, I am a Christian. I never do anything in my summer vacation, or wherever I go, that will injure the influence I have over the girls of my Sunday-school class." The senator bowed, and said, " I honour you ; if there were more Christians like you, more men like myself would become Christians."—*Dr. Pentecost.*

Rebukes should always be dealt in love : never wash a man's face in vitriol. Some persons would burn a house down to get rid of a mouse : the smallest fault is denounced as a great crime, and a good brother is cut off from fellowship, and bad feeling is raised, when a gentle hint would have done the work much more effectually.—*C. H. S.*

CCXXV

€ph. b. 25 —" Husbanns, lobe your tuibes, eben as Christ also lobed the church, and gabe himself for it."

The love of Christ to his church is the pattern for husbands.

It should be a pure, fervent, constant, self-sacrificing love.

The conduct of Jesus was the best proof of his love. " He loved the church, and gave himself for it."

Our conduct should be the genuine outcome of our love.

I. How CHRIST LOVED HIS CHURCH.

He loved his own church with—

1. A love of choice, and special regard.

2. A love of unselfishness : he loved not hers, but her.

3. A love of complacency. He calls her " Hephzibah, my delight is in her."

4. A love of sympathy. Her interests are his interests.

5. A love of communion. He manifests himself to his chosen bride.

6. A love of unity. A loving, living, lasting union is established.

7. A love of immutable constancy. He loves unto the end.

II. How HE PROVED HIS LOVE. "Gave himself for it."

1. He gave himself to his church by leaving heaven and becoming incarnate that he might assume her nature.

2. He gave himself throughout his life on earth by spending all his strength to bless his beloved.

3. He gave himself in death ; the ransom for his church.

4. He gave himself in his eternal life; rising, ascending, reigning, pleading ; and all for the church of his choice.

5. He gave himself in all that he now is as God and man, exalted to the throne, for the endless benefit of his beloved church.

III. How WE SHOULD THINK OF IT.

It is set before us as a love which should influence our hearts.

We should think of it—

1. In a way of gratitude, wondering more and more at such love.

2. In a way of obedience, as the wife obeys the husband.

3. In a way of reverence. Looking up to love so great, so heavenly, so perfect, so divine.

4. In a way of holiness. Rejoicing to be like our Holy Husband.
5. In a way of love. Yielding our whole heart to him.
6. In a way of imitation. Loving him, and others for his sake.

Let us enter into the love of Jesus, enjoy it in our own hearts, and then imitate it in our families.

Concerning Love

Rowland Hill often felt much grieved at the false reports which were circulated of many of his sayings, especially those respecting his publicly mentioning Mrs. Hill. His attentions to her till the close of life were of the most gentlemanly and affectionate kind. The high view he entertained of her may be seen from the following fact:—A friend having informed Mr. Hill of the sudden death of a lady, the wife of a minister, remarked, " I am afraid our dear minister loved his wife too well, and the Lord in wisdom has removed her." " What, sir ? " replied Mr. Hill, with the deepest feeling, "can a man love a good wife too much? Impossible, sir, unless he can love her better than Christ loves the church : ' Husbands, love your wives, *even as* Christ also loved the church, and gave himself for it.' "

"Let all things be done in love," saith the apostle. If all thy actions towards others, then, much more all things that concern thy wife, should be done in love. Thy thoughts should be thoughts of love; thy looks should be looks of love; thy lips, like the honeycomb, should drop nothing but sweetness and love ; thy instructions should be edged with love; thy reprehensions should be sweetened with love; thy carriage and whole conversation towards her should be but the fruit and demonstration of thy love. Oh, how did Christ, who is thy pattern, love his spouse ! His birth, life, and death were but, as it were, a stage whereon the hottest love imaginable, from first to last, acted its part to the life. It was a known, unknown love. Tiberius Gracchus, the Roman, finding two snakes in his bed, and consulting with the soothsayers, was told that one of them must be killed ; yet, if he killed the male, he himself would die shortly; if the female, his wife would die. His love to his wife, Cornelia, was so great, that he killed the male, saith Plutarch, and died quickly.—*George Swinnock.*

The Spanish poet Calderon, in one of his dramas, describes a beautiful Roman girl, Daria by name, eventually a Christian convert and martyr, who declares, while yet a pagan, that she will never love until she finds some one who has died to prove his love for her. She hears of Christ, and her heart is won.

CCXXVI

Eph. bi. 15 —"And your feet shod with the preparation of the gospel of peace."

Christians are meant to be steadfast, active, moving, progressing, ascending, hence their feet are carefully provided for.

They are feeble in themselves, and need protection: their road also is rough, and hence they need the shoe which grace provides.

I. LET US EXAMINE THE SHOES.

1. They come from a blessed Maker. One who is skilful in all arts, and knows by experience what is wanted, since he has himself journeyed through life's roughest ways.

2. They are made of excellent material: "the preparation of the gospel of peace." Well seasoned, soft in wear, lasting long.
   Peace with God as to the past, the future, the present.
   Peace of full submission to the divine mind and will.
   Peace with the Word and all its teachings.
   Peace with one's inner self, conscience, fears, desires, etc.
   Peace with brethren in the church and the family.
   Peace with all mankind : "as much as lieth in you live peaceably with all men": Rom. xii. 18.

3. They are such as none can make except the Lord, who both sends the gospel, and prepares the peace.

4. They are such shoes as Jesus wore, and all the saints.

5. They are such as will never wear out : they are old, yet ever new ; we may wear them at all ages and in all places.

II. LET US TRY THEM ON.

Observe with delight—

1. Their perfect fitness. They are made to suit each one of us

2. Their excellent foothold : we can tread with holy boldness upon our high places with these shoes.

3. Their marching powers for daily duty. No one grows weary or footsore when he is thus shod.

4. Their wonderful protection against trials by the way. "Thou shalt tread on the lion and adder": Ps. xci. 13.

5. Their pleasantness of wear, giving rest to the whole man.

6. Their adaptation for hard work, climbing, ploughing, etc.

7. Their endurance of fire and water: Isa. xliii. 2. By peace of mind we learn to pass through every form of trial.

8. Their fighting qualities. They are really a part of "the whole armour of God." See the chapter in which the text is found.

III. LET US LOOK AT THE BAREFOOTED AROUND US.

The sinner is unshod. Yet he kicks against the pricks. How can he hope to fulfil the heavenly pilgrimage?

The professor is slipshod, or else he wears tight shoes. His fine slippers will soon be worn out. He loves not the gospel, knows not its peace, seeks not its preparation.

The gospel alone supplies a fit shoe for all feet.

To the gospel let us fly at once. Come, poor shoeless beggar!

FASTENINGS

"*Put shoes on his feet*" were among the first words of welcome to the returning prodigal. To be shoeless was in Israel a mark of great disgrace, indicating a lost inheritance, a state of misery and penury. (See Deut. xxv. 10.)

The Chinese advertise shoes which enable the wearer to walk on the clouds. Compare Isa. xl. 31 : "They that wait upon the Lord shall renew their strength. They shall *run*, and not be weary; they shall *walk*, and not faint." "*Run* with patience, looking unto Jesus." (Heb. xii. 1—3.)

"Your feet shod with the preparation of the gospel of peace." (Eph. vi. 15.) The passage has been paraphrased, "Shod with the firm footing of the solid knowledge of the gospel." The word "preparation" signifies *preparedness* or *readiness*. Compare 2 Tim. iv. 2 : "Instant in season, out of season"; also Rom. i. 15 : "I am ready to preach the gospel." This preparedness is well-pleasing to God. "How *beautiful* are thy feet with shoes, O prince's daughter!" (Cant. vii. 1 ; Isa. lii. 7.)

Mrs. Gordon.

Christian in the palace Beautiful.—"The next day they took him, and had him into the armoury, where they showed him all manner of furniture which their Lord had provided for pilgrims, as sword, shield, helmet, breast-plate, all-prayer, and shoes that would not wear out. And there was here enough of this to harness out as many men for the service of their Lord as there be stars in the heaven for multitude."

Bunyan.

None can make a shoe to the creature's foot, so that he shall go easy on a hard way, but Christ; he can do it to the creature's full content. And how doth he do it? Truly, no other way than by underlaying it; or, if you will, lining it with the peace of the gospel. What though the way be set with sharp stones? if this shoe go between the Christian's foot and them, they cannot much be felt.

It is the soldier's shoe that is meant, which, if right, is to be of the strongest make, being not so much intended for finery as for defence.

The gospel shoe will not come on thy foot so long as that foot is swelled with any sinful humour (I mean any unrighteous or unholy practice). This evil must be purged out by repentance, or thou canst not wear the shoe of peace.

The Jews were to eat their passover with their loins girded, their shoes on their feet, and their staff in their hand, and all in haste. (Exod. xii. 11.) When God is feasting the Christian with present comforts, he must have this gospel shoe on; he must not sit down as if he were feasting at home, but stand and eat even as he takes a running meal in an inn on his way, willing to be gone as soon as ever he is a little refreshed for his journey.

The conceited professor, who hath a high opinion of himself, is a man shod and prepared, he thinks; but not with the right gospel shoe. He that cannot take the length of his foot, how can he of himself fit a shoe to it?

Is not thy shoe, Christian, yet on? art thou not yet ready to march? If thou hast it, what hast thou to dread? Canst fear that any stone can hurt thy foot through so thick a sole?—*William Gurnall.*

Paul was thus shod: Rom. viii. 38, "I am persuaded, nothing shall separate me from the love of God." "All things, I know, work together for the good of them that are beloved of God." (Rom. viii. 28.) And this furniture made him go such hard ways cheerfully, in which showers of afflictions did fall as thick as hailstones. This doth make God's children, though not in the letter, yet in some sort, tread upon the adder and the basilisk; yea, to defy vipers, and receive no hurt; whereas, if the feet be bared a little with the absence of this peace, anything causeth us sore smart.—*Paul Bayne.*

CCXXVII

Phil. iv. 4 —"**Rejoice in the Lord alway: and again I say, Rejoice.**"

Joy drives out discord. See how our text follows as a remedy upon a case of disagreement in the church, verses 1 and 2.

Joy helps against the trials of life. Hence it is mentioned as a preparation for the rest of faith which is prescribed in verse 6.

I. THE GRACE COMMANDED. "Rejoice."

 1. It is delightful: our soul's jubilee has come when joy enters.

 2. It is demonstrative: it is more than peace; it sparkles, shines, sings. Why should it not? Joy is a bird; let it fly in the open heavens, and let its music be heard of all men.

 3. It is stimulating, and urges its possessor to brave deeds.

 4. It is influential for good. Sinners are attracted to Jesus by the joy of saints. More flies are caught with a spoonful of honey than with a barrel of vinegar.

 5. It is contagious. Others are gladdened by our rejoicing.

 6. It is commanded. It is not left optional, but made imperative. We are as much commanded to rejoice as to keep the Sabbath.

  It is commanded because joy makes us like God.

  It is commanded because it is for our profit.

  It is commanded because it is good for others.

II. THE JOY DISCRIMINATED. "In the Lord."

 1. As to sphere. "In the Lord." This is that sacred circle wherein a Christian's life should be always spent.

 2. As to object. "In the Lord."

 We should rejoice in the Lord God, Father, Son, and Spirit.

 We should rejoice in the Lord Jesus, dead, risen, &c.

  Not in temporals, personal, political, or pecuniary.

  Nor in special privileges, which involve greater responsibility.

  Nor even in religious successes. "In this rejoice not, that the devils are subject unto you through my word, but rather rejoice that your names are written in heaven": Luke x. 20.

  Nor in self and its doings. Phil. iii. 3.

III. THE TIME APPOINTED. "Always."

 1. When you cannot rejoice in any other, rejoice in God.

 2. When you can rejoice in other things, sanctify all with joy in God

291

3. When you have not before rejoiced, begin at once.
4. When you have long rejoiced, do not cease for a moment.
5. When others are with you, lead them in this direction.
6. When you are alone, enjoy to the full this rejoicing.

IV. THE EMPHASIS LAID ON THE COMMAND. "Again I say, Rejoice."
Paul repeats his exhortation,

1. To show his love to them. He is intensely anxious that they should share his joy.
2. To suggest the difficulty of continual joy. He twice commands, because we are slow to obey.
3. To assert the possibility of it. After second thoughts, he feels that he may fitly repeat the exhortation.
4. To impress the importance of the duty. Whatever else you forget, remember this : Be sure to rejoice.
5. To allow of special personal testimony. "Again I say, Rejoice." Paul rejoiced. He was habitually a happy man.
This epistle to the Philippians is peculiarly joyous.
Let us look it through. The apostle is joyful throughout :
He sweetens prayer with joy : i. 4.
He rejoices that Christ is preached : i. 18.
He wished to live to gladden the church : i. 25.
To see the members likeminded was his joy : ii. 2.
It was his joy that he should not run in vain : ii. 16.
His farewell to them was, "Rejoice in the Lord" : iii. 1.
He speaks of those who rejoice in Christ Jesus : iii. 3.
He calls his converts his joy and crown : iv. 1.
He expresses his joy in their kindness : iv. 4, 10, 18.

To all our friends let us use this as a blessing : "Rejoice in the Lord."
This is only a choicer way of saying, Be happy ; Fare ye well.
"Fare ye well, and if for ever,
Still for ever fare ye well."

JOY-BELLS

It is not an indifferent thing to rejoice, or not to rejoice ; but we are commanded to rejoice, to show that we break a commandment if we rejoice not. Oh, what a comfort is this, when the Comforter himself shall command us to rejoice ! God was wont to say, *Repent,* and not *rejoice,* because men rejoice too much ; but God here commandeth to *rejoice,* as though some men did not rejoice enough : therefore you must understand to whom he speaketh. In Ps. cxlix. 5, it is said, "Let the

292

saints be glad"; not, let the wicked be glad. And in Isa. xl. 1, he saith, "Comfort my people," not, comfort mine enemies, showing to whom this commandment of Paul is sent, "Rejoice evermore."—*Henry Smith.*

The thing whereunto he exhorteth, as ye see, is to rejoice; a thing which the sensual man can quickly lay hold on, who loves to rejoice, and to cheer himself in the days of his flesh; which yet might now seem unreasonable to the Philippians, who lived in the midst of a naughty and crooked nation, by whom they were even hated for the truth's sake which they professed. Mark, therefore, wherein the apostle would they should rejoice, namely, in the Lord; and here the sensual man, that haply would catch hold when it is said, *Rejoice*, by-and-by when it is added, *in the Lord*, will let go his hold. But they that, by reason of the billows and waves of the troublesome sea of this world, cannot brook the speech when it is said, *Rejoice*, are to lay sure holdfast upon it when it is added, *Rejoice in the Lord;* which holdfast once taken, that they might for ever keep it sure, in the third place it is added, *Rejoice in the Lord alway*, to note the constancy that should be in Christian joy.

Henry Airay.

Another note to distinguish this joy in the Lord from all other joys is the fulness and exuberancy of it; for it is more joy than if corn and wine and oil increased. Else what needed the apostle, having said, "Rejoice in the Lord alway," to add, "and again I say, Rejoice"? What can be more than *always*, but still adding to the fulness of our joy, till our cup do overflow?

Upon working days rejoice in the Lord, who giveth thee strength to labour, and feedeth thee with the labour of thy hands. On holidays rejoice in the Lord, who feasteth thee with the marrow and fatness of his house. In plenty, rejoice again and again, because the Lord giveth; in want rejoice, because the Lord taketh away, and as it pleaseth the Lord, so come things to pass.—*Edward Marbury.*

The calendar of the sinner has only a few days in the year marked as festival days; but *every day* of the Christian's calendar is marked by the hand of God as a day of rejoicing.—*Anon.*

'Tis impious in a good man to be sad.

Edward Young.

Napoleon, when sent to Elba, adopted, in proud defiance of his fate, the motto, "*Ubicunque felix.*" It was not true in his case; but the Christian may be truly "happy everywhere" and always.

CCXXVIII

Col. i. 16 —"For by him were all things created, that are in heaven, and that are in earth, visible and invisible, whether they be thrones, or dominions, or principalities, or powers: all things were created by him, and for him."

Any theme which exalts the Saviour is precious to the saints.

This is one in which the preacher cannot hope to do more than to show how vastly his theme is above him.

All things were created by God and for him, yet by Jesus and for him, because he is truly God and one with the Father.

I. CONSIDER THE STATEMENT ITSELF.

   1. Heaven itself was created by and for Christ Jesus.

      There is such a place, as well as such a state, and of that place Jesus is the centre. Enoch and Elijah in their bodies are there, Jesus as man is there, and there all his people will be. God, as a pure Spirit, needed no such place; nor angels, for everywhere they would see God.

      It was created for Jesus, and for the people whom he will bring there to be one for ever with himself.

      It exists by Jesus and for Jesus.

         Everything in heaven prepared by Jesus. He is the designer of it.

         Everything in heaven reflects Jesus. He is the soul of it.

         Everything in heaven praises Jesus. He is the King of it.

   2. The angels. All their ranks were made by him and for him.

      To worship him, and glorify him with their adoration.

      To rejoice with him and in him, as they do when sinners repent.

      To guard Christ's people in life, and bring them to him in death.

      To carry out his purposes of judgment, as with Pharaoh, etc.

      To achieve his purposes of deliverance, as Peter from prison.

   3. This world was made by him to be—

      A place for him to live and die upon.

      A stage for his people to live and act upon.

      A province to be fully restored to his dominion.

      A new world in the ages to come, to bless other worlds, if such there be; and to display, for ever, the glories of Jesus.

   4. All the lower creatures are for Jesus. " And that are in earth."

      They are needful to man, and so to our Lord's system of grace.

      They are illustrations of Christ's wisdom, power, and goodness.

      They are to be treated kindly for his sake.

5. Men were created by and for Christ.

That he might display a special phase of power and skill, in creating spiritual beings embodied in material forms.

That he might become himself one of them.

That he might himself be the head of a remarkable order of beings who know both good and evil, are children of God, are bound to God by ties of gratitude, and are one with his Son.

That for these he might die: to save them, and to make them his companions, friends, and worshippers for ever.

That human thrones, even when occupied by wicked men, might be made to subserve his purpose by restraint or by overruling.

II. REVIEW THE REFLECTIONS HENCE ARISING.

1. Jesus, then, is God. "By him were all things created."

2. Jesus is the clue of the universe; its centre and explanation. All things are to be seen in the light of the cross, and all things reflect light on the cross. For him all things exist.

3. To live to Jesus, then, is to find out the true object of our being, and to be in accord with all creation.

4. Not living to Jesus, we can have no blessing.

5. We can only live *for* him as we live *by* him, for so all things do.

6. It is clear that he must triumph. All is going well. If we look at history from his throne, all things are "for him." "He must reign." Let us comfort one another with these words.

What an honour to be the smallest page in the retinue of such a prince!

WORDS OF HOMAGE

When the Christian martyr Pionius was asked by his judges, "What God dost thou worship?" he replied : "I worship him who made the heavens, and who beautified them with stars, and who has enriched the earth with flowers and trees." "Dost thou mean," asked the magistrates, "Him who was crucified (*illum dicis qui crucifixus est*)?" "Certainly," replied Pionius, "Him whom the Father sent for the salvation of the world." As Pionius died, so died Blandina and the whole host of those who, in the first three centuries, without knowing anything of the Nicene creed, held it implicitly, if not explicitly, and proclaimed it in flames and in dungeons, in famine and in nakedness, under the rack and under the sword.—*Joseph Cook.*

In creation God shows us his hand, but in redemption God gives us his heart.—*Adolphe Monod.*

295

What sublime views does this subject (the creation of angels) furnish us of the greatness of Christ! By him, says the apostle, were all those illustrious beings created, together with all their attributes, importance, and dignity. The character of every workman is seen, of course, in the nature of the work which he has made. If this be insignificant and worthless, it exhibits nothing but the insignificance and worthlessness of the maker. If curious and excellent, if sublime and wonderful, it unfolds strongly and certainly his greatness, wisdom, and glory. Of what faculties are angels the subjects! Of what intelligence, purity, power, loveliness, and elevation of mind! What, then, must be the perfections of him who contrived and formed angels; who with a word called them into being; who preserves, informs, directs, controls, and blesses them for ever! Great and excellent as they are, they are exhibited as "unclean in his sight," and as "charged with folly," before him. How amazing, then, must be the perfection of his character! how great, how wise, how good!—*Timothy Dwight.*

Paul would prevent the shadow of a doubt crossing our minds about our Lord having a right to the divine honours of the Creator. " By him," he says, " all things were created"; and as if an angel, standing at his side when he penned these words, had stooped down to whisper in his ear that men, attempting to rob Jesus of his honour, would rise to throw doubt upon that truth, and explain it away—to make the truth still more plain, he adds, "that are in heaven, and that are in earth." Not content with that, he uses yet more comprehensive terms; and to embrace all the regions of God's universe above the earth and beyond the starry bounds of heaven, he adds, " visible and invisible." Nor leaves his task till, sweeping the highest and the lowest things, men and worms, angels and insects, all into Christ's hands, he adds, " whether they be thrones, or dominions, or principalities, or powers."—*Dr. Guthrie.*

It was well said of a heathen, *Si essem luscinia*—if I were a nightingale I would sing as a nightingale; *si alauda*—if I were a lark I would soar as a lark. Since I am a man, what should I do but know, love, and praise God without ceasing, and glorify my Creator? Things are unprofitable or misplaced when they do not seek or serve their end; therefore, for what use are we meet, if we are unmeet for our proper end? We are like the wood of the vine, good for nothing, not so much as to make a pin whereon to hang anything (Ezek. xv. 2); good for nothing but to be cast into the fire unless it be fruitful. What are we good for if we be not serviceable to the ends for which we were created?
Thomas Manton.

CCXXIX

Col. ii. 6 —"As ye have therefore received Christ Jesus the Lord, so walk ye in him."

There is great safety in going back to first principles.

To make sure of being in the right way, it is good to look back at the entrance gate. Well begun is half done.

The text is addressed, not to the ungodly, nor to strangers, but to those who "have received Christ Jesus the Lord." They have commenced well, let them go on as they have begun.

For the spiritual good and establishment of such in the faith, the apostle longs, and to this end he gives the exhortation.

I. Notice in the text THE FACT STATED. Sincere believers have in very deed "*received* Christ Jesus the Lord."

This is the old gospel word. Here is no evolution from within, but a gift from without heartily accepted by the soul.

This is free-grace language : "received," not earned or purchased.

It is not said that they received Christ's *words*, though that is true, for they prize every precept and doctrine ; but they received Christ.

Carefully observe :

1. The personality of him whom they received, "Christ Jesus the Lord" : his person, his Godhead, his humanity : himself.

Received him into their knowledge.

Received him into their understanding.

Received him into their affections.

Received him into their trust.

Received him as their life at their new birth ; for when they received him he gave them power to become the sons of God.

2. The threefold character in which they received him.

The words of the text, "Christ Jesus the Lord," indicate this. They received him

As Christ, anointed and commissioned of God.

As Jesus, the Saviour, to redeem and sanctify them.

As the Lord, to reign and rule over them with undivided sway.

3. The looking away from self in this saving act of reception.

It is not said, as ye have fought for Jesus and won him, or, studied the truth and discovered Christ Jesus ; but, as ye have "received" him. This strips us of everything like boasting, for all we do is to receive.

4 The blessed certainty of the experience of those to whom Paul wrote: "As ye *have* received Christ Jesus the Lord." They had really received Jesus; they had found the blessing to be real: no doubt remained as to their possession of it.

II. Notice, next, THE COUNSEL GIVEN: "So walk ye in him."
There are four things suggested by that word "walk."
  1. Life. Vitally enjoy the Lord Jesus.
  2. Continuance. Remain in Christ: make him your constant place of daily movement and occupation.
  3. Activity. Busy yourselves, but not with a new way of salvation. Work for Jesus, and with him, and in obedience to him.
  4. Progress. Advance, but ever let your most advanced thought remain in him.

III. Notice, lastly, THE MODEL WHICH IS PRESENTED TO US. We are to walk in Christ Jesus the Lord "as we received him."
And how was that?
  1. We received him gratefully. How we blessed his name for regarding our low estate!
  2. We received him humbly. We had no claim to his grace, and we confessed this, and were lowly.
  3. We received him joyfully. Our first joy was bright as the dew of the morning. Have we lost it?
  4. We received him effectually. We brought forth many spiritual fruits, and abounded in life, faith, love, and every grace.
  5. We received him unreservedly. We made no conditions with him, and we reserved nothing for the flesh.
Thus we should continue to walk in him, evermore in our daily life excelling in all these points.

Alas, some have never received Jesus!
Our closing words must be addressed to such.
If you will not receive Jesus, you refuse mercy here and heaven hereafter. What! will you not receive so great a boon?

EXPLANATORY

Inquirers are not infrequently counselled to give their hearts to Christ, or to consecrate themselves to the Lord. We would not be over-critical with what is well meant; but really this is not the gospel. The good news of grace is, that God hath given to us eternal life and redemption through his Son, and that in order to be saved the sinner has nought to do but to accept it.

But having received the gift of God, and having become partakers of his converting grace, then and therefore the divine obligation for service begins to press upon us. The Lord becomes an asker as soon as we have become recipients. *"As ye have therefore received Christ Jesus the Lord, so walk ye in him"* : let consecration crown conversion, let self-devotement to Christ answer to his self-devotement for you.

Dr. A. J. Gordon.

If you would know how faith is to be exercised in thus abiding in Jesus, to be rooted more deeply and firmly in him, you have only to look back to the time when first you received him. You remember well what obstacles at that time there appeared to be in the way of your believing. There was first your vileness and guilt : it appeared impossible that the promise of pardon and love could be for such a sinner. Then there was the sense of weakness and death : you felt not the power for the surrender and the trust to which you were called. And then there was the future : you dared not undertake to be a disciple of Jesus while you felt so sure that you could not remain standing, but would speedily again be unfaithful and fall. These difficulties were as mountains in your way. And how were they removed? Simply by the word of God. That word, as it were, compelled you to believe that, notwithstanding guilt in the past, and weakness in the present, and un-faithfulness in the future, the promise was sure that Jesus would accept and save you. On that word you ventured to come, and were not deceived : you found that Jesus did indeed accept and save you.

Apply this, your experience in coming to Jesus, to the abiding in him. By faith you became partakers of the initial grace ; by that same faith you can enjoy the continuous grace of abiding in him.

Andrew Murray.

Since they had received the doctrine of Christ, they could not again part with it without convicting themselves either of imprudence, in having mistaken a false doctrine for a true one ; or of instability, in quitting and altering a doctrine which they knew to be good and sufficient when they received it. If your belief be good, why do you change it? If it be otherwise, why did you entertain it? Though it be a heinous sin not to receive the Lord Jesus when he presents himself to us in his gospel, yet it is much more evil to cast him out after having received him ; as it is a greater outrage to thrust a man from your house when you have admitted him, than to shut your doors against him at the first.

Jean Daillé.

CCXXX

Col. iii. 11.—"Where there is neither Greek nor Jew; circumcision nor uncircumcision, Barbarian, Scythian, bond nor free: but Christ is all, and in all.

There are two worlds, the old and the new.

These are peopled by two sorts of manhood, the old man, and the new man, concerning whom see verses 9, 10.

In the first are many things which are not in the second.

In the second are many things which are not in the first.

Our text tells us what there is not, and what there is, in the new man.

Let us begin by asking whether the hearer knows *where* he is; for the text turns on that word "*where*."

I. WHAT THERE IS NOT IN THE NEW.

When we come to be renewed after the image of him that created us, we find an obliteration of

1. National distinctions : "Where there is neither Greek nor Jew."

> Jesus is a man. In the broadest sense he is neither Jew nor Gentile. We see in him no restrictive nationality : and our own peculiar nationality sinks before union with him.

> Jesus is now our nationality, our charter, and our fatherland.

> Jesus is our hero, legislator, ancestor, leader, etc.

> Jesus gives us laws, customs, history, genealogy, prestige, privilege, reliance, power, heritage, conquest, etc.

> Jesus furnishes us with a new patriotism, loyalty, and clanship, which we may safely indulge to the utmost.

2. Ceremonial distinctions : "There is neither circumcision nor uncircumcision." The typical separation is removed.

> The separating rite is abolished, and the peculiar privilege of a nation born after the flesh is gone with it.

> Those who were reckoned far off are brought nigh.

> Both Jew and Gentile are united in one body by the cross.

3. Social distinctions : "There is neither bond nor free."

> We are enabled through divine grace to see that

>> These distinctions are transient.

>> These distinctions are superficial.

>> These distinctions are of small value.

>> These distinctions are non-existent in the spiritual realm.

What a blessed blending of all men in one body is brought about by our Lord Jesus! Let us all work in the direction of unity.

II. WHAT THERE IS IN THE NEW.

"Christ is all and in all;" and that in many senses.

1. Christ is all our culture. In him we emulate and excel the "Greek."
2. Christ is all our revelation. We glory in him even as the "Jew" gloried in receiving the oracles of God.
3. Christ is all our ritual. We have no "circumcision," neither have we seven sacraments, nor a heap of carnal ordinances: he is far more than these. All Scriptural ordinances are of him.
4. Christ is all our simplicity. We place no confidence in the bare Puritanism which may be called "uncircumcision."
5. Christ is all our natural traditions. He is more to us than the freshest ideas which cross the mind of the "Barbarian."
6. Christ is all our unconquerableness and liberty. The "Scythian' had not such boundless independence as we find in him.
7. Christ is all as our Master, if we be "bond." Happy servitude of which he is the head!
8. Christ is our Magna Charta: yea, our liberty itself if we be "free."

In closing we will use the words "Christ is all and in all" as our text for application to ourselves. It furnishes a test question for us.

Is Christ so great with us that he is our all?

Is Christ so broadly and fully with us that he is all in our all?

Is he, then, all in our trust, our hope, our assurance, our joy, our aim, our strength, our wisdom—in a word, "all in all"?

If so, are we living in all for him?

Are we doing all *for* him, because he is all to us?

EMBROIDERIES

What a rich inheritance have all those who are truly interested in Jesus Christ! *Christus meus et omnia.* They possess him that is all in all, and in possessing him they possess all. "I have all things, my brother," saith Jacob to Esau: Gen. xxxiii. 11 (Margin). He that hath him that is all in all cannot want anything. "All things are yours," saith the apostle, "whether things present or things to come, and ye are Christ's": 1 Cor. iii. 22, 23. A true believer, let him be never so poor outwardly, is in truth the richest man in all the world; he hath all in all, and what can be added to all?—*Ralph Robinson.*

Christ is not valued at all unless he be valued above all.—*Augustine.*

He is a path, if any be misled ;
　He is a robe, if any naked be ;
If any chance to hunger, he is bread ;
　If any be a bondman, he is free ;
　If any be but weak, how strong is he !
To dead men life he is, to sick men health,
To blind men sight, and to the needy wealth ;
A pleasure without loss, a treasure without stealth.

Giles Fletcher.

All, then, let him be in all our desires and wishes. Who is that wise merchant that hath heart large enough to conceive and believe as to this ? Let him go sell all his nothings, that he may compass this pearl, barter his bugles for this diamond. Verily, all the haberdash stuff the whole pack of the world hath, is not worthy to be valued with this jewel.

I cannot but reverence the memory of that reverend divine (Mr. Welsh) who, being in a deep muse after some discourse that had passed of Christ, and tears trickling abundantly from his eyes before he was aware, being urged for the cause thereof, he honestly confessed that he wept because he could not draw his dull heart to prize Christ aright. I fear this is a rare mind in Christians, for many think a very little to be quite enough for Jesus, and even too much for him !—*Samuel Ward.*

" At length, one evening, while engaged in a prayer-meeting, the great deliverance came. I received the full witness of the Spirit that the blood of Jesus had cleansed me from all sin. I felt I was nothing, and Christ was all in all. Him I now cheerfully received in all his offices : my Prophet, to teach me ; my Priest, to atone for me ; my King, to reign over me. Oh what boundless, boundless happiness there is in Christ, and all for such a poor sinner as I am ! This happy change took place in my soul March 13th, 1772."—*William Carvosso.*

Dannecker, the German sculptor, spent eight years in producing a face of Christ ; and at last wrought out one in which the emotions of love and sorrow were so perfectly blended that beholders wept as they looked upon it. Subsequently, being solicited to employ his great talent on a statue of Venus, he replied, " After gazing so long into the face of Christ, think you that I can now turn my attention to a heathen goddess ? " Here is the true secret of weanedness from worldly idols, " the expulsive power of a new affection."

　　" I have heard the voice of Jesus,
　　　Tell me not of aught beside ;
　　I have seen the face of Jesus,
　　　All my soul is satisfied."

Dr. A. J Gordon,

CCXXXI

1 **Thess. ii. 13, 14** —"𝔉or this cause also thank we 𝔊od without ceasing, because, when ye received the word of 𝔊od which ye heard of us, ye received it not as the word of men, but as it is in truth, the word of 𝔊od, which effectually worketh also in you that believe.

"𝔉or ye, brethren, became followers of the churches of 𝔊od which in 𝔍udæa are in 𝔠hrist 𝔍esus: for ye also have suffered like things of your own countrymen, even as they have of the 𝔍ews."

Paul unbosoms his heart to the loving church at Thessalonica.

He knew what it was to be worried by the Corinthians and the Galatians, but he found rest when thinking of the Thessalonians.

The most tried ministers have some bright spots.

In setting forth his joyful memories of Thessalonica, Paul gives us a sight of three things.

I. MINISTERS GIVING THANKS. "We also thank God."

Ministers are not always groaning and weeping, though they often do so. They have their time of thanksgiving, as in Paul's case.

1. This followed upon sore travail. See verse 9. Only as we sow in tears do we reap in joy.

2. This was backed by holy living. Dwell upon each point in verses 10 and 11. Unholy ministers will have scant cause for joy.

3. It prevented all self-laudation. They thanked God, and this is the opposite of glorifying self.

4. It was of a social character. "*We* thank God": Paul, and Silas, and Timothy. We hold a fraternal meeting of joy when God blesses us among our beloved people.

5. It was of an abiding character,—"without ceasing." We can never cease praising the Lord for his goodness in saving souls.

6. It cheered them for further service. They wished, according to verse 17, to visit the friends again, and further benefit them.

What a mercy for us all when God's servants are glad about us! Their joy is in our salvation.

II. HEARERS RECEIVING THE WORD. "Ye received the word of God."

Not all receive it. How badly do some treat the gospel!

Not all receive it as did the Thessalonians, for

1. They received the word of God : they heard it calmly, attended to it candidly, considered it carefully.

2. They received the word of God with a hearty welcome. They accepted it by faith, with personal confidence and joy.

3. They did not receive the word of man. It is well to keep the doors locked in that direction. We cannot receive everything; let us reject merely human teaching, and leave the more room in our minds for the Lord's word.

4. They did not receive the gospel as the word of men. Their faith was not based on the clever, eloquent, logical, dogmatical, or affectionate way in which it was preached.

5. They received it as God's revealed word, and therefore received it
    With reverence of its divine character.
    With assurance of its infallibility.
    With obedience to its authority.
    With experience of its sacred power.

6. They received it so that it effectually worked in them. It was practical, efficient, and manifestly operative upon their lives and characters.

III. Converts exhibiting the family likeness.

1. They were like Judæan Christians, the best of them,
   In faith ; in experience ; in afflictions.

2. Yet many of them as heathen began at a great disadvantage.

3. They had never seen the church of God in Judæa, and were no copyists, yet they came to be fac-similes of them.

4. This is a singular confirmation of the divine character of the work.
   The same Lord works in all believers, and in the main the same experience occurs in all the saints, even though they may never have seen each other.
   This similarity of all regenerated men furnishes a valuable set of experimental evidences of the divine origin of conversion.

Let us not be daunted by opposition, for at Thessalonica Paul was persecuted and yet triumphant.

Let us rejoice in the effects of **the** Word everywhere.

Memoranda

There was a minister of the gospel once, a true preacher, a faithful, loving man, whose ministry was supposed to be exceedingly unsuccessful.

After twenty years' labour, he was known to have brought only one soul to Christ. So said his congregation. Poor worker in the trench! his toil was not seen by men, but the eye of God rested upon it. To him, one day, came a deputation from his people, representing to him, respectfully enough, that, inasmuch as God had not seen fit to bless his labours among them, it were better for him to remove to another sphere. They said that he had only been instrumental in the conversion of one sinner. He might do more elsewhere. "What do you say?" said he. "Have I really brought one sinner to Christ?" "Yes," was the reply; "one, but only one." "Thank God," cried he, "for that! Thank God! I have brought one soul to Christ. Now for twenty years' more labour among you! God sparing me, perhaps I may be the honoured instrument of bringing two."—*Calthrop*.

"Whoever made this book," said a Chinese convert, "made me; it tells me the thoughts of my heart."

A celebrated Frenchman said, "I know the Word of God is the sword of the Spirit, because it has pierced me through."

Loskiel's "Account of the Moravian Missions among the North American Indians" has taught me two things. I have found in it a striking illustration of the uniformity with which the grace of God operates on men. *Crantz*, in his "Account of the Missions in Greenland," has shown the grace of God working on a man-fish—on a stupid, sottish, senseless creature, scarcely a remove from the fish on which he lived. *Loskiel* shows the same grace working on a man-devil—a fierce, bloody, revengeful warrior, dancing his infernal war-dance with the mind of a fury. Divine grace brings these men to the same point; it quickens, stimulates, and elevates the Greenlander—it raises him to a sort of new life—it seems almost to bestow on him new senses—it opens his eye, and bends his ear, and rouses his heart; and what it adds, it sanctifies. The same grace tames the high spirit of the Indian—it reduces him to the meekness, and docility, and simplicity of a child. The evidence arising to Christianity from these facts is perhaps seldom sufficient, by itself, to convince the gainsayer; but, to a man who already believes, it greatly strengthens the reason of his belief. I have seen, also, in these books, that the fish-boat, and the oil, and the tomahawk, and the cap of feathers excepted, a Christian minister has to deal with just the same sort of creatures as the Greenlander and the Indian among civilized nations.—*Richard Cecil.*

The Edition of those living Epistles is the same the world over; the binding only may differ.

CCXXXII

2 Thess. iii. 13 —" But ye, brethren, be not weary in well-doing."

Read the two previous verses, and mark the apostle's censure of those who are busy-bodies, " working not at all."

A church should be like a hive of working bees.

There should be order, and there will be order where all are at work.
The apostle condemns disorder in verse 11.

There should be quietness ; and work promotes it : verse 12.

There should be honesty ; and work fosters it.

The danger is, lest we first tire of work, and then fancy that we have done enough, or are discharged from service by our superior importance, or by our subscribing to pay a substitute.   While any strength remains we may not cease from personal work for Jesus.

Moreover, some will come in who are not busy bees, but busy-bodies : they do not work for their own bread, but are surprisingly eager to eat that of others ; these soon cause disturbance and desolation, but they know nothing of " well-doing."

The apostle endeavours to cure this disease, and therefore gives—

I. A SUMMARY OF CHRISTIAN LIFE.   He calls it " well-doing."

1. Religious work is well-doing.   Preaching, teaching, writing books and letters, temperance meetings, Bible-classes, tract-distributing, personal conversation, private prayer, praise, &c.

2. Charitable work is " well-doing."   The poor, the widow and the fatherless, the ignorant, the sick, the fallen, and the desponding, are to be looked after with tender care.

3. Common labour is " well-doing."
This will be seen to be the point in the text, if we read the previous verses. Well-doing takes many forms: among the rest—
Support of family by the husband.
Management of house by the wife.
Assistance in house-work by daughters.
Diligence in his trade by the young man.
Study of his books by the child at school.
Faithful service by domestics in the home.
Honest toil by the day-labourer.

4 Certain labour is " well-doing " in all these senses, since it is common labour used for charitable and religious ends.

Support of aged persons by those who work for them.

Watching over infirm or sick relatives.

Bringing up children in the fear of the Lord.

Work done in connection with the church of God, to enable others to preach the gospel in comfort.

Everything is "well-doing" which is done from a sense of duty, with dependence upon God, and faith in his word; out of love to Christ, in good-will to other workers, with prayer for direction, acceptance, and blessing.

Common actions become holy, and drudgery grows divine when the motive is pure and high.

We now think it will be wise to gather from the epistle—

II. A WARNING AS TO CAUSES OF WEARINESS IN WELL-DOING.

1. Unworthy receivers of charity weary generous workers: verse 10.

2. Idle examples tempt the industrious to idleness: verse 11.

3. Busy-bodies, and disorderly persons in the church, hinder many from their diligent service: verses 11, 12.

4. Troublers, such as "unreasonable and wicked men," dispirit those who would serve the Lord: verse 2.

5. Our own flesh is apt to crave ease, and shun difficulties.

We can make too much of works, and it is equally easy to have too few of them. Let us watch against weariness.

Let us now conclude with—

III. AN ARGUMENT AGAINST WEARINESS IN WELL-DOING. "But ye, brethren, be not weary in well doing."

1. Lose not what you have already wrought.

2. Consider what self-denials others practise for inferior things: soldiers, wrestlers, rowers in boat-race, &c.

3. Remember that the eye of God is upon you, his hand with you, his smile on you, his command over you.

4. Reflect upon the grandeur of the service in itself as done unto the Lord, and to his glorious cause.

5. Think upon the sublime lives of those who have preceded you in this heavenly service.

6. Fix your eye on Jesus, and what he endured.

7. Behold the recompense of reward: the crown, the palm.

If others tire and faint, be not ye weary.

If others meanly loaf upon their fellows, be it yours rather to give than to receive.

If others break the peace of the church, be it yours to maintain it by diligent service, and so to enjoy the blessing of verse 16.

WHETSTONES

A true Christian must be a worker. Industry, or diligence in business, is a prime element in piety; and the industry God demands is the activity of our whole complex nature. Without this a man may be a dreamer, but not a " doer "; and just so far as any faculty of our nature is left unemployed do we come short of a complete Christian character. I must be doing, I—I, my entire self, my hand, my foot, my eye, my tongue, my understanding, my affections—must be all, not only resolving, purposing, feeling, willing, but actively doing. " Let us be doing."
But more than this. I must be " well-doing." The Greek word expresses beauty, and this enters into the apostolic thought. True piety is lovely. Just so far as it comes short in the beautiful, it becomes monstrous. But, as used by Paul, it goes far beyond this, and signifies all moral excellence. Activity is not enough; for activity the intensest may be evil. Lucifer is as active, as constant, and earnest as Gabriel. But the one is a fiend, and the other a seraph. Any activity that is not good is a curse always and only. Better be dead, inert matter—a stone, a clod—than a stinging reptile, or a destroying demon; and herein lies the great practical change in regeneration. It transforms the mere doer into a well-doer. It is not so much a change in the energy as in the direction.—*Charles Wadsworth, D.D.*

The Hebrews have a saying, that God is more delighted in adverbs than in nouns: 'tis not so much the matter that's done, but the matter how 'tis done, that God minds. *Not how much, but how well!* 'Tis the well-doing that meets with a well-done. Let us therefore serve God, not nominally or verbally, but adverbially.—*Ralph Venning.*

Think nothing done while aught remains to do.
Samuel Rogers.

D'Israeli tells the following story of two members of the Port Royal Society. Arnauld wished Nicolle to assist him in a new work, when the latter replied, " We are now old; is it not time to rest?" " Rest!" returned Arnauld, "have we not all eternity to rest in?" So *Gerald Massey* sings—

> " Let me work now, for all Eternity,
> With its immortal leisure, waiteth me."

308

CCXXXIII

1 Tim. i. 15 —"This is a faithful saying, and worthy of all acceptation, that Christ Jesus came into the world to save sinners ; of whom I am chief."

Paul had described his ordination in verse 12.

He then went on to speak of the grace manifested in the call of such a person to the ministry (verse 13), and of the further grace by which he was sustained in that ministry.

Incidentally he was led to mention the message of his ministry.

We may profitably use the text on this occasion. *

I. HOW WE PREACH THE GOSPEL.

1. As a certainty. It is a "faithful saying." *We* do not doubt the truth of our message, or how could we expect *you* to believe it ? We believe, and are sure, because
It is a revelation of God.
It is attested by miracles.
It bears its witness within itself.
It has proved its power upon our hearts.

2. As an everyday truth. It is to us a "saying" or proverb.
The gospel affects us at home, in business, in sickness, in health, in life, in youth and age, in death, &c.

3. As having a common bearing. Therefore a "saying" to be heard by all kinds of people, especially the most sinful.
All have sinned, and need a Saviour.
All who believe in Jesus have a Saviour.
All believers show by their lives that Jesus has saved them.

4. As claiming your attention. "Worthy of all acceptation."
You must believe it to be true.
You must appropriate it to yourself.
You ought to do so, for it is worthy of your acceptance.

II. WHAT GOSPEL DO WE PREACH?

1. The gospel of a person : "Christ Jesus."
He is the Anointed of God : "Christ."
He is the Saviour of men : "Jesus."
He is God and man in one person.
He died, and yet he lives for ever.

Preached at the opening of a mission hall. A simple, popular address was most desirable.

309

2. The gospel of divine visitation.   Jesus came into the world--
     By his birth as a man.
     By his mingling with men.
     By his bearing our sorrows and our sins for us.

3. The gospel for sinners.
     For such Jesus lived and laboured.
     For such he died and made atonement.
     For such he has sent the gospel of pardon.
     For such he pleads in heaven.

4. The gospel of a finished work.
     He finished the work of salvation before he left the world.
     That work continues complete to this day.
     He is ready to apply it to all who come to him.

5. The gospel of effectual deliverance.   "To save sinners."
     Not to half save them.
     Nor to make them salvable.
     Nor help them to save themselves.
     Nor to save them as righteous.
     But to save them wholly and effectually from their sins.

III. WHY DO WE PREACH IT?

1. Because we have been saved by it.

2. Because we are now in sympathy with Jesus, and wish to save
   sinners, even the chief of them.

3. Because we believe it will be a blessing to all of you who hear it.
   If you are saved by it, *you* will be happy, and so shall we.

4. Because we cannot help it, for an inward impulse compels us to
   tell of the miracle of mercy wrought upon us.

Will you not believe a saying so sure?
Will you not accept a truth so gladsome?
Will you not come to a Saviour so suitable?

SAYINGS

A visitor to Rome says, "I was struck with the frequency with which
the priests, and other exhibitors of church curiosities, use the phrase,
"It is said"—*on dit*—when describing relics and rarities.   They do
not vouch for their being what they are reputed to be.   "It is said."
Are they ashamed of their curiosities?   Do they thus try to satisfy their
consciences?   They do not express their personal belief; but—*it is
said*.   Not thus do gospel preachers speak.   "That which we have seen
and heard declare we unto you."

There's a nice word in the text—it is the word "acceptation." It's all provided for you. It's very much like a supper. You'll find the table laid, and everything all ready. You're not expected to bring anything at all. I was once invited out to tea by a poor widow, and I took something in my pocket. But I'll never do it again. It was two cakes ; and, when I brought them out, and laid them on the table, she picked them up and flung them out into the street, and said, " I asked you to tea ; I didn't ask you to provide tea for me." And so with Christ ; he asks, he provides, and he wants nothing but ourselves ; and if we take aught else, he'll reject it. We can only sup with him when we come as we are. Who will accept salvation ? Who'll say,

> " I take the blessing from above,
> And wonder at thy boundless love " ?
> *John Wold Ackrill, in " The Sword and the Trowel."*

Mr. Moody said, " I remember preaching on this subject—Christ as a Deliverer—and walking away, I said to a Scotchman, ' I didn't finish the subject.' ' Ah, man ! you didn't expect to finish, did ye ? It'll take all eternity to finish telling what Christ has done for man.' "

Luther says, " Once upon a time the devil said to me, ' Martin Luther, you are a great sinner, and you will be damned ! ' ' Stop ! Stop ! ' said I ; ' one thing at a time ; I am a great sinner, it is true, though you have no right to tell me of it. I confess it. What next ? ' ' Therefore you will be damned.' ' That is not good reasoning. It is true I am a great sinner, but it is written, " Jesus Christ came to save sinners ; " therefore *I shall be saved !* Now go your way.' So I cut the devil off with his own sword, and he went away mourning because he could not cast me down by calling me a sinner."

The Jews have a saying that the manna tasted to each one precisely like that which he liked best. The gospel is suited to every man, whatever his needs or desires may be.

One of William Carey's last visitors was the Rev. Alexander Duff, who talked with him of his past life, and then knelt down and prayed by his bedside. Leaving the room Mr. Duff thought he heard himself recalled. He turned back, and the dying man addressed him in a whisper, " Mr. Duff, you have been talking about *Doctor* Carey, *Doctor* Carey ; when I am gone, say nothing about Doctor Carey—speak about Doctor Carey's *Saviour.*"

CCXXXIV

1 Tim. i. 16 —"Howbeit for this cause I obtained mercy, that in me first Jesus Christ might shew forth all long-suffering, for a pattern to them which should hereafter believe on him to life everlasting."

The notion is common that Paul's conversion was something uncommon, and not at all to be expected in the usual order of things.

The text flatly contradicts such a supposition : the very reason for his salvation was that he might be a type of other. conversions.

I. IN THE CONVERSION OF PAUL THE LORD HAD AN EYE TO OTHERS.
The fact of his conversion and the mode of it :
1. Would tend to interest, and convince other Pharisees and Jews.
2. Would be used by himself in his preaching as an argument to convert and encourage others.
3. Would encourage Paul as a preacher to hope for others.
4. Would become a powerful argument with him for seeking others.
5. Would, long after Paul's death, remain on record to be the means of bringing many to Jesus.

We are each one saved with an eye to others.
For whose sake are *you* saved ?
Are you making the fullest use of your conversion to this end ?

II. IN HIS ENTIRE LIFE PAUL SPEAKS TO OTHERS.
He was foremost in sin and also in grace, and thus his life speaks to the extremes on each side.
1. In sin. His conversion proves that Jesus receives great sinners.
He was a blasphemer, a persecutor, and injurious.
He went as far as he could in hatred to Christ and his people.
Yet the grace of God changed him and forgave him.
2. In grace. He proved the power of God to sanctify and preserve
He was faithful in ministry, clear in knowledge, fervent in spirit patient in suffering, diligent in service.
And all this notwithstanding what he once was.

The foremost in sin may be saved, and so none are snut out.
These should be and may be foremost in faith and love when saved.

III. In his whole case he presents a cartoon of others.
  1. As to God's longsuffering to him. In his case—
    Longsuffering was carried to its highest pitch.
    Longsuffering so great that *all* the patience of God seemed to be revealed in his one instance.
    Longsuffering concentrated : all the longsuffering that has ever been seen, or ever will be seen in others, met in him.
    Longsuffering which displayed itself in many ways, so as
        To let him live when persecuting saints.
        To allow him the possibility of pardon.
        To call him effectually by grace.
        To give him fulness of personal blessing.
        To put him into the ministry and send him to the Gentiles.
        To keep and support him even unto the end.
  2. As to the mode of his conversion.
  He was saved remarkably, but others will be seen to be saved in like manner if we look below the surface of things.
    Saved without previous preparation on his own part.
    Saved at once out of darkness and death.
    Saved by divine power alone.
    Saved by faith wrought in him by God's own Spirit.
    Saved distinctly, and beyond all doubt.
  Are we not also saved in precisely the same way ?

  It is possible for us to realize in ourselves a full parallel with Paul.
    There is a sad resemblance in our sin.
    There is a similarity in the divine longsuffering towards us.
    There is a likeness in some degree in the revelation, for the Lord Jesus asks us from heaven, " Why persecutest thou me ? "
    Shall there not be a similarity also in the faith ?
    Will we not ask, " Who art thou, Lord ? " and " What wilt thou have me to do ? "

Proof Impressions

The word " pattern," in the original, is expressive—a pattern from which endless copies may be taken. You have heard of stereotype printing : when the types are set up, they are cast—made a fixed thing, so that from one plate you can strike off hundreds of thousands of pages in succession, without the trouble of setting up the types again. Paul says, " That I might be a plate never worn out—never destroyed ; from which proof impressions may be taken to the very end of time." What a splendid thought, that the apostle Paul, having portrayed himself as

313

the chief of sinners, then portrays himself as having received forgiveness for a grand and specific end, that he might be a standing plate, from which impressions might be taken for ever, that no man might despair who had read his biography !—*Dr. Cumming.*

An infidel, during his sickness, became convinced of his wretched condition, and by the assistance of a Sabbath-school teacher was led to the Saviour, and found salvation in his blood. After the change which had passed in his heart, he often spoke of the Saviour's love, and the heaven into which he hoped soon to enter. Finding his life drawing rapidly to a close, he urged the teacher to proceed in his glorious work of doing good ; then, opening his bedroom window, which overlooked a bustling and crowded thoroughfare, as he gazed upon the human forms beneath, summoning his last remaining strength, he cried at the top of his voice, " There is mercy for all ! None need despair, since I, a poor infidel, have obtained mercy." This, his last work, accomplished, exhausted by the effort, he fell back on his bed, and instantly died.

Haughton, in *Bate's Cyclopædia.*

John Newton, speaking of the sudden death of Robinson, of Cambridge, in the house of Dr. Priestly, said : " I think Dr. Priestly is out of the reach of human conviction ; but the Lord can convince him. And who can tell but this unexpected stroke may make some salutary impression upon his mind ? I can set no limits to the mercy or the power of our Lord, and therefore I continue to pray for him. I am persuaded he is not farther from the truth now than I was once." In the same spirit Newton wrote the lines—

> " Come, my fellow sinners, try,
> Jesus' heart is full of love ;
> Oh that you, as well as I,
> May his wondrous mercy prove !
> He has sent me to declare,
> All is ready, all is free ;
> Why should any soul despair,
> When he saved a wretch like me."

Every conversion of a great sinner is a new copy of God's love ; it is a repeated proclamation of the transcendency of his grace. This was his design in Paul's conversion. He sets up this apostle as a white flag to invite rebels to treat with him, and return to their loyalty. As every great judgment upon a grand sinner is as the hanging a man in chains, to deter others from the like practice, so every conversion is not only an act of God's mercy to the convert, but an invitation to the spectators.

Stephen Charnock.

CCXXXV

2 Tim. i. 12 —"**For the which cause I also suffer these things: nevertheless I am not ashamed: for I know whom I have believed, and am persuaded that he is able to keep that which I have committed unto him against that day.**"

Paul, much buffeted and persecuted, is sustained by faith, and by a sense of personal security in Christ Jesus.

The meaning which may be in the text:—the gospel deposited with Paul the Lord Jesus was able to keep until the judgment. This is well worthy of being explained. The gospel is safe in the care of Jesus.

Paul felt great comfort as the result of committing his soul to Jesus.

Let us consider—

I. WHAT HE HAD DONE.

Feeling the value of his soul, knowing its danger, conscious of his own weakness, believing in the grace and power of the Lord Jesus, he had placed his soul in his hands.

1. His soul's case was there for Jesus to heal him as a *Physician*.

2. His soul's calls were there to be supplied by Jesus as a *Shepherd*.

3. His soul's course was there to be directed by Jesus as a *Pilot*.

4. His soul's cause was there to be pleaded by Jesus as an *Advocate*.

5. His soul's care was there to be guarded by Jesus as a *Protector*.

He had committed his soul to Jesus by an act of faith, which act he persevered in continually.

II. WHAT HE KNEW. "I know whom I have believed."

He speaks not of believing *in* him, but of believing him,—a personal faith in a personal Saviour. This trusted One he knew.

1. He knew the Lord Jesus by his personal meeting with him on the road to Damascus, and at other times.

2 By what he had read and heard concerning him, and made his own by meditation thereon.

3. By communion with him. This way is open to all the saints.

4. By experience, through which he had tried and proved his love and faithfulness. He had received a practical education, by which he was made to know his Lord by entering into the fellowship of his sufferings and death.

Have we this personal acquaintance with the Lord?
If so, we shall gladly commit our all to him.

III. WHAT HE WAS SURE OF. "That he is able to keep," &c.

His assurance was reasonable and deliberate, hence he says, "I am persuaded."

Our apostle was persuaded of—

1. The ability of Jesus to keep all souls committed to him.
   He is divine, and therefore omnipotent to save.
   His work is finished, so that he meets all the demands of the law.
   His wisdom is perfect, so that he will ward off all dangers.
   His plea is constant, and ever prevails to preserve his own
2. The ability of Jesus to keep Paul's own soul.
3. The ability of Jesus to keep his soul under the heavy trials which were then pressing upon him. "I suffer . . . I am not ashamed, for I am persuaded that he is able to keep."
4. The ability of Jesus to keep his soul even to the close of all things : "against that day."

Of this Paul was persuaded. Be this our persuasion.

Many would persuade us to the contrary ; but we *know*, and are not therefore to be persuaded into a doubt upon the matter.

IV. WHAT, THEREFORE, HE WAS.

1. Very cheerful. He had all the tone and air of a thoroughly happy man.
2. Very confident. Though a prisoner, he says, "I am not ashamed." Neither of his condition, nor of the cause of Christ, nor of the cross, was he ashamed.
3. Very thankful. He gladly praised the Lord in whom he trusted.
   The text is a confession of faith, or a form of adoration.

Let us seek more knowledge of our Lord, as the Keeper of our souls.
Let us be of that brave persuasion which trusts and is not afraid.

INSTANCES AND ILLUSTRATIONS

When *Dr. James W. Alexander* was dying, his wife sought to comfort him with precious words, as she quoted them to him : "I know in whom I have believed." Dr. Alexander at once corrected her by saying, "Not *in* whom I have believed ; but, ' I know *whom* I have believed.' " He would not even suffer a little preposition to be between his soul and his Saviour.

"I have lost that weary bondage of doubt, and almost despair, which chained me for so many years. I have the same sins and temptations as before, and I do not strive against them more than before, and it is often just as hard work. But whereas I could not before see why I *should* be saved, I cannot now see why I should *not* be saved if Christ died for sinners. On that word I take my stand, and *rest there*."— *F. R. Havergal.*

Justyn Martyr was asked ironically by the Roman prefect if he believed that after his decapitation he would ascend to heaven. He replied: " I am so sure of the grace which Jesus Christ hath obtained for me, that not a shadow of doubt can enter my mind."

Donald Cargill, on the scaffold, July 27th, 1681, as he handed his well-used Bible to one of his friends that stood near, gave this testimony: " I bless the Lord that these thirty years and more I have been at peace with God, and was never shaken loose of it. And now I am as sure of my interest in Christ, and peace with God, as all within this Bible and the Spirit of God can make me. And I am no more terrified at death, or afraid of hell because of sin, than if I had never had sin: for all my sins are freely pardoned and washed thoroughly away through the precious blood and intercession of Jesus Christ."

> Faith, Hope, and Love were questioned what they thought
> Of future glory, which religion taught :
> Now Faith believed it firmly to be true,
> And Hope expected so to find it, too :
> Love answered, smiling, with a conscious glow,
> "Believe? Expect? I know it to be so!"
>
> *John Byrom.*

A child that hath any precious thing given him cannot better secure it than by putting it into his father's hands to keep ; so neither can we better provide for our souls' safety than by committing them to God.

John Trapp.

CCXXXVI

2 Tim. i. 18 —"The Lord grant unto him that he may find mercy of the Lord in that day."

The best method of showing our gratitude to some men for their kindness would be to pray for them.

Even the best of men will be the better for our prayers.

Paul had already prayed for the household of Onesiphorus, and now he concludes by a specially hearty prayer for the good man himself. The repetition of the word "Lord" makes the prayer peculiarly solemn.

Onesiphorus had remembered Paul in his day of peril, and Paul begs the Lord to give him a gracious return in the day of judgment.

Yet the utmost he can ask even for so excellent a man is *mercy*. Even the merciful need mercy; and it is their benediction from the Lord himself that " they shall obtain mercy."

Let us consider this prayer under three heads :—

I. "THAT DAY."

"That day ": it is not specifically described, because well known and much thought of among Christians. Do we sufficiently think of that day? If so, we shall feel our great need to find of the Lord mercy when it comes.

Its date is not given   It would but gratify curiosity.

Its length is not specified.   Will it be a common day? It will be long enough for the deliberate judgment of all men.

Its coming will be solemnly proclaimed.   We shall know it. Ushered in with pomp of angels, sound of trumpet, &c., none will be ignorant of it.

Its glory, the revelation of Jesus from heaven upon the throne of judgment.   This will make it most memorable.

Its event, the assembly of quick and dead, and the last assize.

Its character, excitement of joy or terror.   It will be the day of days, for which all other days were made.

Its personal interest to each one of us will be paramount.

Its revealings of secrets of thought, word, deed, &c., for good or for evil, will be most astounding.

Its decisions will be strictly just, indisputable, unchangeable, &c.

It will be the last day, and henceforth the state of men will be fixed for joy or woe.

How much we shall need mercy in the judgment! Every thought connected with it makes us feel this.   Let us pray about it.

318

II. The mercy.

All will need it.   Assuredly we shall need it ourselves.

To arouse us, let us think of those who will find no mercy of the
Lord in that day :—

Those who had no mercy on others.

Those who lived and died impenitent.

Those who neglected salvation.   How shall they escape?

Those who said they needed no mercy : the self-righteous.

Those who sought no mercy : procrastinators, and the indifferent.

Those who scoffed at Christ, and refused the gospel.

Those who sold their Lord, and apostatized from him.

Those who made a false and hypocritical profession.

III. To-day.

Our address at this moment is to those for whom we would specially
breathe the prayer of the text.

The prospect of judgment for preacher and hearers leads us at once
to pray for you, and at the same time to urge you to seek the
Lord while he may be found.

We would not have you despair as to the future, but hope to find
mercy in the present, that you may find it in " that day."

Remember that now is the accepted time, for—

You are not yet standing at the judgment bar.

You are yet where prayer is heard.

You are where faith will save all who exercise it towards Christ.

You are where the Spirit strives.

You are where sin may be forgiven, at once, and for ever.

You are where grace reigns, even though sin abounds.

To-day is the day of grace ; to-morrow may be a day of another sort,
for you at least, and possibly for all mankind.   The Judge is at the door.
Seek mercy immediately, that mercy may be yours for ever.

Trumpet Notes

I would rather have the gift of a brother's faithful prayers than of his
plentiful substance.   And I feel that when I have given to a brother my
faithful prayers I have given him my best and greatest gift.—*Edward
Irving.*

There is a machine in the Bank of England which receives sovereigns,
as a mill receives grain, for the purpose of determining wholesale whether
they are of full weight.   As they pass through, the machinery, by un-
erring laws, throws all that are light to one side, and all that are of full
weight to another.   That process is a silent but solemn parable for me.

Founded as it is upon the laws of nature, it affords the most vivid similitude of the certainty which characterizes the judgment of the great day. There are no mistakes or partialities to which the light may trust; the only hope lies in being of standard weight before they go in.

William Arnot.

An infidel was introduced by a gentleman to a minister with a remark, " He never attends public worship." "Ah !" said the minister, " I hope you are mistaken." " By no means," said the stranger ; " I always spend Sunday in settling my accounts." " Then, alas !" was the calm, but solemn reply, "you will find, sir, that the day of judgment will be spent in the same manner."—*G. S. Bowes.*

When *Thomas Hooker* was dying, one said to him, " Brother, you are going to receive the reward of your labours." He humbly replied, " Brother, I am going to receive *mercy.*"

By that tremendous phrase, "*eternal* judgment," consider your ways, and be wise! If its true meaning could lighten upon you at this moment, what consternation would strike upon each spirit! Every man, though serene as death before, would spring to his feet, and cry, Tell me, tell me this moment, what I must do !—*Charles Stanford, D.D.*

It is a pathetic tale to tell, and I do not vouch for its absolute truth, that once a famous composer wrote a great anthem to be sung at a festival. He sought to picture the scenes of the final judgment, and introduced a strain of music representing the solemn lamentations of the lost. But no singer was found willing to take such a part. So the wailings and woes were omitted ; and when the passage was reached, the leader simply beat the time in silence till the awful chasm was passed, and the musicians took up gloriously the strains of celestial unison lying on the other side of it—" the shout of them that triumph, and the song of them who feast."—*Dr. C. S. Robinson.*

CCXXXVII

2 Tim. ii. 9 —"**Wherein I suffer trouble, as an evil-doer, even unto bonds; but the word of God is not bound.**"

The Resurrection of Christ was Paul's sheet-anchor. Enlarge upon verse 8, wherein he mentions it as the essence of the gospel.

He himself is suffering and bound, but he is not without comfort.

His great joy is that the Word of God is not bound.

I. IN WHAT SENSES THIS IS TRUE.

The Word of God is not bound—

1. So that it cannot be made known.

> The ministers who preach it may be imprisoned, but not the Word.
>
> The Book which contains it may be burned, but the truth abides.
>
> The doctrine may become almost extinct as to open testimony, and yet it will revive.

2. So that it cannot reach the heart.

> It will not be hindered of its divine purpose
>
> Through the obduracy of the sinner, for grace is omnipotent.
>
> Through absence of the means. The Holy Spirit can reach the conscience without the hearing or reading of the Word.
>
> Through actual derision of it. Even the scoffer and sceptic can yet be convinced and converted.

3. So that it cannot comfort the soul.

> Conviction of sin will not hinder consolation when faith is given.
>
> Constitutional despondency will give way before the light of the Word.
>
> Confirmed despair shall be overcome, even as Samson snapped the cords wherewith he had been bound.

4. So that it cannot be fulfilled.

> Providence will carry out the promise to the individual.
>
> Providence will perform the threat to the rebellious.
>
> Providence will achieve the prophecies of the millennial future.

5. So that it cannot prevail over error.

> Infidelity, Ritualism, Popery, fanaticism, &c., shall not bind the gospel so as to retain their mischievous power over men. The gospel must and will accomplish the purposes of God.

II. For what reasons this is true.

The Word of God cannot be bound, since—

1. It is the voice of the Almighty.

2. It is attended by the energetic working of the Holy Ghost.

3. It is so needful to men. As men will have bread, and you cannot keep it from them, so must they have the truth. The gospel is in such demand that there must be free trade in it.

4. It is in itself a free and unbound thing, the very essence of liberty.

5. It creates such enthusiasm in the hearts wherein it dwells, that men must declare it abroad : it must be free.

III. What other facts are parallel with this?

As the binding of Paul was not the binding of the Word of God, so—

The death of ministers is not the death of the gospel.

The feebleness of workers is not its feebleness.

The bondage of the preacher's mind is not its bondage.

The coldness of men is not its coldness.

The falsehood of hypocrites does not falsify it.

The spiritual ruin of sinners is not the defeat of the gospel.

The rejection of it by unbelievers is not its overthrow.

Rejoice, that the Word of the Lord has free course.

Arouse yourselves to work with it and by it.

Accept its free power and be yourself free at once.

Illustrations

"But the Word of God is not bound." It runs and is glorified (2 Thess. iii. 1), being free and not fettered. "I preach, though a prisoner," saith Paul; so did Bradford and other martyrs. "Within a few days of Queen Mary's reign, almost all the prisons in England were become right Christian schools and churches," saith Mr. Fox, "so that there was no greater comfort for Christian hearts than to come to the prisons to behold their virtuous conversation, and to hear their prayers, preachings, &c." The Earl of Derby's accusation in the Parliament House against Mr. Bradford was, that he did more hurt (so he called good evil) by letters and conferences in prison, than ever he did when he was abroad by preaching.—*John Trapp.*

In a portrait of Tyndale, still preserved in this country, beside the heroic man is a device: a burning book is tied to a stake, while a number of similar books are seen flying out of the fire. The meaning is an historic fact. Tonstal, the Bishop of London, had bought up some scores of Tyndale's Testaments, and burned them. The money paid for them enabled Tyndale to bring out a new and more correct edition.

Towards the close of the last century, before the days of the great Bible Societies, there was, for a season, a woful want of Bibles in America, caused partly by the prevalence of French infidelity, and partly by the general religious apathy which followed the Revolutionary War. In that period a man went into a book-store in Philadelphia and asked to buy a Bible. "I have none," said the bookseller. "There is not a copy for sale in the city : and I can tell you further," said he (for he was of the French way of thinking), "in fifty years there will not be a Bible in the world." The rough answer of the customer was, "There will be plenty of Bibles in the world a thousand years after you are dead and gone to hell."—*The Christian Age.*

When the daughter of the Mayor of Baune had lost her canary bird, her wise parent gave strict orders that all the gates of the town should be shut, that the creature might not escape. The bird was soon over the hills and far away, despite the locking of the gates. When a truth is once known no human power can prevent its spreading; attempts to hinder its progress will be as ineffectual as the mayor's proclamation. As a bird of the air, truth flies abroad on swift wings ; as a ray of light it enters palaces and cottages ; as the unfettered wind it laughs at laws and prohibitions. Walls cannot confine it, nor iron bars imprison it ; it is free, and maketh free. Let every freeman be upon its side, and being so, let him never allow a doubt of its ultimate success to darken his soul.

C. H. S.

The monument in Westminster Abbey to the memory of the two Wesleys bears the sentence, " God buries his workmen, but carries on his work."

Truth is more incompressible than water. If compressed in one way, it will exude through the compressing mass, the more visible through the attempts to compress it.—*Dr. Pusey.*

CCXXXVIII

Titus ii. 10 —" That they may adorn the doctrine of God our Saviour in all things."

The apostle greatly values the doctrine of the gospel, or he would not care so much to have it adorned.

The apostle highly esteems the practical part of religion, hence he regards it as the beauty and ornament of the gospel.

What a wide range of practical instruction we find in this short letter !

With what holy ingenuity is this interwoven with the doctrine !

We are bidden to obey the precept, that we may adorn the doctrine.

We have in our text—

I. A NAME OF ADORNMENT FOR THE GOSPEL. " The doctrine of God our Saviour."

    1. It sets forth its greatness : " doctrine of God."

        Our fall, ruin, sin, and punishment were great.

        Our salvation and redemption are great.

        Our safety, happiness, and hopes are great.

    2. It sets forth its certainty. It is " of God."

        It comes by revelation of God.

        It is guaranteed by the fidelity of God.

        It is as immutable as God himself.

    3. It sets forth its relation to Christ Jesus: " of God our Saviour."

        He is the author of it.

        He is the substance of it.

        He is the proclaimer of it.

        He is the object of it. The gospel glorifies Jesus.

    4. It sets forth its authority.

        The whole system of revealed truth is of God.

        The Saviour himself is God, and hence he must be accepted.

        The gospel itself is divine. God's mind is embodied in the doctrine of the Lord Jesus, and to reject it is to reject God.

Let us believe, honour, defend, and propagate this " doctrine of God our Saviour." What else is so worthy of our love and zeal ?

II. A METHOD OF ADORNMENT FOR THE GOSPEL.

    This is a remarkable verse. Observe

    1. The persons who are to adorn the gospel.

        In Paul's day, bond-servants or slaves.

        In our day, poor servants of the humblest order.

Strange that these should be set to such a task !

Yet the women slaves adorned their mistresses, and both men and women of the poorest class were quite ready to adorn themselves.

From none does the gospel receive more honour than from the poor.

2. The way in which these persons could specially adorn the gospel.
By obedience to their masters.   Verse 9.
By endeavours to please them : "please them well."
By restraining their tongues : " not answering again."
By scrupulous honesty : " not purloining," verse 10.
By trustworthy character : " showing all good fidelity."
All this would make their masters admire the religion of Jesus.

3. The way of adornment of the doctrine in general.
Negatively : it is found
Not in the decoration of the building, the priest, the choir, or the worshippers.
Nor in the attraction of peculiar garb and speech.
Nor in the finery of philosophical thought.
Nor in the tawdriness of rhetorical speech.
Positively : it lies in another direction.
We must adorn it by our godly lives.
Adornment, if really so, is *suitable to beauty*.   Holiness, mercifulness, cheerfulness, etc., are congruous with the gospel.
Adornment is often *a tribute to beauty*.   Such is a godly conversation : it honours the gospel.
Adornment is *an advertisement of beauty*.   Holiness calls attention to the natural beauty of the gospel.
Adornment is *an enhancement of beauty*.   Godliness gives emphasis to the excellence of doctrine.

Let us all endeavour to adorn the gospel, by
Strict integrity in business.
Constant courtesy of behaviour.
Unselfish love to all around us.
Quick forgiveness of injuries.
Abundant patience under trials.
Holy calm and self-possession at all times.

GEMS

Yes, and mark you, this is to be done not as the prerogative of a few grandly gifted spirits, and on some occasion which may lift them proudly up to the gaze of the universe. As found in the text, it was of the power of the poor Cretan slaves the apostle was writing ; of their power, too, not in some tremendous trial, as of torture or martyrdom, to which the cruelty of their masters sometimes subjected their faith, but of their power to do it "in all things"—in the daily, lowly, degrading service of a menial—in the small things as well as the great, in the squalid stall and fold as well as in the splendour of the palace; absolutely, in "all things" to adorn the glorious gospel of God. O blessed bondsmen of Crete ! going forth under the lash and the chain, yet with hearts of faith under their burdens, and smiles of love amid their tears, doing work for God impossible to an angel !— *Charles Wadsworth, D.D.*

We have all heard the story of the girl who said she had been converted, for she now "swept under the mats." Koba, an Indian warrior, recently gave evidence of his conversion by saying, " I pray every day, and hoe onions." An Indian could not give a much better evidence of his sincerity than that. Manual labour is not the chief joy or pride of an Indian warrior.

Fox says, "When people came to have experience of Friends' honesty and faithfulness, and found that their yea was yea, and their nay was nay; and that they kept to a word in their dealings, and that they could not cozen and cheat them ; but that if they sent a child to their shops for anything they were as well used as if they had come themselves, the lives and conversations of Friends did preach. All the enquiry was, Where was a draper, or shopkeeper, or tailor, or shoemaker, or any other tradesman that was a Quaker ?"

A Brahmin wrote to a missionary : "We are finding you out. You are not as good as your Book. If your people were only as good as your Book, you would conquer India for Christ in five years."

Light conceits and flowers of rhetoric wrong the Word more than they can please the hearers; the weeds among the corn make it look gay, but it were all the better they were not amongst it.—*Leighton.*

> All may of thee partake :
>   Nothing can be so mean,
> Which with this tincture (*for thy sake*)
>   Will not grow bright and clean.
>
> A servant with this clause
>   Makes drudgery divine :
> Who sweeps a room, as for thy laws,
>   Makes that and th' action fine.
>
> *George Herbert.*

CCXXXIX

Heb. iv. 12 —"**For the word of God is quick, and powerful, and sharper than any two-edged sword, piercing even to the dividing asunder of soul and spirit, and of the joints and marrow, and is a discerner of the thoughts and intents of the heart.**"

The Word of God is a name for Christ as well as for the Scriptures. The Scriptures are meant in this place, but the Lord Jesus is never dissevered therefrom: indeed, he is the substance of the written Word. Scripture is what it is because the Lord Jesus embodies himself in it. Let us consider from this text—

I. THE QUALITIES OF THE WORD.

   1. It is divine. It is the word of God.

   2. It is living. "The word of God is quick.".
      In contrast to our words, which pass away, God's word lives on
      It has life in itself. It is "the living and incorruptible seed."
      It creates life where it comes.
      It can never be destroyed and exterminated

   3. It is effectual. "Quick, and powerful."
      It carries conviction and conversion.
      It works comfort and confirmation.
      It has power to raise us to great heights of holiness and happiness.

   4. It is cutting. "Sharper than any two-edged sword."
      It cuts all over. It is all edge. It is sharpness itself.
      It wounds more or less all who touch it.
      It kills self-righteousness, sin, unbelief, &c.

   5. It is piercing. "Even to the dividing asunder."
      It forces its way into the hard heart.
      It penetrates the smallest opening, like the arrow which entered between the joints of the harness.

   6. It is discriminating. "To the dividing asunder of soul and spirit."
      It separates things much alike: natural and spiritual religion.
      It divides the outer from the inner: external and internal religion, "joints and marrow."
      It does this by its own penetrating and discerning qualities.

   7. It is revealing. "A discerner of the thoughts and intents of the heart."

It cleaves the man as the butcher cleaves a carcase, and opens
up the secret faculties and tendencies of the soul.

Laying bare thoughts, and intents, and inner workings.

Criticizing them, and putting a right estimate on them.

Tracing their windings, and showing their dubious character.

Approving that which is good, and condemning the evil.

All this we have seen in the preaching of the Word of God.

Have you not felt it to be so?

II. THE LESSONS WHICH WE SHOULD LEARN THEREFROM.

That we do greatly reverence the Word, as truly spoken of God.

That we come to it for quickening for our own souls.

That we come to it for power when fighting the battles of truth.

That we come to it for cutting force to kill our own sins and
to help us in destroying the evils of the day.

That we come to it for piercing force when men's consciences and
hearts are hard to reach.

That we use it to the most obstinate, to arouse their consciences
and convict them of sin.

That we discriminate by its means between truth and falsehood.

That we let it criticize us, and our opinions, and projects, and
acts, and all about us.

Let us keep to this Sword of the Lord, for none other is living and
powerful as this is.

Let us grasp its hilt with firmer grip than ever.

SHARPENERS

All the great conquests which Christ and his saints achieve in this
world are got with this sword; when Christ comes forth against his
enemies this sword is girded on his thigh (Ps. xlv. 3): "Gird thy sword
upon thy thigh, O most mighty"; and his victory over them is ascribed
to it (verse 4), "And in thy majesty ride prosperously because of truth";
that is, the word of truth.

We read of Apollos (Acts xviii. 28), that he "mightily convinced the
Jews"; he did, as it were, knock them down with the weight of his
reasoning. And out of what armoury fetched he the sword with which
he so prevailed? See the same verse, "Showing by the Scriptures that
Jesus was Christ"; and he therefore is said to be "mighty in the
Scriptures" (ver. 24).

Bless God for the efficacy of the word upon thy soul. Did ever its
point prick thy heart, its edge fetch blood of thy lusts? Bless God for
it; you would do as much to a surgeon for lancing a sore, and severing

a putrified part from thy body, though he put thee to exquisite torture in the doing of it. And I hope thou thinkest God hath done thee a greater kindness. . . . There is not another sword like this in all the world, that can cure with cutting; not another arm could use this sword, to have done thus with it, besides the Spirit of God. None could do such feats with Scanderberg's as himself.

The word of God is too sacred a thing, and preaching too solemn a work, to be toyed and played with, as is the usage of some, who make a sermon but matter of wit and fine oratory. If we mean to do good, we must come unto men's hearts, not in word only, but with power. Satan moves not for a thousand squibs and wit-cracks of rhetoric. Draw, therefore, this sword out of your scabbard, and strike with its naked edge; this you will find the only way to pierce your people's consciences, and fetch blood of their sins.—*William Gurnall.*

When the heathen saw the converts reading the book which had produced the change, they enquired if they talked to it. "No," they answered, "it talks to us; for it is the Word of God." "What then!" replied the strangers, "does it speak?" "Yes," rejoined the Christians, "it speaks to the heart."—*Life of Moffat.*

Miss Whateley says, "To rouse the torpid and unexercised mind of a Moslem woman is wonderful, for they are sunk in ignorance and degradation; but while I was reading to one of them a few weeks ago, she exclaimed, 'Why, it is just as if I were out in the dark, and you held a lamp to me, that I might see my way.'"

The *Rev. James Wall*, of Rome, relates the following instances of conversion through the reading of the Scriptures :—One of the converts, when first presented with a New Testament, said, "Very well; it is the very size for me to make my cigarettes," and so he began to smoke it away. He smoked away all the Evangelists, till he was at the Tenth Chapter of John, when it struck him that he must read a bit of it, for if he didn't, there would soon be no more left to read. The first word struck home, and the man read himself into Christ.

A secret society of political conspirators, who sought to achieve their purposes by assassination, were in the habit of placing a Bible (as a blind) on the table of the room where they met for deliberation; and one night, when there happened to be little business to transact, and they were all rather sleepy, a member of the society opened the Bible, and saw a verse that went right to his heart. He soon returned to the book, and read more of it; and now he was a very earnest follower of the Lord Jesus.—*Missionary Herald.*

CCXL

Heb. iv. 16 —"*Let us therefore come boldly unto the throne of grace, that we may obtain mercy, and find grace to help in time of need.*"

Prayer occupies a most important place in the life of the Christian.
His vigour, happiness, growth, and usefulness depend thereon.
In Scripture the utmost encouragements are held out to prayer.
This verse is one of the sweetest of invitations to prayer.

I. HERE IS OUR GREAT RESORT DESCRIBED :—"The throne of grace."
Once it was called "the mercy-*seat*," but now "the throne."
In drawing near to God in prayer, we come—

1. To God as a King, with reverence, confidence, and submission.
2. To one who gives as a King : therefore we ask largely and expectantly. He has riches of grace and power.
3. To one who sits upon a throne "of grace," on purpose to dispense grace. It is his design, his object in displaying himself as King.
4. To one who in hearing prayer is enthroned and glorified. Grace is at its utmost when believers pray : it is grace on the throne.
5. To one who even in hearing prayer acts as a sovereign, but whose sovereignty is all of grace.

To the throne of the great God poor sinners are invited to come. Oh, the privilege of having audience with the King of Grace!

II. HERE IS A LOVING EXHORTATION :—"Let us come."
It is the voice of one who goes with us. It is an invitation—

1. From Paul, a man like ourselves, but an experienced believer who had much tried the power of prayer.
2. From the whole church speaking in him.
3. From the Holy Spirit; for the apostle spake by inspiration. The Spirit, making intercession in us, says, "Let us come."

Let us not be indifferent to this sympathetic call. At once let us draw near to God.

III. HERE IS A QUALIFYING ADVERB:—"Let us come boldly."
Not proudly, presumptuously, nor with the tone of demand, for it is the throne; yet "boldly," for it is the throne *of grace.*

330

By this adverb, "boldly," is meant—

1. We may come constantly, at all times.
2. We may come unreservedly, with all sorts of petitions.
3. We may come freely, with simple words.
4. We may come hopefully, with full confidence of being heard.
5. We may come fervently, with importunity of pleading.

IV. HERE IS A REASON GIVEN FOR BOLDNESS:—" Let us *therefore* come."

1. "That we may obtain mercy, and find grace:" not that we may
utter good words; but may actually obtain blessings.
We may come when we need great mercy, because of our sin.
We may come when we have little grace.
We may come when we are in great need of more grace.

2. There are many other reasons for coming at once, and boldly.
Our character may urge us. We are invited to come for "mercy,"
and therefore undeserving sinners may come.
The character of God encourages us to be bold.
Our relation to him as children gives us great freedom.
The Holy Spirit's guidance draws us near the throne.
The promises invite us by their greatness, freeness, sureness, &c.
Christ is already given to us, and therefore God will deny us
nothing.
Our former successes at the throne give us solid confidence.

3. The great reason of all for bold approach is in Jesus.
He once was slain, and the mercy-seat is sprinkled with his blood.
He is risen and has justified us by his righteousness.
He has ascended and taken possession of all covenant blessings
on our behalf. Let us ask for that which is our own.
He is sympathetic, tender, and careful for us; we *must* be heard.

Let us come to the throne, when we are sinful, to find mercy.
Let us come to the throne, when we are weak, to find help.
Let us come to the throne, when we are tempted, to find grace.

EXPOSITIONS

When God enacts laws, he is on a throne of legislation : when he
administers these laws, he is on a throne of government : when he tries
his creatures by these laws, he is on a throne of judgment : but when
he receives petitions, and dispenses favours, he is on a *throne of grace.*

The idea of a throne inspires awe, bordering upon terror. It repels
rather than invites. Few of us could approach it without trembling.
But what is the throne of the greatest earthly monarch that ever swayed

a sceptre? The God we address is the King of kings. In his eye an Alexander is a worm; yea, all nations before him are less than nothing and vanity. How can we approach his infinite majesty? Blessed be his name, he is on a throne of grace; and we are allowed, and even commanded, to come to it *boldly.*—*William Jay.*

It is styled a throne of *grace*, because God's gracious and free favour doth there accompany his glorious majesty. Majesty and mercy do there meet together. This was, under the law, typified by the ark. At each end thereof was an angel, to set forth God's glorious majesty. The cover of it is styled a "mercy-seat": Exodus xxv. 17, 18.

William Gouge.

A holy boldness, a chastened familiarity, is the true spirit of right prayer. It was said of Luther that, when he prayed, it was with as much reverence as if he were praying to an infinite God, and with as much familiarity as if he were speaking to his nearest friend.

G. S. Bowes.

This word *boldly* signifies liberty without restraint. You may be free, for you are welcome. You may use freedom of speech. The word is so used, Acts ii. 29, and iv. 13. You have liberty to speak your minds freely; to speak all your heart, your ails, and wants, and fears, and grievances. As others may not fetter you in speaking to God by prescribing what words you should use; so you need not restrain yourselves, but freely speak all that your condition requires.—*David Clarkson.*

A petitioner once approached Augustus with so much fear and trembling that the emperor cried, "What, man! do you think you are giving a sop to an elephant?" He did not care to be thought a hard and cruel ruler. When men pray with a slavish bondage upon them, with cold, set phrases, and a crouching solemnity, the free Spirit of the Lord may well rebuke them. Art thou coming to a tyrant? Holy boldness, or at least a childlike hope, is most becoming in a Christian.

Obtaining mercy comes first; then finding grace to help in time of need. You cannot reverse God's order. You will not find grace to help in time of need till you have sought and found mercy to save. You have no right to reckon on God's help and protection and guidance, and all the other splendid privileges which he promises to "the children of God by faith in Jesus Christ," until you have this first blessing, the mercy of God in Christ Jesus; for it is "*in*" Jesus Christ that all the promises of God are yea and Amen.—*F. R. Havergal.*

CCXLI

𝕳𝖊𝖇. 𝖛. 2 —"𝕿𝖆𝖍𝖔 𝖈𝖆𝖓 𝖍𝖆𝖛𝖊 𝖈𝖔𝖒𝖕𝖆𝖘𝖘𝖎𝖔𝖓 𝖔𝖓 𝖙𝖍𝖊 𝖎𝖌𝖓𝖔𝖗𝖆𝖓𝖙, 𝖆𝖓𝖉 𝖔𝖓 𝖙𝖍𝖊𝖒 𝖙𝖍𝖆𝖙 𝖆𝖗𝖊 𝖔𝖚𝖙 𝖔𝖋 𝖙𝖍𝖊 𝖜𝖆𝖞."

Men who are ignorant should not be met with scorn, nor fault-finding, nor neglect, for they need compassion.

We should lay ourselves out to bear with such for their good.

A disciple who has been taught all that he knows by a gracious Saviour should have compassion on "the ignorant."

A wanderer who has been restored should have compassion on "them that are out of the way."

A priest should have compassion on the people with whom he is one flesh and blood, and assuredly our Lord, who is our great High Priest, has abundant compassion upon the ignorant.

Let us think of his great pity towards them.

I. WHAT IS THIS IGNORANCE?

It is moral and spiritual, and deals with eternal things.

1. It is fearfully common among all ranks.

2. It leaves them strangers to themselves.
   They know not their own ignorance.
   They are unaware of the heart's depravity.
   They are unconscious of the heinousness of their actual sin.
   They dream not of their present and eternal danger.
   They have not discovered their inability for all that is good.

3. It leaves them unacquainted with the way of salvation.
   They choose other ways.
   They have a mixed and injurious notion of the one way.
   They often question and cavil at this one and only way.

4. It leaves them without the knowledge of Jesus.
   They know not his person, his offices, his work, his character his ability, his readiness to save them.

5. It leaves them strangers to the Holy Spirit.
   They perceive not his inward strivings.
   They are ignorant of regeneration.
   They cannot comprehend the truth which he teaches.
   They cannot receive his sanctification.

6. It is most ruinous in its consequences.
   It keeps men out of Christ.
   It does not excuse them when it is wilful, as it usually is,

II. What is there in this ignorance which is liable to provoke us, and therefore demands compassion?

1. Its folly. Wisdom is worried with the absurdities of ignorance.
2. Its pride. Anger is excited by the vanity of self-conceit.
3. Its prejudice. It will not hear nor learn; and this is vexatious.
4. Its obstinacy. It refuses reason; and this is very exasperating.
5. Its opposition. It contends against plain truth, and this is trying.
6. Its density. It cannot be enlightened : it is profoundly foolish.
7. Its unbelief. Witnesses to divine truth are denied credence.
8. Its wilfulness. It chooses not to know. It is hard teaching such.
9. Its relapses. It returns to folly, forgets and refuses wisdom, and this is a sore affliction to true love.

III. How our Lord's compassion towards the ignorant is shown.
" He can have compassion on the ignorant."

This he clearly shows—

1. By offering to teach them.
2. By actually receiving them as disciples.
3. By instructing them little by little, most condescendingly.
4. By teaching them the same things over again, patiently.
5. By never despising them notwithstanding their dulness.
6. By never casting them off through weariness of their stupidity.

To such a compassionate Lord let us come, ignorant as we are.

For such a compassionate Lord let us labour among the most ignorant, and never cease to pity them.

Notes

It is a sad thing for the blind man who has to read the raised type when the tips of his fingers harden, for then he cannot read the thoughts of men which stand out upon the page; but it is far worse to lose sensibility of soul, for then you cannot peruse the book of human nature, but must remain untaught in the sacred literature of the heart. You have heard of the " iron duke," but an iron Christian would be a very terrible person : a heart of flesh is the gift of divine grace, and one of its sure results is the power to be very pitiful, tender, and full of compassion.—*C. H. S.*

Ignorance is the devil's college.—*Christmas Evans.*

What the Papists cry up as the mother of devotion, we cry down as the father of superstition,— *William Secker.*

That there should one man die ignorant who had capacity for knowledge, this I call a tragedy. Were it to happen more than twenty times in the minute, as by some computations it does, what a line of tragedies! The miserable fraction of science which our united mankind, in a wide universe of nescience, has acquired, why is not this, with all diligence, imparted to all?—*Thomas Carlyle.*

Utter ignorance is a most effectual fortification to a bad state of the mind. Prejudice may perhaps be removed ; unbelief may be reasoned with; even demoniacs have been compelled to bear witness to the truth; but the stupidity of confirmed ignorance not only defeats the ultimate efficacy of the means for making men wiser and better, but stands in preliminary defiance to the very act of their application. It reminds us of an account, in one of the relations of the French Egyptian Campaigns, of the attempt to reduce a garrison posted in a bulky fort of mud. Had the defences been of timber, the besiegers might have set fire to and burnt them; had they been of stone, they might have shaken and ultimately breached them by the battery of their cannon, or they might have undermined and blown them up. But the huge mound of mud had nothing susceptible of fire or any other force ; the missiles from the artillery were discharged but to be buried in the dull mass ; and all the means of demolition were baffled.—*John Foster.*

In *Eyesight, Good and Bad*, by Dr. R. B. Carter, the writer says "Nothing is more common than for defective sight to be punished as obstinacy or stupidity. For my own part, I have long learned to look upon obstinate and stupid children as mainly artificial productions, and shall not readily forget the pleasure with which I heard from the master of the great elementary school at Edinburgh, where twelve hundred children attend daily, that his fundamental principle of management was that there were no naughty boys and no boobies."

I used to reproach myself for *religious stupidity* when I was not well; but I see now that God is my kind Father, not my hard taskmaster expecting me to be full of life and zeal when physically exhausted. It takes long to learn such lessons. One has to penetrate deeply into the heart of Christ to begin to know its tenderness and sympathy and forbearance.

> The love of Jesus—what it is
> Only His *sufferers* know.
>   *Elizabeth Prentiss.*

CCXLII

Heb. b. 8 —"Though he were a Son, yet learned he obedience by the things which he suffered."

It is always consoling to us to behold the footsteps of our Lord.

When we see him tried, we cheerfully submit to the like trial.

When we perceive that in his case an exception to the rule of chastening might have been expected, and yet none was made, we are encouraged to bear our sufferings patiently.

When we see the great Elder Brother put to more rather than less of trial, we are fully drawn to obey the will of God by submission.

I. SONSHIP DOES NOT EXEMPT FROM SUFFERING.

1. Not even Jesus, as a Son, escaped suffering.

He was *the* Son, peculiarly, and above all others.

He was the honoured and beloved first-born.

He was the faithful and sinless Son.

He was soon to be the glorified Son in an eminent sense.

2. No honour put upon sons of God will exempt them from suffering.

3. No holiness of character, nor completeness of obedience, can exempt the children of God from the school of suffering.

4. No prayer of God's sons, however earnest, will remove every thorn in the flesh from them.

5. No love in God's child, however fervent, will prevent his being tried.

The love and wisdom of God ensure the discipline of the house for all the heirs of heaven without a single exception.

II. SUFFERING DOES NOT MAR SONSHIP.

The case of our Lord is set forth as a model for all the sons of God.

1. His poverty did not disprove his Sonship. Luke ii. 12.

2. His temptations did not shake his Sonship. Matt. iv. 3.

3. His endurance of slander did not jeopardize it. John x. 36.

4. His fear and sorrow did not put it in dispute. Matt. xxvi. 39.

5. His desertion by men did not invalidate it. John xvi. 32.

6. His being forsaken of God did not alter it. Luke xxiii. 46.

7. His death cast no doubt thereon. Mark xv. 39. He rose again, and thus proved his Father's pleasure in him. John xx. 17.

Never was there a truer, or lovelier, or more beloved Son than the sufferers. "A man of sorrows, and acquainted with grief."

III. Obedience has to be learned even by sons.

Even he in whom there was no natural depravity, but perfect, inherent purity, had to learn obedience.

1. It must be learned experimentally.
    What is to be done and suffered can only be learned in the actual exercise of obedience.
    How it is done must be discovered by practice.
    The actual doing of it is only possible in trial.

2. It must be learned by suffering.
    Not by words from the most instructive of teachers. .
    Nor by observation of the lives of others.
    Nor even by perpetual activity on our own part. This might make us fussy rather than obedient : we *must* suffer.

3. It must be learned for use in earth and in heaven.
    On earth by sympathy with others.
    In heaven by perfect praise to God growing out of experience.

IV. Suffering has a peculiar power to teach true sons.

It is a better tutor than all else, because—

1. It touches the man's self ; his bone, his flesh, his heart.

2. It tests his graces, and sweeps away those shams which are not proofs of obedience, but pretences of self-will.

3. It goes to the root, and tests the truth of our new nature. It shows whether repentance, faith, prayer, etc., are mere importa tions, or home-grown fruits.

4. It tests our endurance, and makes us see how far we are established in the obedience which we think we possess. Can we say, " Though he slay me, yet will I trust in him " ?

The anxious question—Am I a son ?
The aspiring desire—Let me learn obedience.
The accepted discipline—I submit to suffer.

Blossomings of the Rod

Corrections are pledges of our adoption, and badges of our sonship. One Son God hath without sin, but none without sorrow. As God corrects none but his own, so all that are his shall be sure to have it ; and they shall take it for a favour too. 1 Cor. xi. 32.—*John Trapp.*

I bear my willing witness that I owe more to the fire, and the hammer, and the file, than to anything else in my Lord's workshop. I sometimes question whether I have ever learned anything except through th rod. When my school-room is darkened, I see most.—*C. H S.*

If aught can teach us aught, Affliction's looks,
  Making us look unto ourselves so near,
Teach us to know ourselves beyond all books,
  Or all the learned schools that ever were.

This mistress lately pluck'd me by the ear,
  And many a golden lesson hath me taught ;
Hath made my senses quick, and reason clear,
  Reform'd my will, and rectified my thought.

Sir John Davies.

"I never," said Luther, "knew the meaning of God's word, until I came into affliction. I have always found it one of my best schoolmasters." On another occasion, referring to some spiritual temptation on the morning of the preceding day, he said to a friend (Justin Jonas), "Doctor, I must mark the day ; I was yesterday at school.' In one of his works, he most accurately calls affliction "the theology of Christians"—"Theologium Christianorum." "I have learned more divinity," said Dr. Rivet, confessing to God of his last days of affliction —"in these ten days that thou art come to visit me, than I did in fifty years before. Thou teachest me after a better manner than all those doctors, in reading whom I spent so much time."—*Charles Bridges.*

A minister was recovering from a dangerous illness, when one of his friends addressed him thus, "Sir, though God seems to be bringing you up from the gates of death, yet it will be a long time before you will sufficiently retrieve your strength, and regain vigour enough of mind to preach as usual." The good man answered : "You are mistaken, my friend : for this six weeks' illness has taught me more divinity than all my past studies and all my ten years' ministry put together."

New Cyclopædia of Anecdote.

Not to be unhappy is unhappiness,
And misery not to have known misery ;
For the best way unto discretion is
The way that leads us by adversity ;
And men are better showed what is amiss
By the expert finger of calamity
Than they can be with all that fortune brings,
Who never shows them the true face of things.

Samuel Daniel.

CCXLIII

Ħeb. x. 9 —"Ħe taketh away the first, that he may establish the second."

The way of God is to go from good to better.
This excites growing wonder and gratitude.
This makes men desire, and pray, and believe, and expect.
This aids man in his capacity to receive the best things.
The first good thing is removed, that the second may the more fitly come.
Upon this last fact we will meditate, noticing—

I. THE GRAND INSTANCE. First came the Jewish sacrifices, and then came Jesus to do the will of God.

1. The removal of instructive and consoling ordinances.
While they lasted they were of great value, and they were removed because, when Jesus came—
They were needless as types.
They would have proved burdensome as services.
They might have been dangerous as temptations to formalism.
They would have taken off the mind from the substance which they had formerly shadowed forth.

2. The establishment of the real, perfect, everlasting atonement.
This is a blessed advance; for
No one who sees Jesus regrets Aaron.
No one who knows the simplicity of the gospel wishes to be brought under the perplexities of the ceremonial law.
No one who feels the liberty of Zion desires to return to the bondage of Sinai.

Beware of setting up any other ordinances; for this would be to build again what God has cast down; if not to do even worse.
Beware of imagining that the second can fail as the first did. The one was "taken away"; but the other is *established* by God himself.

II. INSTANCES IN HISTORY. These are many. Here are a few—

1. The earthly paradise has been taken away by sin; but the Lord has given us salvation in Christ, and heaven.
2. The first man has failed; behold the Second Adam.
3. The first covenant is broken, and the second gloriously takes its place.

339

4. The first temple, with its transient glories, has melted away; but the second and spiritual house rises beneath the eye and hand of the Great Architect.

III. INSTANCES IN EXPERIENCE.

1. Our first righteousness is taken away by conviction of sin; but the righteousness of Christ is established.
2. Our first peace has been blown down as a tottering fence; but we shelter in the Rock of Ages.
3. Our first strength has proved worse than weakness; but the Lord is our strength and our song, he also has become our salvation.
4. Our first guidance led us into darkness; now we give up self, superstition, and philosophy, and trust in the Spirit of our God.
5. Our first joy died out like thorns which crackle under a pot; but now we joy in God.

IV. INSTANCES TO BE EXPECTED.

1. Our body decaying shall be renewed in the image of our risen Lord.
2. Our earth passing away, and its elements being dissolved, there shall be new heavens and a new earth.
3. Our family removed one by one, we shall be charmed by the grand reunion in the Father's house above.
4. Our all being taken away, we find more than all in God.
5. Our life ebbing out, the eternal life comes rolling up in a full tide of glory.

Let us not grieve at the taking away of the first.
Let us expect the establishment of the second.

MELIORA

The Law is a Gospel pre-figured, and the Gospel a Law consummated.
Bishop Hall.

The sin-destroyer being come, we are no longer under the sin-revealer.
Martin Boos.

No need of prophets to inquire :
The Sun is risen—the stars retire :
The Comforter is come, and sheds
His holy unction on our heads.
Josiah Conder.

When Alexander went upon a hopeful expedition, he gave away his gold; and when he was asked what he kept for himself, he answered,

"Spem majorum et meliorum"—the hope of greater and better things. . . . A Christian's motto always is, or always should be, Spero meliora—I hope for better things.—*Thomas Brooks, in "The Best Things reserved till Last."*

On a cold, windy March day, a gentleman stopped at an apple-stand, whose proprietor was a rough-looking Italian. He alluded to the severe weather, when, with a cheerful smile and tone, the Italian replied: "Yes, pritty cold; but *by-and-by*—tink of dat!" In other words, the time of warm skies, flowers, and songs, was near, and was to be thought of. The humble vendor little thought of the impression made by his few words. "By-and-by—think of that!"

The Jewish rabbins report (how truly is uncertain) that when Joseph, in the times of plenty, had gathered much corn in Egypt, he threw the chaff into the river Nile, that so, flowing to the neighbouring cities and nations more remote, they might know what abundance was laid up, not for themselves alone, but for others also. So God, in his abundant goodness, to make us know what glory there is in heaven, hath thrown some husks to us here in this world, that so, tasting the sweetness thereof, we might aspire to his bounty that is above, and draw out this happy conclusion to the great comfort of our precious souls—that if a little earthly glory do so much amaze us, what will the heavenly do? If there be such glory in God's footstool, what is there in his throne? If he give us so much in the land of our pilgrimage, what will he not give us in our own country? If he bestoweth so much on his enemies, what will he not give to his friends?—*John Spencer.*

There are certain words which, occurring frequently, are like a bunch of keys, and enable us to unlock the treasures in this epistle. Such a key is "*better*"; and we find the Lord Jesus described as being better than angels (i. 4; illustrated in John v. 4—6), better than Moses (iii.), Joshua (iv.), and Aaron (vii.); his blood speaking better things than that of Abel (xii. 24); himself the Surety of a better testament, established upon better promises (vii. 22; viii. 6). The old covenant based upon man's *promise* (Exod. xix. 8; xxiv. 7, 8) was broken in forty days; but the *performance* by the Son of God was the foundation of the better covenant. "The two tables of the testimony were in the *hand* of Moses" (Exod. xxxii. 15; Gal. iii. 19), but God's law is within the *heart* of our Surety (Ps. xl. 8; compare Deut. x. 1, 2). That word was spoken by angels (Heb. ii. 2; Acts vii. 53); but this by him who is "so much *better* than angels."—*E. A. H. (Mrs. Gordon).*

CCXLIV

Heb. xii. 13.—" And make straight paths for your feet, lest that which is lame be turned out of the way; but let it rather be healed."

We sometimes meet with those who are fleet of foot and joyous of spirit. Would to God that all were so! But as they are not, the lame must be considered.

The road should be cleared for tottering steps.

Our desire is that the whole band may reach the journey's end in safety.

I, IN ALL FLOCKS THERE ARE LAME SHEEP.

   1. Some are so from their very nature and birth.
      Ready to despond and doubt.
      Ready to disbelieve and fall into error.
      Ready to yield to temptation, and so to prove unstable.
      Unready and feeble in all practical duties.

   2. Some have been ill-fed. This brings on a foot-rot and lameness.
      Many are taught false doctrine.
      Many more receive indefinite, hazy doctrine.
      Many others hear light, unsubstantial, chaffy doctrine.

   3. Some have been worried, and so driven to lameness.
      By Satan, with his insinuations and temptations.
      By persecutors, with their slander, taunting, ridicule, etc.
      By proud professors, unkindly pious, severely critical, etc.
      By a morbid conscience, seeing evil where there is none.

   4. Some have grown weary through the roughness of the road.
      Exceeding much ignorance has enfeebled them.
      Exceeding much worldly trouble has depressed them.
      Exceeding much inward conflict has grieved them.
      Exceeding much controversy has worried them.

   5. Some have gradually become weak.
      Backsliding by neglect of the means of grace.
      Backsliding through the evil influence of others.
      Backsliding through pride of heart and self-satisfaction.
      Backsliding through general coldness of heart.

   6. Some have had a terrible fall.
      This has broken their bones so as to prevent progress.
      This has snapped the sinew of their usefulness,
      This has crippled them as to holy joy.

II. The rest of the flock must seek their healing.

1. By seeking their company, and not leaving them to perish by the way through neglect, contempt, and despair.

2. By endeavouring to comfort them and to restore them. This can be done by the more experienced among us; and those who are unfit for such difficult work can try the next plan, which is so plainly mentioned in our text.

3. By making straight paths for our own feet.
   By unquestionable holiness of life.
   By plain gospel teaching in our own simple way.
   By manifest joy in the Lord.
   By avoiding all crooked customs which might perplex them.
   By thus showing them that Jesus is to us "The way, the truth, and the life." No path can be more straight than that of simple faith in Jesus.

III. The Shepherd of the flock cares for such.

1. Their fears: they conclude that he will leave them.
2. The reason: to do so would be by far the easier plan for him.
3. Their dread: if he did so, they must inevitably perish.
4. Their comfort: he has provided all the means of healing the lame.
5. Their hope: he is very gentle and tender, and wills not that any one of them should wander and perish.
6. Their confidence: healing will win him much honour and grateful affection; wherefore we conclude that he will keep them.

Let us be careful to cause no offence or injury to the weakest.

Let us endeavour to restore such as are out of the way, and comfort those who are sorely afflicted.

Sheep-Lore.

Sheep are liable to many diseases, many of them are weak and feeble; these a good shepherd taketh pity of, and endeavours to heal and strengthen. So the saints of God are subject to manifold weaknesses, temptations, and afflictions, which moved the Almighty to great compassion, and sorely to rebuke the shepherds of Israel for their cruelty and great remissness towards his flock: "The diseased have ye not strengthened, neither have ye healed that which was sick," etc. And therefore he saith he would himself take the work into his own hands; "I will bind up that which was broken, and will strengthen that which was sick," etc.—*Benjamin Keach.*

Many preachers in our days are like Heraclitus, who was called "*the dark doctor.*" They affect sublime notions, obscure expressions, uncouth phrases, making plain truths difficult, and easy truths hard. "They darken counsel with words without knowledge": Job xxxviii. 2. Studied expressions and high notions in a sermon, are like Asahel's carcase in the way, that did only stop men and make them gaze, but did no ways profit them or better them. It is better to present Truth in her native plainness than to hang her ears with counterfeit pearls. — *Thomas Brooks.*

Now Mr. Feeble-mind, when they were going out at the door, made as if he intended to linger : the which, when Mr. Great-heart espied, he said, " Come, Mr. Feeble-mind, pray do you go along with us ; I will be your conductor, and you shall fare as the rest."

Feeble-mind : " Alas ! I want a suitable companion : you are all lusty and strong ; but I, as you see, am weak : I choose, therefore, rather to come behind, lest, by reason of my many infirmities, I should be both a burden to myself and to you. I am, as I said, a man of a weak and feeble mind, and shall be offended and made weak at that which others can bear. I shall like no laughing : I shall like no gay attire : I shall like no unprofitable questions. Nay, I am so weak a man as to be offended with that which others have a liberty to do. I do not know all the truth : I am a very ignorant Christian man. Sometimes, if I hear any rejoice in the Lord, it troubles me because I cannot do so too. It is with me as it is with a weak man among the strong, or as with a sick man among the healthy, or as 'a lamp despised'; so that I know not what to do. 'He that is ready to slip with his feet is as a lamp despised in the thought of him that is at ease ': Job xii. 5."

" But, brother," said Mr. Great-heart, " I have it in commission to 'comfort the feeble-minded,' and 'to support the weak.' You must needs go along with us : we will wait for you ; we will lend you our help ; we will deny ourselves of some things, both opinionate and practical, for your sake ; we will not enter into 'doubtful disputations' before you ; we will be 'made all things' to you, rather than you shall be left behind."—*John Bunyan.*

It should be between a strong saint and a weak as it is between two lute strings that are tuned one to another ; no sooner one is struck but the other trembles ; no sooner should a weak saint be struck, but the strong should tremble. " Remember them that are in bonds, as bound with them ": Heb. xiii. 3.—*Thomas Brooks.*

𝔥𝔢𝔟. 𝔵𝔦𝔦. 25 —" See that ye refuse not him that speaketh. For if they escaped not who refused him that spake on earth, much more shall not we escape, if we turn away from him that speaketh from heaven."

Jesus still speaks to us in the gospel.
What a privilege to hear such a voice, with such a message !
What cruel sin to refuse Jesus a hearing !
Here is a most urgent exhortation to yield him reverent attention.

I. THERE IS NEED OF THIS EXHORTATION FROM MANY CONSIDERATIONS.

1. The excellence of the word.   It claims obedient attention.
2. The readiness of Satan to prevent our receiving the divine word.
3. Our own indisposition to receive the holy, heavenly message.
4. We have rejected too long already.   It is to be feared that we may continue to do so ; but our right course is to hearken at once.
5. The word comes in love to our souls ; let us therefore heed it, and render love for love.

II. THERE ARE MANY WAYS OF REFUSING HIM THAT SPEAKETH.

1. Not hearing.   Absence from public worship, neglect of Bible-reading.   "Turn away from him."
2. Hearing listlessly, as if half asleep, and unconcerned.
3. Refusing to believe.   Intellectually believing, but not with the heart.
4. Raising quibbles.   Hunting up difficulties, favouring unbelief.
5. Being offended.   Angry with the gospel, indignant at plain speech, opposing honest personal rebuke.
6. Perverting his words.   Twisting and wresting Scripture.
7. Bidding him depart.   Steeling the conscience, trifling with conviction, resorting to frivolous company for relief.
8. Reviling him.   Denying his Deity, hating his gospel, and his holy way.
9. Persecuting him.   Turning upon his people as a whole, or assailing them as individuals.

III. THERE ARE MANY CAUSES OF THIS REFUSING.

1. Stolid indifference, which causes a contempt of all good things.

2. Self-righteousness, which makes self an idol, and therefore rejects the living Saviour.

3. Self-reliant wisdom, which is too proud to hear the voice of God.

4. Hatred of holiness, which prefers the wilful to the obedient, the lustful to the pure, the selfish to the divine.

5. Fear of the world, which listens to threats, or bribes, or flatteries, and dares not act aright.

6. Procrastination, which cries "to-morrow," but means "never."

7. Despair and unbelief, which declare the gospel to be powerless to save, and unavailable as a consolation.

IV. REFUSING TO HEAR CHRIST, THE HIGHEST AUTHORITY IS DESPISED. "Him that speaketh from heaven."

1. He is of heavenly nature, and reveals to us what he has known of God and heaven.

2. He came from heaven, armed with heavenly authority.

3. He speaks from heaven at this moment by his eternal Spirit in Holy Scripture, the ordinances and the preaching of the gospel.

4. He will speak from heaven at the judgment.
He is himself God, and therefore all that he saith hath divinity within it.

V. THE DOOM TO BE FEARED IF WE REFUSE CHRIST.
Those to whom Moses spake on earth, who refused him, escaped not.

1. Let us think of their doom, and learn that equally sure destruction will happen to all who refuse Christ.
Pharaoh and the Egyptians.
The murmurers dying in the wilderness.
Korah, Dathan, and Abiram.

2. Let us see how some have perished in the church.
Judas, Ananias and Sapphira, etc.

3. Let us see how others perish who remain in the world, and refuse to quit it for the fold of Christ.
They shall not escape by Annihilation, nor by Purgatory, nor by Universal Restitutions.
They shall not escape by infidelity, hardness of heart, cunning, or hypocrisy. They have refused the only way of escape, and therefore they must perish for ever.

Instead of refusing, listen, learn, obey.
Instead of the curse, you shall gain a blessing.

WARNING WORDS

Our blessed Lord is represented as "now speaking from heaven" to Christians generally; and even if we were, contrary to all just reason, to confine the reference to the persons to whom the Epistle was immediately written, he is said to speak to multitudes who never saw or heard him in the days of his flesh. This could be only by the agency of inspired men, whose commission to teach and command "in the name of Christ" was proved by miracles. Those miracles they attributed to him, as is plain from many passages in the Acts and the Epistles. Thus Christ stands in the very position of power, authority, and action, continually ascribed to Jehovah in the Old Testament, *speaking by his prophets.* "This," observes Michaelis, "is saying of Christ the greatest thing that can be said."—*Dr. J. Pye Smith.*

We seem to have done with the Word as it has passed through our ears; but the Word, be it remembered, will never have done with us, till it has judged us at the last day.—*Judge Hale.*

A nobleman, skilled in music, who had often observed the Hon. and Rev. Mr. Cadogan's inattention to his performance, said to him one day, 'Come, I am determined to make you feel the force of music; pay particular attention to this piece." It was accordingly played. "Well, what do you say now?" "Why, just what I said before." "What! can you hear this and not be charmed? Well, I am quite surprised at your insensibility. Where are your ears?" "Bear with me, my lord," replied Mr. Cadogan, "since I, too, have had my surprise. I have often, from the pulpit, set before you the most striking and affecting truths; I have sounded notes that might have raised the dead; I have said, 'Surely he will feel now,' but you never seemed to be charmed with my music, though infinitely more interesting than yours. I, too, have been ready to say, with astonishment, 'Where are his ears?'"

One of the modern thinkers had been upholding the doctrine of universal salvation at a certain house with much zeal. A child who had listened to his pestilent talk was heard to say to his companion, "We can now steal, and lie, and do wicked things, for there is no hell when we die." If such preachers gain much power in this country we shall not need to raise the question of a hell hereafter, for we shall have one here.—*C. H. S.*

347

CCXLVI

Heb. xiii. 5 —"He hath said, I will never leave thee, nor forsake thee.

Here is a divine word, directly from God's own mouth : " For himself hath said." (See Revised Version.)

Here is a promise which has been frequently made "He hath said": This promise occurs again and again.

Here are some of the fat things full of marrow. The sentence is as full of meaning as it is free from verbiage.

Here is the essence of meat, the quintessence of medicine.

May the Holy Spirit show us the treasure hid in this matchless sentence!

I. VIEW THE WORDS AS A QUOTATION.

The Holy Spirit led Paul to quote from the Scriptures, though he could have spoken fresh words.

Thus he put honour on the Old Testament.

Thus he taught that words spoken to ancient saints belong to us.

Our apostle quotes the sense, not the exact words, and thus he teaches us that the spirit of a text is the main thing.

We find the words which Paul has quoted—

In Gen. xxviii. 15, "I will not leave thee, until I have done that which I have spoken to thee of." Spoken to Jacob when quitting home, and thus to young saints setting out in life.

In Deut. xxxi. 8, "He will be with thee, he will not fail thee, neither forsake thee." To Joshua, and so to those who have lost a leader, and are about to take the lead themselves, and to enter upon great wars and fightings, in which courage will be tried.

In 1 Chron. xxviii. 20, "He will not fail thee, nor forsake thee, until thou hast finished all the work." To Solomon, and thus to those who have a weighty charge upon them, requiring much wisdom. We build a spiritual temple.

In Isa. xli. 10, "Fear thou not; for I am with thee." To Israel, and so to the Lord's tried and afflicted people.

II. VIEW THEM AS A HOUSEHOLD WORD FROM GOD.

1. They are peculiarly a saying of God : "He hath said." This has been said, not so much by inspiration as by God himself.

2. They are remarkably forcible from having five negatives in them in the Greek.

348

3. They relate to God himself and his people. "I" . . . "thee."
4. They ensure his presence and his help. He would not be with us, and be inactive.
5. They guarantee the greatest good. God with us means all good.
6. They avert a dreadful evil which we deserve and might justly fear; namely, to be deserted of God.
7. They are such as he only could utter and make true. Nobody else can be with us effectually in agony, in death, in judgment.
8. They provide for all troubles, losses, desertions, weaknesses, difficulties, places, seasons, dangers, etc., in time and eternity.
9. They are substantiated by the divine love, immutability, and faithfulness.
10. They are further confirmed by our observation of the divine proceeding to others and to ourselves.

III. VIEW THEM AS A MOTIVE FOR CONTENTMENT. "Let your conversation be without covetousness, and be content with such things as ye have."
These most gracious words—
Lead us to live above visible things when we have stores in hand.
Lead us to present satisfaction however low our stores may be.
Lead us to see provision for all future emergencies.
Lead us into a security more satisfactory, sure, ennobling, and divine, than all the wealth of the Indies could bestow.
Lead us to reckon discontent a kind of blasphemy of God.
Since God is always with us, what can we want besides?

IV. VIEW THEM AS A REASON FOR COURAGE. "So that we may boldly say, The Lord is my helper, and I will not fear what man shall do unto me."
1. Our Helper is greater than our foes. "Jehovah is my helper."
2. Our foes are entirely in his hand. "I will not fear what man shall do."
3. If permitted to afflict us, God will sustain us under their malice.
What a blessed deliverance from fretting and from fearing have we in these few words!
Let us not be slow to follow the line of things which the Spirit evidently points out to us.

NOTES ON "NOTS"
Lord, the apostle dissuadeth the Hebrews from covetousness with this argument, because God said, "I will not leave thee, nor forsake thee."

349

Yet I find not that God ever gave this promise to all the Jews; but he spake it only to Joshua, when first made commander against the Canaanites: yet this (without violence to the analogy of faith) the apostle applieth to all good men in general. Is it so, that we are heirs apparent to all promises made to thy servants in Scripture? Are the charters of grace granted to them good to me also? Then will I say with Jacob, "I have enough." But because I cannot entitle myself to thy promises to them except I imitate their piety to thee, grant I may take as much care in following the one as comfort in the other.—*Thomas Fuller.*

Our friend, Dr. William Graham, of Bonn, has lately departed this life, and we are told that on his death-bed one said to him, "He hath said, 'I will never leave thee, nor forsake thee,'" to which the good man replied, with his dying breath, "Not a doubt of it! Not a doubt of it!"—*C. H. S., in the Sword and the Trowel,* 1884.

It is right to be contented with what we have, never with what we are.—*Mackintosh.*

I have read, says *Brooks,* of a company of poor Christians who were banished into some remote part; and one standing by, seeing them pass along, said that it was a very sad condition these poor people were in, to be thus hurried from the society of men, and made companions with the beasts of the field. "True," said another, "it were a sad condition indeed if they were carried to a place where they should not find their God. But let them be of good cheer, God goes along with them, and will exhibit the comforts of his presence whithersoever they go."

A heathen sage said to one of his friends, "Do not complain of thy misfortunes, as long as Cæsar is thy friend!" What shall we say to those whom the Prince of the kings of the earth calls his sons and his brethren? "I will never leave thee, nor forsake thee!" Ought not these words to cast all fear and care for ever to the ground? He who possesses him, to whom all things belong, possesseth all things.

F. W. Krummacher.

The soul that on Jesus has leaned for repose
I will not, I will not desert to his foes;
That soul though all hell should endeavour to shake,
I'll never, no never, no never forsake.

George Keith.

CCXLVII

James i. 12 —"𝕭lessed is the man that endureth temptation: for when he is tried, he shall receive the crown of life, which the Lord hath promised to them that love him."

To be *blessed* is to be happy, favoured, prosperous, etc.

But it has a secret, sacred emphasis all its own; for the favour and prosperity are such as only God himself can bestow.

Who would not desire to be blessed of God?

Most men mistake the whereabouts of blessedness.

It is not bound up with wealth, rank, power, talent, admiration, friendship, health, pleasure, or even with a combination of all these.

It is often found where least expected : amid trials, temptations, etc.

I. THE BLESSED IN THIS LIFE.

   1. Blessedness is not in our text connected with ease, freedom from trial, or absence of temptation.

      Untested treasures may be worthless ; not so those which have endured the fire. No man may reckon himself blessed if he has to fear that a trial would wither all his excellence.

   2. Blessedness belongs to those who endure tests.

      These have faith, or it would not be tried ; and faith is blessed.

      These have life which bears trials ; and the spiritual life is blessed.

      These possess uprightness, purity, truth, patience ; and all these are blessed things.

   3. Blessedness belongs to those who endure trials out of love to God. The text speaks of "them that love him."

      He that has love to God finds joy in that love.

      He also finds blessedness in suffering for that love.

   4. Blessedness belongs to those who are proved true by trial.

      After the test comes approval. "When he hath been approved" is the rendering of the Revised Version.

      After the test comes assurance of our being right. Certainty is a most precious commodity.

   5. Blessedness comes out of patient experience.

      Blessedness of thankfulness for being sustained.

      Blessedness of holy dependence under conscious weakness.

      Blessedness of peace and submission under God's hand.

      Blessedness of fearlessness as to result of further trial.

      Blessedness of familiarity with God enjoyed in the affliction.

      Blessedness of growth in grace through the trial.

He who, being tested, is supported in the ordeal, and comes out of the trial approved, is the blessed man.

II. THE BLESSED IN THE LIFE TO COME.

Those who have endured trial inherit the peculiar blessedness—

1. Of being crowned. How crowned if never in the wars?
   Crowned because victorious over enemies.
   Crowned because appreciated by their God.
   Crowned because honoured of their fellows.
   Crowned because they have kept the conditions of the award.

2. Of attaining the glory and "crown of life" by enduring trial, thus only can life be developed till its flower and crown appear.
   By trial brought to purest health of mind.
   By trial trained to utmost vigour of grace.
   By trial developed in every part of their nature.
   By trial made capable of the highest glory in eternity.

3. Of possessing a living crown of endless joy. "Crown of life" or living crown: amaranthine, unfading.
   If such fierce trials do not kill them, nothing will.
   If they have spiritual bliss, it can never die.
   If they have heavenly life, it will always be at its crowning point.

4. Of receiving this life-crown from God.
   His own promise reveals and displays it.
   His peculiar regard to those who love him doubly ensures it.
   His own hand shall give it.

Let us encounter trial cheerfully.

Let us wait for the time of approval patiently.

Let us expect the crown of life most joyfully, and gather courage from the assurance of it.

EXTRACTS

"*Blessed*"; that is, already blessed. They are not miserable as the world judgeth them. It is a Christian paradox, wherein there is an allusion to what is said (Job v. 17). "Behold, happy is the man whom God correcteth"; it is a wonder, and therefore he calleth the world to see it. *Behold!* So the apostle, in an opposition to the judgment of the world, saith, *Blessed.*

Afflictions do not make the people of God miserable. There is a great deal of difference between a Christian and a man of the world: his best estate is vanity (Psalm xxxix. 5); and a Christian's worst is happiness. He that loveth God is like a die; cast him high or low, he is still upon a square: he may be sometimes afflicted, but he is always happy.—*Thomas Manton.*

Times of affliction often prove times of great temptations, and therefore afflictions are called temptations.—*Thomas Brooks.*

The most durable and precious metal in the ancient arts was the Corinthian bronze, which was said to have first been caused by the fusing of all the precious metals when Corinth was burned. The most precious products of experience are got in the fire of trial.—*John Legge.*

An old sailor was asked for what purpose shoals and rocks were created, and the reply was, "That sailors may avoid them." A Christian philosopher, using that axiom, upon being asked for what purpose trials and temptations are sent, answered, "That we may overcome and use them." The true dignity of life is not found in escaping difficulties, but in mastering them for Christ's sake and in Christ's strength.

Dean Stanley.

Many were the sorts of crowns which were in use amongst the Roman victors; as first, *corona civica,* a crown made of oaken boughs, which was given by the Romans to him that saved the life of any citizen in battle against his enemies. 2. *Obsidionalis,* which was of grass, given to him that delivered a town or city from siege. 3. *Muralis,* which was of gold, given to him that first scaled the wall of any town or castle. 4. *Castralis,* which was likewise of gold, given to him that first entered the camp of the enemy. 5. *Navalis,* and that also of gold, given to him that first boarded the ship of an enemy. 6. *Ovalis* (and that of myrtle), which was given to those captains that subdued any town or city, or that won any field easily, without blood. 7. *Triumphalis,* which was of laurel, given to the chief general or consul who, after some signal victory, came home triumphing. These, with many others, as imperial, regal, and princely crowns (rather garlands or coronets than crowns), are not to be compared to the crown of glory which God hath prepared for those that love him. Who is able to express the glory of it; or to what glorious thing shall it be likened? If I had the tongue of men and angels, I should be unable to decipher it as it worthily deserveth. It is not only a crown of glory, but hath divers other titles of pre-eminency given unto it, of which all shall be true partakers that are godly; a crown of righteousness, by the imputation of Christ's righteousness; a crown of life, because those that have it shall be made capable of life eternal; a crown of stars, because they that receive it shall shine as stars for ever and ever.—*John Spencer.*

> The same who crowns the conqueror, will be
> A coadjutor in the agony.

Robert Herrick.

CCXLVIII.

James iv. 6 —" But he giveth more grace."

Practical as is the Epistle of James, the apostle does not neglect to extol the grace of God, as unevangelical preachers do in these times.

We err if we commend the fruits regardless of the root from which they spring. Every virtue should be traced to grace.

We must clearly point out the fountain of inward grace as well as the stream of manifest service which flows from it.

The principle of grace produces the practice of goodness, and none can create or preserve that principle but the God of all grace.

If we fail anywhere, it will be our wisdom to get more grace.

See the bounty of God—ever giving, and ever ready to give more!

I. OBSERVE THE TEXT IN ITS CONNECTION.

    1. It presents a contrast. "But he giveth more grace."

        Two potent motives are confronted. "The spirit that dwelleth in us lusteth to envy"; on God's part this is met by "but he giveth more grace."

    2. It suggests a note of admiration.

        What a wonder that when sin aboundeth, grace still more abounds!

        When we discover more of our weakness, God gives more grace.

    3. It hints at a direction for spiritual conflict.

        We learn where to obtain the weapons of our warfare: we must look to him who gives grace.

        We learn the nature of those weapons: they are not legal, nor fanciful, nor ascetical, but gracious—"he giveth more grace."

        We learn that lusting after evil must be met by the fulfilment of spiritual desires and obtaining more grace.

    4. It encourages us in continuing the conflict.

        As long as there is one passion in the believing soul that dares to rise, God will give grace to struggle with it.

        The more painfully we mourn the power of sin, the more certainly will grace increase if we believe in Jesus for salvation.

    5. It plainly indicates a victory.

        "He giveth more grace" is a plain promise that—

        God will not give us up; but that he will more and more augment the force of grace, so that sin must and shall ultimately yield to its sanctifying dominion.

Glory be to God, who, having given grace, still goes on to give more and more grace till we enter into glory! There is no stint or limit to the Lord's increasing gifts of grace.

II. Observe the general truth of the text.

God is ever on the giving hand. The text speaks of it as the Lord's way and habit: "He giveth more grace."
1. He giveth new supplies of grace.
2. He giveth larger supplies of grace.
3. He giveth higher orders of grace.
4. He giveth more largely as the old nature works more powerfully.
This should be—
1. A truth of daily use for ourselves.
2. A promise daily pleaded for others.
3. A stimulus in the contemplation of higher or sterner duties, and an encouragement to enter on wider fields.
4. A solace under forebodings of deeper trouble in common life.
5. An assurance in prospect of the severe tests of sickness and death.
Seeing it is the nature of God to give more and more grace, let us have growing confidence in him.

III. Bring it home by special appropriation.

1. My spiritual poverty, then, is my own fault, for the Lord giveth more grace to all who believe for it.
2. My spiritual growth will be to his glory, for I can only grow because he gives more grace. Oh, to grow constantly!
3. What a good God I have to go to! Let me rejoice in the present and hope for the future. Since the further I go the more grace shall I know, let me proceed with dauntless courage.

Brethren, let us trust the liberality of God, try it by prayer, prove it by faith, bear witness to it with zeal, and praise it with grateful joy.

Encouragements

When Lord North, during the American war, sent to the Rev. Mr. Fletcher, of Madeley (who had written on that unfortunate war, in a manner that had pleased the minister), to know what he wanted, he sent him word, that he wanted but one thing, which it was not in his lordship's power to give him, and that was *more grace.—John Whitecross.*

When a man gives a flower, it is a perfect gift; but the gift of grace is rather the gift of a flower *seed.*

355

When Matthew Henry was a child he received much impression from a sermon on the parable of the "mustard-seed." On returning home, he said to his child sister, "I think I have received a grain of grace." It was the seed of the Commentary "cast upon the waters."

Charles Stanford.

I have grace every day! every hour! When the rebel is brought, nine times a-day, twenty times a-day, for the space of forty years, by his prince's grace, from under the axe, how fair and sweet are the multiplied pardons and reprievals of grace to him! In my case here are multitudes of multiplied redemptions! Here is plenteous redemption! I defile every hour, Christ washeth; I fall, grace raiseth me; I come this day, this morning, under the rebuke of justice, but grace pardoneth me; and so it is all along, till grace puts me into heaven.—*Samuel Rutherford.*

Were you to rest satisfied with any present attainments to which you have reached, it would be an abuse of encouragement. It would be an evidence that you know nothing of the power of divine grace in reality, for

"Whoever says, I want *no more*,
Confesses he has *none*."

Those who have seen their Lord, will always pray, "I beseech thee, show me thy glory." Those that have once tasted that the Lord is gracious, will always cry, "Evermore give us this bread to eat."

William Jay.

A little grace will bring us to heaven hereafter, but great grace will bring heaven to us now.—*An old Divine.*

Oh, what a sad thing it is when Christians are what they always were! You should have more grace; your word should be, *ego non sum ego*—I am not the same I, or, *nunc oblita mihi*—now my old courses are forgotten; or, as the apostle, 1 Peter iv. 3, "The time past may suffice to have walked in the lusts of the flesh."—*Thomas Manton.*

"Have you on the Lord believed?
Still there's more to follow;
Of his grace have you received?
Still there's more to follow;
Oh, the grace the Father shows!
Still there's more to follow!
Freely he his grace bestows;
Still there's more to follow!"

356

CCXLIX

1 Peter i. 9 —Receiving the end of your faith, even the salvation of your souls.

The greater benefits of salvation are usually classed among things to come, but indeed a large portion of them may be received here and now.

I. WHAT OF SALVATION IS RECEIVED HERE?

1. The whole of it by the grip of faith, and the grace of hope.
2. The absolute and final pardon of sin is ours at this moment.
3. Deliverance from slavish bondage, and from a sense of awful distance from God is a present relief.

    Peace, reconciliation, contentment, fellowship with God, and delight in God, we enjoy at this hour.
4. Rescue from the condemning power of sin is now complete.
5. Release from its dominion is ours. It can no longer command us at its will, nor lull us to sleep by its soothing strains.
6. Conquest over evil is given to us in great measure at once.

    Sins are conquerable. No one should imagine that he must necessarily sin because of his constitution or surroundings.

    Holy living is possible. Some have reached a high degree of it. Why not others?
7. Joy may become permanent in the midst of sorrow.

The immediate heritage of believers is exceedingly great.

Salvation is ours at this day, and with it "all things."

II. HOW IS IT RECEIVED?

1. Entirely from Jesus, as a gift of divine grace.
2. By faith, not by sight or feeling. We believe to see, and this is good. To require to see in order to believe is vicious.
3. By fervent love to God. This excites to revenge against sin, and so gives present purification. This also nerves us for consecrated living, and thus produces holiness.
4. By joy in the Lord. This causes us to receive peace unspeakable, not to be exaggerated, nor even uttered. Too great, too deep to be understood, even by those who enjoy it.

Much of heaven may be enjoyed before we reach it.

357

III. HAVE YOU RECEIVED IT, AND HOW MUCH?

   1. You have heard of salvation, but hearing will not do.

   2. You profess to know it, but mere profession will not do.

   3. Have you *received* pardon? Are you sure of it?

   4. Have you been made holy? Are you daily cleansed in your walk?

   5. Have you obtained rest by faith and hope and love?

Make these inquiries as in God's sight.

If the result is unsatisfactory, begin at once to seek the Lord.

Look for the appearing of the Lord as the time for receiving in a fuller sense "the end of your faith."

BREVIATES

An evangelist said in my hearing : " He that believeth *hath* everlasting life. H A T H—that spells '*got it*.'" It is an odd way of spelling, but it is sound divinity.—*C. H. S.*

This is the certainty of their hope, that it is as if they had already received it. If the promise of God and the merit of Christ hold good, then they who believe in him, and love him, are made sure of salvation. The promises of God in Christ "are not yea and nay ; but they are in him yea, and in him amen." Sooner may the rivers run backward, and the course of the heavens change, and the frame of nature be dissolved, than any one soul that is united to Jesus Christ by faith and love can be severed from him, and so fall short of the salvation hoped for in him ; and this is the matter of their rejoicing.—*Archbishop Leighton.*

To fall into sin is a serious thing even though the guilt of it be forgiven. A boy who had often been disobedient was made by his father to drive a nail into a post for each offence. When he was well-behaved for a day he was allowed to draw out one of the nails. He fought against his temper bravely, and at last all the nails were gone from the post, and his father praised him. "Alas, father," said the lad, "the nails are all gone, but the holes are left !" Even after forgiveness it will require a miracle of grace to recover us from the ill effects of sin.

In St. Peter's, at Rome, I saw monuments to James III., Charles III., and Henry IX., kings of England. These potentates were quite unknown to me. They had evidently a name to reign, but reign they did not : they never received the end of their faith. Are not many professed Christians in the same condition?—*C. H. S.*

CCL

1 Peter iv. 18.—"If the righteous scarcely be saved, where shall the ungodly and the sinner appear?"

"Scarcely saved" points out the difficulty of salvation.

Some think it easy to begin by believing; but the prophet cries, "Who hath believed?" and Jesus asks, "When the Son of man cometh, shall he find faith on the earth?"

Some may also think it easy to persevere to the end, but the godly are hard put to it to keep their faces Zionward.

It is no light thing to be saved: omnipotent grace is needed.

It is no trifling thing to be lost, but it can be done by neglect.

I. THE FACT: "*The righteous scarcely are saved.*"

    1. From the connection we conclude that the righteous are saved with difficulty because of the strictness of divine rule. "The time is come that judgment must begin at the house of God."

    There is equity and fitness in this speciality of examination.

    These tests are many, varied, repeated, applied by God himself.

    Good corn endures the sickle, the flail, the fan, the sieve, the mill, the oven.

    The great test of all is the omniscient judgment of the jealous God. What grace will be needed to pass that ordeal!

    2. From the experience of saints we come to the same conclusion.

    They find many saving acts to be hard, as for instance—

    To lay hold on Christ simply, and as sinners.

    To overcome the flesh from day to day.

    To resist the world with its blandishments, threats, and customs.

    To vanquish Satan and his horrible temptations.

    To perform needful duties in a humble and holy spirit.

    To reach to gracious attainments and to continue in them.

    To pass the tribunal of their own awakened and purified conscience, and to receive a verdict of acquittal there.

    3. From the testimony of those who are safely landed.

    "These are they which came out of great tribulation."

II. THE INFERENCE FROM THE FACT: "*Where shall the ungodly and the sinner appear?*"

    1. If even the true coin is so severely tested, what will become of "reprobate silver"?

2. If saints scarcely reach heaven, what of the ungodly?
   What can they do who have no God?
   What can they do who have no Saviour?
   What can they do who are without the Spirit of God?
   What without prayer, the Word, the promise of God, &c.?
   What without diligence? When the tradesman, though careful, is losing all his capital, what of the spendthrift?
   What without truth? When the fire consumes houses strongly built, what must become of wood, hay, stubble?
3. If saints are so sorely chastened, what will justice mete out to the openly defiant sinner?

III. ANOTHER INFERENCE. *Where will the mere professor appear?*
If the truly godly have a hard fight for it—
   The formalist will find ceremonies a poor solace.
   The false professor will be ruined by his hypocrisy.
   The presumptuous will find his daring pride a poor help.
   He who trusted to mere orthodoxy of creed will come to a fall.
   Height of office will do no more than increase responsibility.

IV. ANOTHER INFERENCE. *Then the tempted soul may be saved.*
It seems that even those who are truly saints are saved with difficulty : then we may be saved, though we have a hard struggle for it.
   Uprising corruption makes us stagger.
   A persecuting world tries us sorely.
   Fierce temptations from without cause us perplexity.
   Loss of inward joys brings us to a stand.
   Failure in holy efforts tests our faith.
But in all this we have fellowship with the righteous of all ages.
They are saved, and so shall we be.

V. ANOTHER INFERENCE. *How sweet will heaven be!*
There the difficulties will be ended for ever.
There the former trials will contribute to the eternal bliss.

ENFORCEMENTS

When the apostle uses the phrase—"*If the righteous scarcely be saved,*" he does not, assuredly, mean that there is any doubt about the absolute and infinite sufficiency of the ground of their salvation ; or that there is any uncertainty in the result ; or that there is any stinted-ness or imperfection in the final enjoyment; or that, when believers come to stand before the judgment-seat at last, it will go hard with them, so that they may barely come off with acquittal, the poised balance vibrating in long uncertainty, and barely turning on the favourable side, the justifying righteousness of their Lord forming no more than a counterpoise, and hardly that, to their demerits. He means none of these things. *His language refers to the difficulty of bringing them through* to their final salvation ; to the necessity of employing the rod and furnace; the process, in many instances severe, of correction and purification ; of bringing them " to the wealthy place through the fire and the water"; of their " entering the kingdom through much tribulation"; of their being "chastened of the Lord, that they might not be condemned with the world." If "fiery trial" be required, and his hatred of sin and his love to his children will not allow him to withhold it, to purge out the remaining alloy of their holiness, what must his enemies have to look for from his abhorrence of evil, in whom sin is not the mere alloy of a better material, *but all is sin together ?*

Dr. Wardlaw.

There is much ado to get Lot out of Sodom, to get Israel out of Egypt. It is no easy matter to get a man out of the state of corruption.—*Richard Sibbes.*

Of this I am assured, that no less devotion than that which carried the martyrs through the flames, will carry us unpolluted through this present world.— *Mrs. Palmer.*

Do you grieve and murmur that you must be saved with difficulty ? Ungrateful creatures ! you had deserved certain damnation. The vengeance of God might have appeared armed for your destruction ; and he might long ago have sworn in his wrath that you should never enter into his rest. And will you complain of the Lord's leadings because he does not always strew your path with roses ?

Dr. Doddridge.

" *Where shall the ungodly and the sinner appear ?* Surely nowhere. Not before saints and angels, for holiness is their trade. Not before God, for he is of "more pure eyes than to behold them." Not before Christ, for he shall come in flaming fire rendering vengeance. Not in heaven, for it is an undefiled inheritance.—*John Trapp.*

Where shall he appear, when to the end that he might not appear, he would be glad to be smothered under the weight of the hills and mountains, if they could shelter him from appearing ?—*Archbishop Leighton.*

CCLI

1 Peter b. 1 —"The elders which are among you I exhort, who am also an elder, and a witness of the sufferings of Christ, and also a partaker of the glory that shall be revealed."

The apostle's care. He was anxious that the elders should tend the flock of God, and make themselves ensamples to it.

The apostle's gentleness. "I exhort": not command, &c.

The apostle's humility—"also an elder." He does not insist upon his apostleship, though this was much the greater office.

The apostle's wisdom—"also an elder." In this capacity he would have most weight with them in his exhortation.

Besides this, he mentioned two other characters, and calls himself "a witness of the sufferings of Christ, and a partaker of the glory that shall be revealed."

I. A WITNESS OF THE SUFFERINGS OF CHRIST.

So far as possible, let us be witnesses with Peter.

1. An eye-witness of those sufferings. Apostles must have seen Jesus. He had seen the passion and death of our Lord.

In this we cannot participate, nor need we desire to do so.

2. A faith-witness of those sufferings.
He had personally believed on Jesus at the first.
He had further believed through after-communion with him.

3. A testifying witness of those sufferings.
He bore witness to their bitterness when borne by Jesus.
He bore witness to their importance as an atonement.
He bore witness to their completeness as a satisfaction.
He bore witness to their effect in perfect salvation.

4. A partaking witness of those sufferings.
In defence of truth he suffered from opposers.
In winning others he suffered in the anguish of his heart.
In serving his Lord he suffered exile, persecution, death.

What he witnessed in all these ways became a motive and a stimulus for his whole life.

II. A PARTAKER OF THE GLORY TO BE REVEALED.

It is important to partake in all that we preach, or else we preach without vividness and assurance.

1. Peter had enjoyed a literal foretaste of the glory on the holy mount. We, too, have our earnests of eternal joy.

362

2. Peter had not yet *seen* the glory which shall be revealed, and yet he had partaken of it in a spiritual sense : our participation must also be spiritual. Peter had been a spiritual partaker in the following ways—

By faith in the certainty of the glory.

By anticipation of the joy of the glory.

By sympathy with our Lord, who has entered into glory.

3. Peter had felt the result of faith in that glory—

In the comfort which it yielded him.

In the heavenliness which it wrought in him.

In the courage with which it endowed him.

These two things, his witnessing and his partaking, made our apostle intense in his zeal for the glory of God. Because he had seen and tasted of the good word, he preached it with living power and vivid speech. All preachers need to be witnesses and partakers.

These made him urgent with others to "feed the flock of God." Such a man could not endure triflers.

These are the essentials for all eminently useful and acceptable service. The Lord will only bless witnesses and partakers.

Hints

I remember a story which runs thus :—To a saint who **was** praying the evil spirit showed himself radiant with royal robes, and crowned with a jewelled diadem, and said, " I am Christ—I am descending on the earth—and I desire first to manifest myself to thee." The saint kept silence, and looked on the apparition ; and then said, " I will not believe that Christ is come to me save in that state and form in which he suffered : he must wear the marks of the wounds and the cross." The false apparition vanished. The application is this : Christ comes not in pride of intellect or reputation for ability. These are the glittering robes in which Satan is now arraying himself. Many false spirits are abroad, more are issuing from the pit : the credentials which they display are the precious gifts of mind, beauty, richness, depth, originality. Christian, with the saint, look hard at them in silence, and ask them for the print of the nails.—*Dr. J. S. Howson.*

'Tis a very sad thing when preachers are like printers, who compose and print off many things, which they neither understand, nor love, nor experience ; all they aim at is money for printing, which is their trade. It is also sad when ministers are like gentlemen ushers, who bring ladies to their pews, but go not in themselves—bring others to heaven, and themselves stay without.—*Ralph Venning.*

CCLII

2 **Peter ii. 9**—"**The Lord knoweth how to deliver the godly out of temptations, and to reserve the unjust unto the day of judgment to be punished.**"

"The Lord knoweth." Our faith in the superior knowledge of God is a great source of comfort to us—

> In reference to perplexing doctrines.
> In reference to puzzling prophecies.
> In reference to amazing promises.
> In reference to distressing providences.
> In reference to grievous temptations.
> In our entrance upon an unknown world in the last solemn article in death.

The government of this world and the next is in the hands of the all-knowing One, who cannot be mistaken, nor taken at unawares.

I. THE LORD'S KNOWLEDGE IN REFERENCE TO CHARACTER.

> 1. He knows the godly—
> > Under trial, when they are not known to others.
> > Under temptation, when scarcely known to themselves.
>
> 2. He knows the unjust—
> > Though they may make loud professions of piety.
> > Though they may be honoured for their great possessions.

No error either as to partiality or severity is made by God.

II. THE LORD'S KNOWLEDGE IN REFERENCE TO THE GODLY.

A people knowing, fearing, trusting, loving God.

He knows how to let them suffer, and yet to deliver them in the most complete and glorious manner.

> 1. His knowledge answers better than theirs would do.
> 2. His knowledge of their case is perfect. Before, in, and after temptation he knows their sorrows.
> 3. He knows in every case how to deliver them.
> 4. In every case there must therefore be a way of escape.
> 5. He knows the most profitable way of deliverance for themselves.
> 6. He knows the way which will be most glorifying to himself.
> 7. His knowledge should cause them to trust in him with holy confidence, and never to sin in order to escape.

364

III. The Lord's knowledge in reference to the unjust.

They are unjust in all senses, for they are—
    Not legally just by keeping the law;
    Nor evangelically just through faith in Jesus;
    Nor practically just in their daily lives.

The Lord knows best—

1. How to deal with them from day to day.
2. How to reserve them under restraints. He makes it possible to reprieve them, and yet to maintain law and order.
3. How to punish them with unrest and fears even now.
4. How and when to strike them down when their iniquities are full.
5. How to deal with them in judgment, and throughout the future state. The mysteries of eternal doom are safe in his hand.

Two fine illustrations of the Lord's dealings with the righteous and the wicked may be found in Acts xii., in connection with Peter's life.

Peter in prison was unexpectedly set free.

Herod on the throne was eaten of worms.

BREVIA

On the headstone of a little grave containing a little child which was washed ashore during the gales, without any clue to birth, name, or parentage, was placed the epitaph : " God knows."—*Leisure Hour.*

" *The Lord knoweth how.*" It is set down indefinitely : no man, no apostle, no angel, can know all the means of God's delivering his : it is enough that he himself knows. This gives a check to all saucy inquirers that will not believe help from the Lord, unless he tells them how . . . Deliverance we look for : how or when the Lord will deliver thee or me, that is in his own bosom, and in the breast of his Privy Counsellor, Jesus Christ.—*Thomas Adams.*

In the *Life and Letters of G. Ticknor,* a remark is made to the effect, that when in Brussels, and conversing with some of the *élite* of society there, he could not avoid constantly remembering that two of the high-minded intellectual persons with whom he was sitting were under sentence of death if found within the grasp of Austria. We cannot forget that many around us are now "under condemnation," and are "reserved until the day of judgment."

CCLIII

1 John iii. 2 —"**It doth not yet appear what we shall be: but we know that when he shall appear, we shall be like him; for we shall see him as he is.**"

The present condition of the believer, notwithstanding its imperfection, is a state of much joy and honour. Looked at in the light of faith it is sublime, for "now are we the sons of God."

We are near to God's heart as his children.

We nestle under the wings of God for protection.

We abide in his pavilion for communion.

We are fed in his pasture for provision.

For all this, our earthly existence is not a life which we would desire to be perpetual. It is as a traveller's pilgrimage, a sailor's voyage, a soldier's warfare ; and we look forward to its end with joyful expectation.

We will let the text divide itself verbally.

I. "IT DOTH NOT YET APPEAR WHAT WE SHALL BE."

At present we are veiled, and travel through the world *incognito*.

　1. Our Master was not made manifest here below.

　　His glory was veiled in flesh.

　　His Deity was concealed in infirmity.

　　His power was hidden under sorrow and weakness.

　　His riches were buried under poverty and shame.

The world knew him not, for he was made flesh.

　2. We are not fit to appear in full figure as yet.

　　The son is treated as a servant while under age.

　　The heir is kept a pensioner till his majority.

　　The prince serves as a soldier before he reaches the throne.

We must needs have an evening before our morning, a schooling before our college, a tuning before the music is ready.

　3. This is not the world to appear in.

　　There are none to appreciate us, and it would be as though kings showed their royalty at a wake, or wise men discoursed philosophy before fools.

　　A warring and waiting condition like the present would not be a fit opportunity for unveiling.

　4. This is not the time in which to appear in our glory.

　　The winter prepares flowers, but does not call them forth.

The ebb-tide reveals the secrets of the sea, but many of our rivers no gallant ship can then sail.

To everything there is a season, and this is not the time of glory.

II. "BUT WE KNOW THAT WHEN HE SHALL APPEAR."

1. We speak of our Lord's manifestation without doubt.   "We know."
2. Our faith is so assured that it becomes knowledge.

He will be manifest upon this earth in person.

He will be manifest in perfect happiness.

He will be manifest in highest glory.

He will appear surely, and so we speak of it as a date for our own manifesting—"when he shall appear."

Oh the hope, the glory, the bliss, the fulness of delight which cluster around this great appearing!

III. "WE SHALL BE LIKE HIM."

We shall then be as manifested, and as clearly seen, as he will be.

The time of our open presentation at court will have come.

1. Having a body like his body.

Sinless, incorruptible, painless, spiritual, clothed with beauty and power, and yet most real and true.

2. Having a soul like his soul.

Perfect, holy, instructed, developed, strengthened, active, delivered from temptation, conflict, and suffering.

3. Having such dignities and glories as he wears.

Kings, priests, conquerors, judges, sons of God.

We must be made in a measure like him now, or else we shall not be found so at his appearing.

IV. "WE SHALL SEE HIM AS HE IS."

1. This glorious sight will perfect our likeness.
2. This will be the result of our being like him.
3. This will be evidence of our being like him, since none but the pure in heart can see God.

The sight will be ravishing.

The sight will be transforming and transfiguring.

The sight will be abiding, and a source of bliss for ever.

Behold what glories come out of our being the sons of God!

Let us not rest till by faith in Jesus we receive power to become sons of God, and then let us go on to enjoy the privileges of sonship.

367

God showed *power* in making us creatures, but *love* in making us sons. Plato gave God thanks that he had made him a man, and not a beast; but what cause have they to adore God's love, who hath made them children ! The apostle puts an *ecce* to it, *Behold !—Thomas Watson.*

And here, reader, wonder not if I be at a loss ; and if my apprehensions receive but little of that which is in my expressions. If to the beloved disciple that durst speak and enquire into Christ's secrets, and was filled with his revelations, and saw the New Jerusalem in her glory, and had seen Christ, Moses, and Elias in part of theirs ; if it did not appear to him what we shall be, but only in general, that when Christ appears, we shall be like him, no wonder if I know little.—*Richard Baxter, in " The Saint's Everlasting Rest."*

Such divine, God-given glimpses into the future reveal to us more than all our thinking. What intense **truth**, what divine meaning there is in God's creative word : " Let us make man in our image, after our likeness" ! To show forth the likeness of the Invisible, to be partaker of the divine nature, to share with God his rule of the universe, is man's destiny. His place is indeed one of unspeakable glory. Standing between two eternities, the eternal purpose in which we were predestinated to be conformed to the image of the first-born Son, and the eternal realization of that purpose when we shall be like him in his glory. We hear the voice from every side : O ye image-bearers of God ! on the way to share the glory of God and of Christ, live a Godlike, live a Christlike life !—*Andrew Murray.*

A converted blind man once said, " Jesus Christ will be the first person I shall ever see, for my eyes will be opened in heaven."

> Then shall we see Thee as Thou art,
> For ever fix'd in no unfruitful gaze,
> But such as lifts the new-created heart,
> Age after age, in worthier love and praise.
>
> *John Keble.*

" You are going to be with Jesus, and to see him as he is," said a friend to Rowland Hill on his deathbed. " Yes," replied Mr. Hill with emphasis, " and I shall be *like* him ; *that* is the crowning point."

To see him as he is, and in himself, is reserved till we shall have better eyes : these eyes we have are carnal and corruptible, and cannot see God till they have put on incorruption.—*Sir Richard Baker.*

> One view of Jesus as he is
> Will strike all sin for ever dead.
>
> *W. Cowper.*

CCLIV

1 John iii. 3 —"And every man that hath this hope in him purifieth himself, even as he is pure."

The Christian is a man whose main possessions lie in reversion.

Most men have a hope, but his is a peculiar one; and its effect is special, for it causes him to purify himself.

I. THE BELIEVER'S HOPE. "Everyone that hath this hope in him."

1. It is the hope of being like Jesus.
   Perfect, Glorious, Conqueror over sin, death and. hell.
2. It is based upon divine love.   See verse 1.
3. It arises out of sonship.   "Called the sons of God."
4. It rests upon our union to Jesus.   "When he shall appear."
5. It is distinctly hope in *Him*.   "We shall be like him," etc.
6. It is the hope of his second Advent.

II. THE OPERATION OF THAT HOPE.   "Purifieth."

It does not puff up, like the conceit of Pharisees.

It does not lead to loose living, like the presumption of Antinomians.

It shows us what course is grateful, is congruous to grace, is according to the new nature, and is preparatory to the perfect future.

1. The believer purifies himself from—
   His grosser sins.   From evil company, etc.
   His secret sins, neglects, imaginings, desires, murmurings, etc.
   His besetting sins of heart, temper, body, relationship, etc.
   His relative sins in the family, the shop, the church, etc.
   His sins arising out of his nationality, education, profession, etc
   His sins of word, thought, action, and omission.
2. He does this in a perfectly natural way.
   By getting a clear notion of what purity really is.
   By keeping a tender conscience, and bewailing his faults.
   By having an eye to God and his continual presence.
   By making others his beacons or examples.
   By hearing rebukes for himself, and laying them to heart.
   By asking the Lord to search him, and practising self-examination.
   By distinctly and vigorously fighting with every known sin.
3. He sets before him Jesus as his model.   "He purifieth himself, even as HE is pure."

369

Hence he does not cultivate one grace only.

Hence he is never afraid of being too precise.

Hence he is simple, natural, and unconstrained.

Hence he is evermore aspiring after more and more holiness

III. THE TEST OF THAT HOPE. "He purifieth himself."

Actively, personally, prayerfully, intensely, continually, he aims at the purification of himself, looking to God for aid.

Some defile themselves wilfully.

Some take things as they are.

Some believe that they need no purifying.

Some talk about purity, but never strive after it.

Some glory in that which is a mere counterfeit of it.

The genuine Hoper does not belong to any of these classes : he really and successfully purifies himself.

What must it be to be without a good hope?

How can there be hope where there is no faith?

Grace adopts us; adoption gives us hope; hope purifies us, till we are like the Firstborn.

ANIMATING WORDS

1. First, *The Workman.* "Every one that hath this hope in him," every one that looks to be like the Lord Jesus in the Kingdom of Glory is the man that must set about this task. 2. Secondly, *The work* is a work to be wrought by himself. He is a part of the Lord's husbandry, and he must take pains as it were to plough his own ground, to weed his own corn, he must purify himself; this is his present and personal work. 3. Thirdly, the *pattern* by which he must be directed is the Lord Jesus: his purity. Take him for a pattern and instance; look unto him that is the author and finisher of our faith; as you have seen him do, so do you; as he is pure, so labour you to express in your lives the virtue of him who hath redeemed you.—*Richard Sibbes.*

Then thou comportest with thy hopes of salvation when thou labourest to be as holy in thy conversation as thou art high in thy expectation This the apostle urgeth from the evident fitness of the thing, 2 Pet. iii. 11 : "What manner of persons ought ye to be in all holy conversation and godliness, looking for and hastening unto the coming of the day of God?" Certainly, it becomes such to be holy, even to admiration, who look for such a blessed day : we hope then to be like the angels in glory, and therefore should, if possible, live now like angels in holiness. Every believing soul is Christ's spouse. The day of conversion is the day of espousals, wherein she is betrothed by faith to Christ, and, as such, lives in hopes for the marriage-day, when he shall come and fetch her home to his father's house, as Isaac did Rebekah to his mother's tent, there to dwell with him, and live in his sweet embraces of love, world without end. Now, would the bride have the bridegroom find her in sluttery and vile raiment? No, surely: "Can a bride forget her attire?" Jer. ii. 32. Was it ever known that a bride forgot to have her wedding clothes made against the marriage-day, or to put them on when she looks for her bridegroom's coming? Holiness is the raiment of needle-work in which, Christian, thou art to be brought to thy King and husband: Ps. xlv. 14. Wherefore is the wedding-day put off so long, but because this garment is so long a-making? When this is once wrought, and thou art ready dressed, then that joyful day comes. Remember how the Holy Spirit wordeth it in the Book of Revelation, "the marriage of the Lamb is come, and his wife hath made herself ready:" Rev. xix. 7.—*William Gurnall.*

A good hope, through grace, animates and gives life to action, and purifies as it goes; like the Highland stream that dashes from the rock, and purifies itself as it pursues its course to the ocean.—*H. G. Salter.*

The Christian needs Christ in his redemption as the object of Faith, for salvation; Christ himself the object of Love, for devotion and service; and Christ in his coming glory, the object of Hope, for separation from the world.—*W. Haslam.*

The biographer of Hewitson says of him: "He not only believed in the speedy appearing, but loved it, waited for it, watched for it. So mighty a motive power did it become, that he ever used to speak of it afterwards as *bringing with it a kind of second conversion.*"

A. J. Gordon, D.D.

CCLV

1 John iii. 14 — "𝔚e know that we have passed from death unto life, because we love the brethren."

The spiritual things which we speak of are matters of knowledge. John, in almost every verse of this epistle, uses the words "we know." The philosophical distinction between believing and knowing is mere theory. "We know and have believed."

I. WE KNOW THAT WE WERE DEAD.

1. We were without feeling when law and gospel were addressing us.
2. Without hunger and thirst after righteousness.
3. Without power of movement towards God in repentance.
4. Without the breath of prayer, or pulse of desire.
5. With signs of corruption; some of them most offensive.

II. WE KNOW THAT WE HAVE UNDERGONE A SINGULAR CHANGE.

1. The reverse of the natural change from life to death.
2. No more easy to describe than the death change would be.
3. This change varies in each case as to its outward phenomena, but it is essentially the same in all.
4. As a general rule its course is as follows—
   It commences with painful sensations.
   It leads to a sad discovery of our natural weakness.
   It is made manifest by personal faith in Jesus.
   It operates on the man by repentance and purification.
   It is continued by perseverance in sanctification.
   It is completed in joy, infinite, eternal.
5. The period of this change is an era to be looked back upon in time and through eternity with grateful praise.

III. WE KNOW THAT WE LIVE.

1. We know that we are not under condemnation.
2. We know that faith has given us new senses, grasping a new world, enjoying a realm of spiritual things.
3. We know that we have new hopes, fears, desires, delights, etc.
4. We know that we have been introduced into new surroundings and a new spiritual society: God, saints, angels, etc.
5. We know that we have new needs; such as heavenly breath, food, instruction, correction, etc.
6. We know that this life guarantees eternal bliss.

IV. WE KNOW THAT WE LIVE, BECAUSE WE LOVE. "We love the brethren."

1. We love them for Christ's sake.
2. We love them for the truth's sake.
3. We love them for their own sake.
4. We love them when the world hates them.
5. We love their company, their example, their exhortations.
6. We love them despite the drawbacks of infirmity, inferiority, etc.

Let us prove our love by our generosity.
Thus shall we supply ourselves with growing evidences of grace.

LOVE-LINES

Just as in his gospel he rescues the word *logos* from antichristian uses, so in this Epistle he rescues the word "*know*," and aims at making his "little children" Gnostics in the divine sense. Knowledge is excellent, but the path to it is not through intellectual speculation, however keen and subtle, but through faith in Jesus Christ and subjection to him, according to those most Johannine words in the Gospel of Matthew: "Neither knoweth any man the Father save the Son, and he to whomsoever the Son will reveal him."—*Dr. Culross.*

The Christian apologist never further misses the mark than when he refuses the testimony of the Agnostic to himself. When the Agnostic tells me he is blind and deaf, dumb, torpid, and dead to the spiritual world, I must believe him. Jesus tells me that. Paul tells me that. Science tells me that. He knows nothing of this outermost circle; and we are compelled to trust his sincerity as readily when he deplores it as if, being a man without an ear, he professed to know nothing of a musical world, or being without taste, of a world of art. The nescience of the Agnostic philosophy is the proof from experience that to be carnally minded is death.—*Professor Henry Drummond.*

The world always loves to believe that it is impossible to know that we are converted. If you ask them, they will say, "I am not sure; I cannot tell"; but the whole Bible declares we may receive, and know that we have received, the forgiveness of sins.—*R. M. McCheyne.*

In the writings of Paul, "Faith in the Lord Jesus, *and* love to all the saints," constitute a well-understood and oft-recurring sequence. It is a straitening about that upper spring of faith that makes the streams of love fail in their channels. — *W. Arnot.*

No outward mark have we to know
  Who thine, O Christ, may be,
Until a Christian love doth show
  Who appertains to thee :
For knowledge may be reached unto,
  And formal justice gained,
But till each other love we doe,
  Both faith and workes are feigned.

George Wither, 1588—1667.

Yes, brethren in Christ have all one common Father, one common likeness, one object of faith, love, and adoration ; one blessed hope, one present employment ; alike in trials, alike in prayer. They lean upon the same hand, appear daily before the same mercy-seat, feed at the same table. How much all these things link them together, not in profession only, but in heart ! Hence this is a decisive test : " We know that we have passed from death unto life, because we love the brethren."

D. Katterns.

In the early days of Christianity, when it triumphed over the old heathenism of the Roman world, it founded a new society bound together by this holy mutual love. The catacombs of Rome bear remarkable testimony to this gracious brotherhood. There were laid the bodies of members of the highest Roman aristocracy, some even of the family of the Cæsars, side by side with the remains of obscure slaves and labourers. And in the case of the earliest graves the inscriptions are without a single allusion to the position in society of him who was buried there : they did not trouble themselves whether he had been a consul or a slave, a tribune of the legion or a common soldier, a patrician or an artisan. It sufficed that they knew him to have been a believer in Christ, a man who feared God. They cared not to perpetuate in death the vain distinctions of the world ; they had mastered the glorious teaching of the Lord, " One is your master, even Christ, and all ye are brethren."—*E. De Pressensé.*

CCLVI

1 John iii. 20, 21 —" For if our heart condemn us, God is greater than our heart, and knoweth all things.

"Beloved, if our heart condemn us not, then have we confidence toward God."

The fault of many is that they will not lay spiritual things to heart at all, but treat them in a superficial manner. This is foolish, sinful, deadly. We ought to put our case upon serious trial in the court of our own conscience.

Certain of a better class are satisfied with the verdict of their hearts, and do not remember the higher courts; and therefore either become presumptuous, or are needlessly distressed. We are about to consider the judgments of this lower court. Here we may have—

I. A CORRECT VERDICT AGAINST OURSELVES.

Let us sum up the process.

1. The court sits under the King's arms, to judge by royal authority. The charge against the prisoner is read. Conscience accuses, and quotes the law as applicable to the points alleged.

2. Memory gives evidence. As to the fact of sin in years past, and of sin more lately committed. *Items* mentioned. Sabbath sins. Transgressions of each one of the ten commandments. Rejection of the gospel. Omissions in a thousand ways. Failure in motive, spirit, temper, etc.

3. Knowledge gives evidence that the present state of mind and heart and will is not according to the Word.

4. Self-love and pride urge good intents and pious acts in stay of proceedings. Hear the defence! But alas! it is not worth hearing. The defence is but one of "the refuges of lies."

5. The heart, judging by the law, condemns. Henceforth the man lives as in a condemned cell under fear of death and hell.

If even our partial, half-enlightened heart condemns, we may well tremble at the thought of appearing before the Lord God.

The higher court is more strictly just, better informed, more authoritative, and more able to punish. God knows all. Forgotten sin, sins of ignorance, sins half seen are all before the Lord.

What a terrible case is this! Condemned in the lower court, and sure to be condemned in the higher!

II. An incorrect verdict against ourselves.

The case as before. The sentence apparently most clear.
But when revised by the higher court it is reversed, for good reasons.

1. The debt has been discharged by the man's glorious Surety.
2. The man is not the same man; though he sinned he has died to sin, and he now lives as one born from above.
3. The evidences in his favour, such as the atonement and the new birth, were forgotten, undervalued, or misjudged in the lower court; hence he was condemned. Sentence of condemnation does not stand when these matters are duly noted.
4. The evidence looked for by a sickly conscience was what it could not find, for it did not exist, namely, natural goodness, perfection, unbroken joy, etc. The judge was ignorant, and legally inclined. The verdict was therefore a mistaken one. An appeal clears the case: "God is greater than our heart, and knoweth all things."

III. A correct verdict of acquittal.

Our heart sometimes justly "condemns us not."
The argument for non-condemnation is good: the following are the chief items of evidence in proof of our being gracious—

1. We are sincere in our profession of love to God.
2. We are filled with love to the brethren.
3. We are resting upon Christ, and on him alone.
4. We are longing after holiness.

The result of this happy verdict of the heart is that we have—

Confidence towards God that we are really his.
Confidence as to our reconciliation with God by Jesus Christ.
Confidence that he will not harm us, but will bless us.
Confidence in prayer that he will accept and answer.
Confidence as to future judgment that we shall receive the gracious reward at the last great day.

IV. An incorrect verdict of acquittal.

1. A deceived heart may refuse to condemn, but God will judge us all the same. He will not allow self-conceit to stand.
2. A false heart may acquit, but this gives no confidence Godward.
3. A deceitful heart pretends to acquit while in its centre it condemns.

If we shrink now, what shall we do in judgment?
What a waking, to find ourselves condemned at the last!

When Sir Walter Raleigh had laid his head upon the block, says an eloquent divine, he was asked by the executioner whether it lay aright. Whereupon, with the calmness of a hero and the faith of a Christian, he returned an answer, the power of which we all shall feel when our head is tossing and turning on death's uneasy pillow —" It matters little, my friend, how the head lies, providing the heart be right."—*Steele.*

As Luther says : " Though conscience weigh us down, and tell us God is angry, yet God is greater than our heart. The conscience is but one drop ; the reconciled God is an ocean of consolation."
Critical English Testament.

A seared conscience thinks better of itself, a wounded worse than it ought : the former may account all sin a sport, the latter all sport a sin ; melancholy men, when sick, are ready to conceive any cold to be the cough of the lungs, and an ordinary pustule to be no less than a plague-sore. So wounded consciences conceive sins of infirmity to be sins of presumption, sins of ignorance to be sins of knowledge, apprehending their case to be far more dangerous than it is indeed.—*Thomas Fuller.*

Conscience works after the manner so beautifully set forth in the ring that a great magician, according to an Eastern tale, presented to his prince. The gift was of inestimable value, not for the diamonds and rubies and pearls that gemmed it, but for a rare and mystic property in the metal. It sat easily enough on the finger in ordinary circumstances, but as soon as its wearer formed a bad thought, designed or committed a bad action, the ring became a monitor. Suddenly contracting, it pressed painfully on his finger, warning him of sin. Such a ring, thank God, is not the peculiar property of kings ; the poorest of us, those that wear none other, may possess and wear this inestimable jewel ; for the ring of the fable is just that conscience which is the voice of God within us, which is his law, engraven by the finger of God, not on Sinai's granite tables, but on the fleshy tablets of the heart, which, enthroned as a sovereign in every bosom, commends us when we do right, and condemns us when we do wrong.—*Dr. Guthrie.*

The spirit of man, that candle of the Lord, often gives but a faint and glimmering light ; but the Spirit of God snuffs it, that it may burn brighter.—*Benjamin Beddome.*

CCLVII

1 John b. 4 —"For whatsoever is born of God overcometh the world: and this is the victory that overcometh the world, even our faith."

What is meant by this world?

The power of sin all around us : the influence which operates towards evil, and makes the commandments and purposes of God grievous to society. The Prince of this world has much to do with this evil power.

This world is our foe, and we must fight with it.

We must contend till we overcome the world, or it will overcome us.

I. The conquest itself : " overcometh the world."

We are not to be litigious, eager to contradict everybody.

We are not, however, to be cowardly, and anxious to flee the fight.

We mingle among men of the world, but it must be as warriors who are ever on the watch, and are aiming at victory.   Therefore—

1. We break loose from the world's customs.

2. We maintain our freedom to obey a higher Master in all things.
    We are not enslaved by dread of poverty, greed of riches, official command, personal ambition, love of honour, fear of shame, or force of numbers.

3. We are raised above circumstances, and find our happiness in invisible things : thus we overcome the world.

4. We are above the world's authority.   Its ancient customs or novel edicts are for its own children : we do not own it as a ruler, or as a judge.

5. We are above its example, influence, and spirit.   We are crucified to the world, and the world is crucified to us.

6. We are above its religion.   We gather our religion from God and his Word, not from human sources.

As one in whom this conquest was seen, read the story of Abraham. Think of him in connection with his quitting home, his lonely wanderings, his conduct towards Lot, Sodom and her king, Isaac, etc.

II. The conquering nature.—" Whatsoever is born of God."

1. This nature alone will undertake the contest with the world.

2. This nature alone can continue it.   All else wearies in the fray.

378

3. This nature is born to conquer. God is the Lord, and that which is born of him is royal and ruling.

It is not an amendment of the former creation.

It is not even a new creation without relationship to its **Creator**; but it is a birth from God, with eminence of descent, infusing similarity of nature, and conferring rights of heirship.

The Creator cannot be overcome, nor those born of him.

Jesus, the firstborn, never was defeated, nor will those conformed to him fail of ultimate triumph.

The Holy Spirit in us must be victorious, for how should he be vanquished? The idea would be blasphemous.

III. The conquering weapon : " even our faith."

We are enabled to be conquerors through regarding—

1. The unseen reward which awaits us.

2. The unseen presence which surrounds us. God and a cloud of witnesses hold us in full survey.

3. The mystic union to Christ which grace has wrought in us. Resting in Jesus we overcome the world.

4. The sanctifying communion which we enjoy with the unseen God.

In these ways faith operates towards overcoming sin.

IV. The speciality of it—" This is *the* victory."

1. For salvation, finding the rest of faith.

2. For imitation, finding the wisdom of Jesus, the Son of God.

3. For consolation, seeing victory secured to us in Jesus.

Behold your conflict—born to battle.

Behold your triumph—bound to conquer.

War-cries

When a traveller was asked whether he did not admire the admirable structure of some stately building, " *No*," said he, "*for I have been at Rome, where better are to be seen every day.*" O believer, if the world tempt thee with its rare sights and curious prospects, thou mayst well scorn them, having been, by contemplation, in heaven, and being able, by faith, to see infinitely better delights every hour of the day! "This is the victory that overcometh the world, even our faith."

Feathers for Arrows.

The danger to which Christians are exposed from the influence of the visible course of things, or the world (as it is called in Scripture), is a principal subject of St. John's General Epistle. He seems to speak of the world as some False Prophet, promising what it cannot fulfil, and gaining credit by its confident tone. Viewing it as resisting Christianity, he calls it the "Spirit of Antichrist," the parent of a numerous progeny of evil, false spirits like itself, the teachers of all lying doctrines, by which the multitude of men are led captive. The antagonist of this great tempter is the Spirit of Truth, which is "greater than he that is in the world"; its victorious antagonist, because gifted with those piercing Eyes of Faith which are able to scan the world's shallowness, and to see through the mists of error into the glorious kingdom of God beyond them. "This is the victory that overcometh the world," says the text, "even our faith."—*J. H. Newman.*

The believer not only overcomes the world in its deformities, but in its seeming excellences. Not in the way that Alexander and other conquerors overcame it, but in a much nobler way; for they, so far from overcoming the world, were slaves to the world. The man who puts ten thousand other men to death does not overcome the world. The true conqueror is he who can say with Paul, "Thanks be to God, who giveth us the victory through our Lord Jesus Christ," and, "Who shall separate us from the love of Christ? Shall tribulation? etc." "Nay, in all these things we are more than conquerors, through him that loved us." Such an one has recourse, by faith, to an infallible standard—the Word of God: indeed, there is no other. He detects the world, and will not be imposed upon by it. When he is tempted to take the world's good things as his portion, he rejects them; because he has something better in hand. Thus, faith in Christ overcometh the corrupt influence, the inordinate love, the slavish fear, the idolatry, the friendship, the false wisdom, and the maxims of the world: it overcometh not only the folly, but the very religion of the world, as far as it is a false religion. The Christian has hold of a superior influence, and engages superior strength. Doubtless, says he, I have great enemies to attack but greater is he that is with me than he that is in the world.

Richard Cecil.

It is asserted of this elegant creature (the Bird of Paradise) that it always flies against the wind; as, otherwise, its beautiful but delicate plumage would be ruffled and spoiled. Those only are Birds of Paradise, in a spiritual sense, who make good their way against the wind of worldliness; a wind always blowing in an opposite direction to that of heaven.—*J. D. Hull.*

Believers, forget it not! you are the soldiers of *the Overcomer.*

J. H. Evans.

CCLVIII

3 John 2 —"𝔅𝔢𝔩𝔬𝔟𝔢𝔡, 𝔍 𝔴𝔦𝔰𝔥 𝔞𝔟𝔬𝔳𝔢 𝔞𝔩𝔩 𝔱𝔥𝔦𝔫𝔤𝔰 𝔱𝔥𝔞𝔱 𝔱𝔥𝔬𝔲 𝔪𝔞𝔶𝔢𝔰𝔱 𝔭𝔯𝔬𝔰𝔭𝔢𝔯 𝔞𝔫𝔡 𝔟𝔢 𝔦𝔫 𝔥𝔢𝔞𝔩𝔱𝔥, 𝔢𝔳𝔢𝔫 𝔞𝔰 𝔱𝔥𝔶 𝔰𝔬𝔲𝔩 𝔭𝔯𝔬𝔰𝔭𝔢𝔯𝔢𝔱𝔥."

The gospel made a marvellous change in John. Once he could call fire from heaven on opposers; now, having received the Holy Ghost, he is full of love and kind desires.

The gospel makes the morose, cheerful; the gay, serious; the revengeful, loving. Coming to such an one as John, it made him the mirror of love.

A man's private letters often let you into the secrets of his heart.

Instance Rutherford, Kirke White, Cowper, and John Newton.

In this letter, John gratefully wishes Gaius every blessing, and above all things better health.

Health is an invaluable mercy; it is never properly valued till lost.

But John puts soul-prosperity side by side with it.

Man has two parts; the one corporeal and earthy, the other immaterial and spiritual. How foolish is the man who thinks of his body, and forgets his soul; neglects the tenant, and repairs the house; prizes the earthern vessel, and despises the treasure!

I. WE WILL EXAMINE THE WORDS OF THE TEXT.

1. "I wish"; more correctly, as in the margin, "I pray." Prayer is a wish sanctified. Turn your wishes into prayers.

2. "That thou mayest prosper." We may ask for prosperity for our friends; especially if, like Gaius, they serve God and his cause with their substance.

3. "And be in health." This is necessary to the enjoyment of prosperity. What would all else be without it?

4. "Even as thy soul prospereth." We are startled at this wish: the spiritual health of Gaius is made the standard of his outward prosperity! Dare we pray thus for many of our friends?

Dare we pray thus for ourselves? What would be the result if such a prayer were answered? Picture our bodies made like our souls.

Some would have fever, others paralysis, others ague, etc.

Let us bless God that the body is not the invariable index of the soul.

Few would care to have their spiritual condition expressed in their external condition.

II. WE WILL MENTION THE SYMPTOMS OF ILL-HEALTH.

1. A low temperature.

Lukewarmness is an ill sign.   In business, such a man will make
but little way; in religion, none at all.
This is terrible in the case of a minister.
This is dangerous in the case of a hearer.

2. A contracted heart.
While some are latitudinarian, others are intolerant, and cut off
all who do not utter their Shibboleth.
If we do not love the brethren, there is something wrong with us.

3. A failing appetite as to spiritual food.

4. A difficulty in breathing.
When prayer is an irksome duty, everything is wrong with us.

5. A general lethargy: unwillingness for holy service, want of heart, etc.

6. An ungovernable craving for unhealthy things.   Some poor
creatures will eat dirt, ashes, etc.   Some professors are ill in a
like way, for they seek grovelling amusements and pursuits.

III. WE WILL SUGGEST MEANS OF RECOVERY.

We will not here dwell upon the means God uses, though he is the
great Physician ; but we will think of the regimen we must use for
ourselves.

1. Seek good food.   Hear a gospel preacher.   Study the Word.

2. Breathe freely.   Do not restrain prayer.

3. Exercise yourself unto godliness.   Labour for God.

4. Return to your native air : breathe the atmosphere of Calvary.

5. Live by the sea.   Dwell near to God's all-sufficiency.

6. If these things fail, here is an old prescription: "*Carnis et
Sanguinis Christi.*"   This taken several times a day, in a draught
of the tears of repentance, is a sure cure.

God help you to practise the rules of the heavenly Physician !

IV. WE WILL CONCLUDE WITH AN EXHORTATION.

Brother Christian, is it a small matter to be weak and feeble? Thou
needest all thy vigour.   Go to Calvary, and recruit thyself.

Sinner, thou art dead, but life and health are in Christ !

NOTA MEDICA

An ancient Roman wished that he had a window in his breast that
all might see his heart, but a sage suggested that in such a case he
would have urgent need of shutters, and would keep them closed.   We
could not afford to wear the signs of our spiritual condition where all
could see.   We should then need all our blood for blushing.—*C.H.S.*

Sin is called in Scripture by the names of diseases. It is called the plague of the heart: 1 Kings viii. 38. There are as many diseases of the soul as there are of the body. Drunkenness is a spiritual dropsy; security is a spiritual lethargy; envy is a spiritual canker; lust is a spiritual fever: Hos. vii. 4. Apostasy or backsliding is the spiritual falling sickness; hardness of heart is the spiritual stone; searedness of conscience is a spiritual apoplexy; unsettledness of judgment is a spiritual palsy; pride a spiritual tumour; vainglory a spiritual itch. There is not any sickness of the body but there is some distemper of the soul that might be paralleled with it, and bear the name of it.—*Ralph Robinson.*

The fact of the Scriptures furnishing nutriment and upbuilding to the soul is the most real experience of which we have knowledge. None of us, " by taking thought, can add one cubit unto his stature." But how many, by taking in God's great thoughts, feeding on them, and inwardly digesting them, have added vastly to their spiritual stature !

A. J. Gordon, D.D.

If a portrait were taken of a person in strong, vigorous health, and another was taken of the same man after a severe illness, or when he had been almost starved to death, or weakened by confinement, we should scarcely recognize them as the likeness of the same man, the dear old friend we loved ! Still greater would be the change could we draw the *spiritual* portrait of many a once hearty, vigorous saint of God, whose soul has been starved for want of the proper spiritual nourishment, or by feeding upon " ashes " instead of bread.—*G. S. Bowes.*

Oh, that our friends were well in soul ! We are not sufficiently concerned about this best of health ! When they are well in soul we are grieved to see them ailing in body; and yet this is often the case. The soul is healed, and the body is still suffering ! Well, it is by far the smaller evil of the two ! If I must be sick, Lord, let the mischief light on my coarser nature, and not on my higher and diviner part !—*C.H.S.*

CCLIX

Jude 24, 25 —"Now unto him that is able to keep you from falling, and to present you faultless before the presence of his glory with exceeding joy,

"To the only wise God our Saviour, be glory and majesty, dominion and power, both now and ever. Amen."

We will joyfully praise the Lord with Jude's doxology.

It is well to be called full often to adoring praise, and the specific statement of the reason for praise is helpful to fervour of gratitude.

Our great danger is falling and faultiness.

Our great safety is divine ability and faithfulness, by which we are kept from stumbling so as to dishonour our Lord.

I. LET US ADORE HIM WHO CAN KEEP US FROM FALLING.

1. We need keeping from falling, in the sense of preservation from—
   Error of doctrine ; which is rife enough in this age.
   Error of spirit : such as want of love, or want of discernment, or unbelief, or credulity, or fanaticism, or conceit.
   Outward sin.   Alas, how low may the best fall !
   Neglect of duty : ignorance, idleness, want of thought.
   Backsliding.   Into this state we may insensibly descend.

2. None but the Lord can keep us from falling.
   We cannot keep ourselves without him.
   No place guarantees security : the church, the closet, the communion-table—all are invaded by temptation.
   No rules and regulations will secure us from stumbling.   Stereotyped habits may only conceal deadly sins.
   No experience can eradicate evil, or protect us from it.

3. The Lord can do it.   He is "able to keep," and he is "the only wise God, our Saviour."   His wisdom is part of his ability.
   By teaching us so that we fall not into sins by ignorance.
   By warning us : this may be done by our noting the falls of others, or by inward monitions, or by the Word.
   By providence, affliction, etc., which remove occasions of sinning.
   By a bitter sense of sin, which makes us dread it as a burnt child dreads the fire.
   By his Holy Spirit, renewing in us desires after holiness.

4. The Lord will do it.   According to the Revised Version he is "The only God our Saviour."   He will assuredly save.

384

From final falls, and even from stumblings (see *R. V.*), his divine power can and will keep us.

II. Let us adore him who will present us in his courts faultless.

   1. None can stand in those courts who are covered with fault.

   2. None can deliver us from former guilt, or keep us from daily faultiness in the future, but the Saviour himself.

   3. He can do it as our Saviour. He is divinely wise to sanctify.

   4. He will do it. We should not be exhorted to praise him for an ability which he would not use.

   5. He will do it "with exceeding joy," both to himself and to us.

III. Let us adore him with highest ascriptions of praise.

   1. Presenting our praise through Jesus, who is himself our Lord. (*R. V.*)

   2. Wishing him glory, majesty, dominion and power.

   3. Ascribing these to him as to the past, for he is "before all time." (*R. V.*)

   4. Ascribing them to him "now."

   5. Ascribing them to him "for ever."

   6. Adding to this adoration, and to the adoration of all his saints, our own fervent "Amen." Heartily consenting to all his praise.

Come let us praise our Guardian *now*, in memory of past upholdings. Let us praise him in foretaste of what he will do for us. Let us praise him with "exceeding joy."

A Statement and an Instance

We cannot stand a moment longer than God upholdeth us; we are as a staff in the hand of a man; take away the hand, and the staff falleth to the ground: or rather, as a little infant in the nurse's hand (Hosea xi. 3); if we are left to our own feet, we shall soon fall. Created grace will never hold out against so many difficulties. One of the fathers bringeth in the flesh, saying, *Ego deficiam*, I shall fail; the world, *Ego decipiam*, I will deceive them; the devil, *Ego eripiam*, I will sweep them away; but God saith, *Ego custodiam*, I will keep them, I will never fail them, nor forsake them. There lieth our safety.—*Thomas Manton.*

Philip Dickerson, an aged Baptist minister, who died October 22nd, 1882, just before his death, said, "Seventy years ago the Lord took me into his service without a character. He gave me a good character, and by his grace I have kept it."

CCLX

Rev. i. 7 —"**Behold, he cometh with clouds ; and every eye shall see him, and they also which pierced him : and all kindreds of the earth shall wail because of him. Even so Amen.**"

The doxology which precedes our text is most glorious.

It runs well in the Revised Version : " To him that loved us and loosed us."

Keeping to our Authorized Version, we can get the alliteration by reading " loved us and laved us."

To him who has made us kings, is himself a King, and is coming into his kingdom : to him be glory.

Our adoration is increased by our expectation. " He cometh."

Our solemnity in praise is deepened by the hope that our expectation will be speedily realized. The coming is in the present tense.

John, who once heard the voice, " Behold the Lamb of God ! " now utters the voice, " Behold, he cometh ! "

I. OUR LORD JESUS COMES.

1. This fact is worthy of a note of admiration—" Behold ! "

2. It should be vividly realized till we cry, " Behold, he cometh ! "

3. It should be zealously proclaimed. We should use the herald's cry, " Behold ! "

4. It is to be unquestioningly asserted as true. Assuredly he cometh.
    It has been long foretold. Enoch. Jude 14.
    He has himself warned us of it. " Behold, I come quickly ! "
    He has made the sacred supper a token of it. " Till he come."
    What is to hinder his coming ? Are there not many reasons for it ?

5. It is to be viewed with immediate interest.
    " Behold ! " for this is the grandest of all events.
    " He cometh," the event is at the door.
    " He," who is your Lord and Bridegroom, comes.
    He is coming even now, for he is preparing all things for his advent, and thus may be said to be on the road.

6. It is to be attended with a peculiar sign—" with clouds."
    The clouds are the distinctive tokens of his Second Advent.
    The tokens of the divine presence. " The dust of his feet."
    The pillar of cloud was such in the wilderness.

386

The emblems of his majesty.

The ensigns of his power.

The warnings of his judgment. Charged with darkness and tempest are these gathered clouds.

II. OUR LORD'S COMING WILL BE SEEN OF ALL.

1. It will be a literal appearance. Not merely every mind shall think of him, but "Every eye shall see him."
2. It will be beheld by all sorts and kinds of living men.
3. It will be seen by those long dead.
4. It will be seen by his actual murderers, and others like them.
5. It will be manifest to those who desire not to see the Lord.
6. It will be a sight in which *you* will have a share.

Since you must see him, why not at once look to him and live?

III. HIS COMING WILL CAUSE SORROW. "All kindreds of the earth shall wail because of him."

1. The sorrow will be very general. "All kindreds of the earth."
2. The sorrow will be very bitter. "Wail."
3. The sorrow proves that men will not be universally converted.
4. The sorrow also shows that men will not expect from Christ's coming a great deliverance.

    They will not look to escape from punishment.

    They will not look for Annihilation.

    They will not look for Restoration.

    If they did so, his coming would not cause them to wail.
5. The sorrow will in a measure arise out of his glory, seeing they rejected and resisted him. That glory will be against them.
6. The sorrow will be justified by the dread result. Their fears of punishment will be well grounded. Their horror at the sight of the great Judge will be no idle fright.

To his Lord's coming the believer gives his unfeigned assent, whatever the consequences.

Can you say, " Even so, Amen " ?

ADVENT THOUGHTS

Even so, Lord Jesus, come quickly! In the meanwhile, it is not heaven that can keep thee from me : it is not earth that can keep me from thee : raise thou up my soul to a life of faith with thee : let me even enjoy thy conversation, whilst I expect thy return.—*Bishop Hall.*

"*Every eye shall see him.*" Every eye; the eye of every living man, whoever he is. None will be able to prevent it. The voice of the trumpet, the brightness of the flame, shall direct all eyes to HIM; shall fix all eyes upon him. Be it ever so busy an eye, or ever so vain an eye, whatever employment, whatever amusement it had the moment before, will then no longer be able to employ it, or to amuse it. The eye will be lifted up to Christ, and will no more look down upon money, upon books, upon land, upon houses, upon gardens. Alas ! these things will then all pass away in a moment; and not the eyes of the living alone, but also all the eyes that have ever beheld the sun, though but for a moment : the eyes of all the sleeping dead will be awakened and opened. The eyes of saints and sinners of former generations. The eyes of Job, according to those rapturous words of his, which had so deep and so sublime a sense, " I know that my Redeemer liveth, and that he shall stand in the last day on the earth : in my flesh I shall see God, whom my eyes shall behold, and not another." The eyes of Balaam, of which he seems to have had an awful foreknowledge when he said, " I shall see him, but not now ; I shall behold him, but not nigh " Your eyes and mine. O awful thought ! Blessed Jesus ! May we not see thee as through tears ; may we not then tremble at the sight !—*Dr. Doddridge.*

"And the Lord turned, and looked upon Peter. . . . And Peter went out and wept bitterly." So shall it be, but in a different sense, with sinners at the day of judgment. The eye of Jesus as their judge shall be fixed upon them, and the look shall awake their sleeping memories, and reveal their burdens of sin and shame—countless and cursed crimes, denials worse than Peter's, since life-long and unrepented of, scoffings at love that wooed them, and despisings of mercy that called them—all these shall pierce their hearts as they behold the look of Jesus. And they shall go out and flee from the presence of the Lord—go out never to return, flee even into the outer darkness, if so be they may hide them from that terrible gaze. And they shall weep bitterly—weep as they never wept before, burning, scalding tears, such as earth's sorrow never drew—weep never to be comforted, tears never to be wiped away. Their eyes shall be fountains of tears, not penitential and healing, but bitter and remorseful—tears of blood—tears that shall rend the heart in twain, and deluge the soul in fathomless woe.—*Anon.*

CCLXI

Rev. xi. 19 —"And the temple of God was opened in heaven, and there was seen in his temple the ark of his testament: and there were lightnings, and voices, and thunderings, and an earthquake, and great hail."

It may not be easy to work out the connection of the text; but taken by itself it is eminently instructive.

Much that is of God we fail to see : to us the temple of God in heaven is still in a measure closed.

There is need that it be opened to us by the Holy Spirit.

Jesus has rent the veil, and so laid open, not only the holy place, but the Holy of holies; and yet by reason of our blindness it still needs laying open, so that its treasures may be seen.

There are minds that even now see the secret of the Lord. We all shall do so above ; and we may do so in a measure while below.

Among the chief objects which are to be seen in the heavenly temple is the ark of the covenant of God. This means that the covenant is always in the mind of God, and that his most holy and most secret purposes have a reference to that covenant.

It is "covenant," not testament (see the Revised Version, which is the better translation in this place).

I. THE COVENANT IS ALWAYS NEAR TO GOD. "There was seen in his temple the ark of his covenant."

Whatever happens, the covenant stands secure.

Whether we see it or not, the covenant is in its place, near to God.

The covenant of grace is for ever the same, for—

1. The God who made it changes not.

2. The Christ who is its Surety and Substance changes not.

3. The love which suggested it changes not.

4. The principles on which it is settled change not.

5. The promises contained in it change not ; and, best of all,

6. The force and binding power of the covenant change not.

It is, it must be, for ever where God at first placed it.

II. THE COVENANT IS SEEN OF SAINTS. "There was seen in his temple."

We see in part, and blessed are we when we see the covenant.

We see it when—

1. By faith we believe in Jesus as our Covenant-head.

389

2. By instruction we understand the system and plan of grace.

3. By confidence we depend upon the Lord's faithfulness, and the promises which he has made in the covenant.

4. By prayer we plead the ovenant.

5. By experience we come to perceive covenant-love running as a silver thread through all the dispensations of providence.

6. By a wonderful retrospect we look back when we arrive in heaven, and see all the dealings of our faithful covenant God.

III. THE COVENANT CONTAINS MUCH THAT IS WORTH SEEING.

The ark of the covenant may serve us as a symbol.

In it typically, and in the covenant actually, we see—

1. God dwelling among men : as the ark in the tabernacle, in the centre of the camp.

2. God reconciled, and communing with men upon the mercy-seat.

3. The law fulfilled in Christ : the two tables in the ark.

4. The kingdom established and flourishing in him : Aaron's rod.

5. The provision made for the wilderness : for in the ark was laid up the golden pot which had manna.

6. The universe united in carrying out covenant purposes, as typified by the cherubim on the mercy-seat.

IV. THE COVENANT HAS SOLEMN SURROUNDINGS. "There were lightnings, and voices, and thunderings," etc.

It is attended by—

1. The sanctions of divine power—confirming.

2. The supports of eternal might—accomplishing.

3. The movements of spiritual energy—applying its grace.

4. The terrors of eternal law—overthrowing its adversaries.

Study the covenant of grace.

Fly to Jesus, who is the Surety of it.

REMARKS OF SOUND DIVINES

The great glory of the covenant is the certainty of the covenant ; and this is the top of God's glory, and of a Christian's comfort, that all the mercies that are in the covenant of grace are "the sure mercies of David," and that all the grace that is in the covenant is sure grace, and that all the glory that is in the covenant is sure glory, and that all the external, internal, and eternal blessings of the covenant are sure blessings.

Thomas Brooks.

The covenant stands unchangeable. Mutable creatures break their leagues and covenants, and when they are not accommodated to their interests, snap them asunder, like Samson's cords. But an unchangeable God keeps his: "The mountains shall depart, and the hills be removed; but my kindness shall not depart from thee, nor shall the covenant of my peace be removed" (Isa. liv. 10).—*Stephen Charnock.*

The ark was an especial type of Christ, and it is a very fit one; for in a chest or coffer men put their jewels, plate, coin, treasure, and whatsoever is precious, and whereof they make high account. Such a coffer men use to have in the house, where they dwell continually, in the chamber where they lie, even by their bedside : because his treasure is in his coffer, his heart is there also. Thus in Christ "are hid all the treasures of wisdom and knowledge" (Col. ii. 3). He is "full of grace and truth" (John i. 14). "It pleased the Father that in him should all fulness dwell" (Col. i. 19). Hereupon Christ is "the Son of God's love" (Col. i. 13); "his elect in whom his soul delighteth" (Isa. xlii. 1); and he is "ever at the right hand of God" (Heb. x. 12).—*William Gouge.*

A friend calling on the Rev. Ebenezer Erskine, during his last illness, said to him, "Sir, you have given us many good advices; pray, what are you now doing with your own soul?" "I am doing with it," said he, "what I did forty years ago; I am resting on that word, '*I am the Lord thy God*'; and on this I mean to die." To another he said, "The covenant is my charter, and if it had not been for that blessed word, '*I am the Lord thy God*,' my hope and strength had perished from the Lord."—*Whitecross.*

The rainbow of the covenant glitters above, lightnings of wrath issue from below. This is the fire that breaks forth from the sanctuary to consume those who profane its laws. It is the wrath of the Lamb that bursts from the altar upon those who trample under foot his blood. It is the savour of death unto death to those who have rejected the gospel as a savour of life unto life. It is the reply of Christ to those who command him upon their own authority to come down from his lofty elevation, and commit himself into their hands. "If I be a man of God, let fire come down from heaven and consume you." Humiliation brings Christ himself from heaven to earth; imperiousness brings down consuming fire. From the same temple, in which some behold the ark of the covenant, lightnings, voices, thunderings, earthquake, and great hail, descend upon those who have profaned its courts with their abominations.—*George Rogers.*

CCLXII

Rev. xvi. 8, 9 —"And the fourth angel poured out his vial upon the sun; and power was given unto him to scorch men with fire.

"And men were scorched with great heat, and blasphemed the name of God, which hath power over these plagues: and they repented not to give him glory."

What forces God has at his disposal, since all *angels* serve him! These bring forth the vials of his wrath.

What power these beings have over nature; for on the sun the angel empties his bowl, and men are scorched with fire!

No men are beyond the power of the judgments of God. He can reach them by any medium. He can make ill effects flow from our best blessings : in this case burning heat poured from the sun.

The judgments of God do not of themselves produce true repentance; for these men "repented not to give him glory."

I. THEY MAY PRODUCE *A* REPENTANCE.

1. A carnal repentance caused by fear of punishment. Cain.

2. A transient repentance which subsides with the judgment. Pharaoh.

3. A superficial repentance which retains the sin. Herod.

4. A despairing repentance which ends in death. Judas.

There is nothing about any of these which gives glory to God.

II. THEY DO NOT PRODUCE *THE* REPENTANCE WHICH GIVES GOD GLORY.

True repentance glorifies God—

1. By acknowledging his omniscience, and the wisdom of his warnings, when we confess the fact and folly of sin.

2. By admitting the righteousness of his law, and the evil of sin.

3. By confessing the justice of the Lord's threatenings, and bowing before his throne in reverent submission.

4. By owning that it lies with the sovereign mercy of God further to punish us, or graciously to forgive us.

5. By accepting the grace of God as presented in the Lord Jesus.

6. By seeking sanctification so as to live in holy gratitude, in accordance with favour received.

In the case before us in the chapter, the men under the plague went from bad to worse, from impenitence to blasphemy; but where there is godly sorrow sin is forsaken.

III. THEY INVOLVE MEN IN GREATER SIN WHEN THEY DO NOT SOFTEN.
1. Their sin becomes more a sin of knowledge.
2. Their sin becomes more a sin of defiance.
3. Their sin becomes a sin of falsehood before God. Vows broken,. resolutions forgotten : all this is lying unto the Holy Ghost.
4. Their sin becomes a sin of hate towards God. They even sacrifice themselves to spite their God.
5. Their sin becomes more and more deliberate, costly, and stubborn.
6. Their sin is thus proven to be engrained in their nature.

IV. THEY ARE TO BE LOOKED UPON WITH DISCRETION.
Hasty generalization will lead us into great errors in reference to divine judgments.
1. Used by the grace of God, they tend to arouse, impress, subdue, humble, and lead to repentance.
2. They may not be regarded as of themselves beneficial.
Satan is not bettered by his misery.
The lost in hell grow more obdurate through their pains.
Many wicked men are the worse for their poverty.
Many sick are not really penitent, but are hypocritical.
3. When we are not under judgment and terror, we should repent.
Because of God's long-suffering and goodness.
Because we are not now distracted by pain.
Because now we can think of the sin apart from the judgment,. and are more likely to be honest in repentance.
Because we shall find it sweeter and nobler to be drawn than to be like "dumb driven cattle."

Be it our one aim " to give HIM glory."
Begin with this object in repentance, continue in it by faith, rise nearer to it in hope, abide in it by zeal and love.

FROM GREAT AUTHORS
Trees may blossom fairly in the spring, on which no fruit is to be found in the harvest ; and some have sharp soul exercises which are nothing but foretastes of hell.—*Boston.*

Richard Sibbes says, "We see, by many that have recovered again, that have promised great matters in their sickness, that it is hypocritical repentance, for they have been worse after than they were before." *Dr. Grosart* adds, by way of illustration, the testimony of a prison chaplain, to the effect that of " *reprieved* " criminals who, in the shadow of the gallows, had manifested every token of apparent penitence and *heart*-change, the number whose subsequent career gave evidence of reality is as 1 to 500, perhaps as awful a fact as recent criminal statistics reveal.

I believe it will be found that the repentance of most men is not so much sorrow for sin as sin, or real hatred of it, as sullen sorrow that they are not allowed to sin.—*Adam's Private Thoughts.*

There is no repentance in hell. They are scorched with heat, and blaspheme God's name, but repent not to give him glory. They curse him for their pains and sores, but repent not of their deeds. True repentance ariseth from faith and hope ; but there can be no faith of releasement where is certain knowledge of eternal punishment : knowledge and sense exclude faith. There can be no hope of termination where be chains of desperation. There shall be a desperate sorrow for pain, no penitent sorrow for sin. None are now saved but by the blood of the Lamb ; but when the world is ended, that fountain is dried up. The worm of conscience shall gnaw them with this remorse, bringing to their minds the cause of their present calamities : how often they have been invited to heaven, how easily they might have escaped hell. They shall weep for the loss of the one and gain of the other, not for the cause of either, which were repentance. . . . They suffer, and they blaspheme.—*Thomas Adams.*

How awful to read, "men blasphemed God because of the plague of the hail " ! How true it is that affliction makes good men better, and bad men worse ! Wrath converts no man. It is grace that saves. The chastisement that does not soften hardens. Judgments lead men to blaspheme ; and the greater the plague, the more they blaspheme. What a solemn, but truthful, representation of the consequence of oft-neglected warnings ! See the employment of man in the future state— in heaven, to praise ; in hell, to blaspheme.—*George Rogers.*

CCLXIII

Reb. xix. 9 —" And he saith unto me, Write, Blessed are they which are called unto the marriage supper of the Lamb."

Amazed by what he saw and heard, John might have failed to write but he was warned to do so on this occasion, because of—

The value of the statements herein recorded.

Their absolute certainty, as sure promises and true sayings of God.

The necessity of keeping such facts in remembrance throughout all time for the comfort of all those who look for the Lord's appearing.

This fact, that men shall partake of the marriage supper of the Lamb, might seem too good to be true if it were not specially certified by order of the Lord, under the hand and seal of the Spirit of God.

In the historical order, the false harlot-church is to be judged (see previous chapter), and then the true bride of Christ is to be acknowledged and honoured.

In meditating upon this august marriage festival, we shall note—

I. The description of the Bridegroom.

The inspired apostle speaks of him as "the Lamb."

This is John's special name for his Lord. Perhaps he learned it from hearing the Baptist cry, by the Jordan, " Behold the Lamb."

What we learn early abides with us late.

John uses this name continually in this Book of the Revelation.

The last book of the Bible still reveals Jesus in this character as the Lamb of God.

In this passage the marriage of the Lamb may even seem incongruous as a figure : but John looks at the sense, and not at the language.

He wishes us above all things to remember that as the sacrifice for sin our Lord appears in his glory; and that as a Lamb he will manifest himself in the consummation of all things when his church is perfected.

1. As the Lamb he is the one everlasting sacrifice for sin : he will not be other than this in his glory.

2. As the Lamb, suffering for sin, he is specially glorious in the eyes of the angels and all other holy intelligences : and so in his joyous day he wears that character.

3. As the Lamb he most fully displayed his love to his church; and so he appears in this form on the day of his love's triumph.

4. As the Lamb he is best loved of our souls. Behold, how he loved us even to the death!

Ever as a victim for sin he rejoices to display himself to the universe.

II. THE MEANING OF THE MARRIAGE SUPPER.

In the evening of time, in the end of the gospel day, there shall be—

1. The completion and perfection of the church. "His bride hath made herself ready."

2. The rising of the church into the nearest and happiest communion with Christ in his glory. "The marriage of the Lamb is come." The espousals lead up to this.

3. The fulfilment of the long expectations of both.

4. The open publication of the great fact of mutual love and union.

5. The overflowing of mutual delight and joy. "Be glad and rejoice."

6. The grandest display of magnificent munificence in a banquet.

7. The commencement of an eternally unbroken rest. "He shall rest in his love." The church, like Ruth, shall find rest in the house of her husband.

III. THE PERSONS WHO ARE CALLED TO IT.

Not those who have the common call and reject it, but—

1. Those who are so called as to accept the invitation.

2. Those who now possess the faith which is the token of admission.

3. Those who love Bridegroom and bride.

4. Those who have on the wedding garment of sanctification.

5. Those who watch with lamps burning.

These are they which are called to the marriage supper.

IV. THE BLESSEDNESS WHICH IS ASCRIBED TO THEM.

1. They have a prospect which blesses them even now.

2. They have great honour in being called to such a future.

3. They will be blessed indeed when at that feast, for—

Those who are called will be admitted.

Those who are admitted will be married.

Those who are married to Jesus will be endlessly happy. How many a marriage leads to misery! but it is not so in this case.

Alas, some are not thus blessed!

To be unblest is to be accursed.

MARRIAGE MUSIC

As they that have invited a company of strangers to a feast do stay till the last be come, so there will not be a glorious coming of Christ until all the elect be gathered into one body. And then shall be the coming of all comings, which is the glorious coming of Christ, to take us to himself.—*Richard Sibbes.*

How blessed it will be to those "called" ones, to "sit down" at "the marriage supper of the Lamb!" Then will "the King sit indeed at his table," and "the spikenard will send forth the smell thereof."

He who once hung so sad upon the cross for every one, will look around that bright company, and in every white robe, and in every lighted countenance, he will behold the fruit of his sufferings. He will "see of the travail of his soul, and will be satisfied." It will be the eternal union of God fulfilled in its deepest counsel—a people given to Christ from before all worlds; and that they are, that day, all chosen—all gathered—all washed—all saved—and not one of them is lost!

James Vaughan.

We dare not say that our Lord will love us more than he loves us now, but he will indulge his love for us more; he will manifest it more, we shall see more of it, we shall understand it better; it will appear to us as though he loved us more. He will lay open his whole heart and soul to us, with all its feelings, and secrets, and purposes, and allow us to know them, as far at least as we can understand them, and it will conduce to our happiness to know them. The love of this hour will be the perfection of love. This marriage-feast will be the feast, the triumph, of love—the exalted Saviour showing to the whole universe that he loves us to the utmost bound love can go, and we loving him with a fervour, a gratitude, an adoration, a delight, that are new even in heaven.

The provisions made by him for our enjoyment will astonish us. Conceive of a beggar taken for the first time to a splendid monarch's table, and this at a season of unusual splendour and rejoicing. How would he wonder at the magnificence he would see around him, and the profusion of things prepared for his gratification; some altogether new to him, and others in an abundance and an excellence he had never thought of! So will it be with us in heaven. We shall find it a feast and a monarch's feast. It will have delights for us, of which we have no conception; and the pleasures we anticipate in it will be far higher and more abundant than our highest expectations have ever gone. We shall have a provision made for us, which will befit, not *our* rank and condition, but the rank and condition, the greatness, the magnificence, of a glorious God.—*Charles Bradley.*

CCLXIV

Reb. xix. 9 —" And he saith unto me, These are the true sayings of God."

These words relate to that which immediately precedes them.

    The judgment of the harlot church. Verse 2.

    The glorious and universal reign of Christ. Verse 6.

    The sure reward and glory of Christ with his saved ones in the glorious period at the last. Verses 7, 8.

    The existence, beauty, purity, simplicity, and glory of the church.

    The union of Christ and the church in love, joy, glory.

    The blessedness of all who have to do with this union.

The subjects thus referred to make up a summary of what the Lord has said upon future human history.

The words before us we shall use as expressing—

I. A RIGHT ESTIMATE OF HOLY SCRIPTURE.

    1. These words which we find in the Old and New Testaments are true. Free from error, certain, enduring, infallible.

    2. These are divine words. Infallibly inspired, so as to be, in very truth "the sayings of God "

    3. These words are thus true and divine in opposition to

    Words of man. These may or may not be true.

    Pretended words of God. False prophets and men with addled intellects profess to speak in the name of God ; but they lie.

    4. These words are all of them truly divine. " These are the true sayings of God."

    Neither too severe to be true, nor too terrible to be uttered by a God of love, as some dare to say.

    Nor too good to be true, as tremblers fear.

    Nor too old to be true, as novelty-hunters affirm.

    Nor too simple to be truly divine, as the worldly-wise insinuate.

    5. These words are a blessing to us for that reason.

    What else can guide us if we have no sure revelation from God ?

    How can we understand the revelation if it is not all true? How could we discriminate between the truth and the error on subjects so much beyond us ?

II. THE RESULT OF FORMING SUCH AN ESTIMATE.

If you believe that " these are the true sayings of God,"

1. You will listen to them with attention, and judge what you hear from preachers by this infallible standard.
2. You will receive these words with assurance.
   This will produce confidence of understanding.
   This will produce rest of heart.
3. You will submit with reverence to these words, obey their precepts, believe their teachings, and value their prophecies.
4. You will expect fulfilment of divine promises under difficulties.
5. You will cling to revealed truth with pertinacity.
6. You will proclaim it with boldness.

III. OUR JUSTIFICATION FOR FORMING SUCH AN ESTIMATE.
In these days we may be accused of bibliolatry, and other new crimes; but we shall hold to our belief in inspiration, for—
1. The Scriptures are what they profess to be—the word of God.
2. There is a singular majesty and power in them; and we see this when the truth of God is preached.
3. There is a marvellous omniscience in Scripture, which is perceived by us when it unveils our inmost souls.
4. They have proven themselves true to us.
   They warned us of the bitter fruit of sin, and we have tasted it.
   They told us of the evil of the heart, and we have seen it.
   They told us of the peace-giving power of the blood, and we have proved it by faith in Jesus.
   They told us of the purifying energy of divine grace : we are already instances of it, and desire to be more so.
   They assured us of the efficacy of prayer, and it is true.
   They assured us of the upholding power of faith in God, and by faith we have been upheld in trial.
   They assured us of the faithfulness of God to his people as shown in providence, and we have experienced it. All things have worked together for our good hitherto.
5. The witness of the Holy Spirit in our hearts confirms our faith in Holy Scripture. We believe, and are saved from sin by believing. Those words must be truly divine which have wrought in us such gracious results.

What follows upon this? We believe all the Scripture.
We now accept as true sayings of God —
   The proclamation that our Lord is coming.
   The doctrine that the dead will be raised at his call.

The fact that there will be a judgment of the quick and dead.
The truth that saints will enjoy eternal life, and that
Sinners will go away into everlasting punishment.

WORTH QUOTING

Whence but from heaven could men unskill'd in arts,
In several ages born, in several parts,
Weave such agreeing truths? or how, or why
Should all conspire to cheat us with a lie?
Unask'd their pains, ungrateful their advice,
Starving their gain, and martyrdom their price.

Dryden.

Of most things it may be said, "Vanity of vanity, all is vanity"; but
of the Bible it may be truly said, "Verity of verity, all is verity."

Arrowsmith.

The True is the one asbestos which survives all fire, and comes out
purified.—*Thomas Carlyle.*

A young man had fallen into loose habits, and was living a wild, fast
life. Late hours were frequent with him, and he would pay no regard
to the remonstrances of a Christian father. At last it came to a point.
The father told his son that he must either leave his home or conform
to rules. He followed his old ways, went into lodgings, and was rather
pleased to be free from the restraint he felt at home. After a while he
picked up some young companions who professed infidel opinions, and
soon, like them, he even scoffed at religion, and made light of all his
parents had taught him. But the prayers of his father and mother
followed him, and in a remarkable way were abundantly answered. One
night the young fellow lay awake and began to think. "I tell people,"
said he to himself, "that there is no truth in the Bible, but there must
be truth somewhere, and if not there, where is it? I wonder what the
Bible says about truth."

In this way he was led to go to the Scriptures, and read every
passage where truth is spoken of. The Bible became its own witness.
It so took hold of him that he was persuaded that it was the very Word
of the Living God. He was convinced of the evil of his past life, and
was led to see Jesus as the Way, the Truth, and the Life. His whole
future was the reverse of his former course.—*G. Everard.*